On Bobwhites

NUMBER TWENTY-SEVEN:
W. L. Moody, Jr., Natural History Series

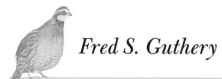

Fred S. Guthery

ON $\mathscr{B}$OBWHITES

Texas A&M University Press
COLLEGE STATION

LIBRARY OF CONGRESS CATALOGING-IN-PUBLICATION DATA

Guthery, Fred S.
    On bobwhites / Fred S. Guthery. — 1st ed.
        p.   c.m. — (W. L. Moody, Jr., natural history series : no. 27)
    Includes index.
    ISBN 0-89096-915-9 (cloth)
    1. Bobwhite.   I. Title.   II. Series.
QL696.G27G88   2000
598.6'273—dc21   99-41820
                                                                    CIP

Contents

List of Illustrations   *vii*
Preface   *ix*

Part One: LIFE AND TIMES   1
1. The Family Tree   *3*
2. Flight   *7*
3. Death Webs   *11*
4. Red Gopher Mounds   *16*
5. Loafing Coverts   *20*
6. Thermal Brinkmanship   *23*
7. Gular Flutter   *26*
8. Postmortem of a Dead Season   *28*
9. Fat Bobwhites   *34*
10. Food Choices   *36*
11. The Question of Water   *40*
12. Another Shot of Water   *42*
13. Fire Ants   *45*

Part Two: MANAGEMENT   51
14. The Value of a Seed   *53*
15. Food Management for Bobwhite Chicks   *56*
16. The Thanksgiving Syndrome   *59*
17. Thoughts on Supplementation   *63*
18. Prescribed Burning   *68*
19. The QUAILity of CRP Fields   *72*
20. The Economics of Bobwhite Management   *75*
21. Weird-year Management   *78*
22. Management Makes a Difference   *81*
23. Effective Management   *85*
24. Aldo Leopold on Bobwhites   *87*
25. Slack Zones   *92*
26. Robots and Quail Management   *96*
27. Space, Time, and Relativity   *99*

28. *Counting Bobwhites*   103

29. *Pen-reared Bobwhites*   108

   Part Three: POPULATIONS AND HARVEST   *113*

30. *Changes in Latitudes, Changes in Attitudes*   115

31. *Eight Hundred Million Heartbeats*   118

32. *Die-offs*   121

33. *Key Variables in Quail Production*   124

34. *To Gemini and Cancer*   126

35. *The Great Wisconsin Quail Irruption*   129

36. *The Occurrence of Multiple Broods*   132

37. *Implications of Third Broods*   136

38. *The Mysteries of Density*   138

39. *When 2 + 2 = 0*   142

40. *Minimum Requirements of Habitat and Population Size*   144

41. *The Stiff Spring of Density Dependence in Quail Populations*   146

42. *From Austin and Other Capitols*   149

43. *A Trilogy on Quail Harvest Management*   151

44. *The Thinking Bobwhite*   161

45. *The Role of Random Variation in Population Dynamics*   164

   Part Four: ISSUES AND PHILOSOPHIES   *167*

46. *A Pattern of Ecological Havoc*   169

47. *Perspectives on Grazing*   172

48. *Hot Habitat*   176

49. *La Perdiz Mascarita*   181

50. *The Misleading of America*   184

51. *Spike Memes*   187

52. *Watercolor Equations*   190

53. *Habitat Loss and Quail Decline*   193

54. *Falling into Cracks*   197

55. *The Value of Mistakes*   201

   Index   205

Illustrations

1. The bobwhite family tree consists of 4 distinct species and about 46 subspecies *4*
2. Properties of the average bobwhite flight *8*
3. Bobcat *12*
4. Sharp-shinned hawk *12*
5. Tepee shelters and brush piles may increase the amount of habitat available *22*
6. When drought and heat cause reproductive failure in bobwhite populations, rewards of the hunt are limited largely to companionship *32*
7. Bobwhite chicks require high levels of protein in their diet *57*
8. Research has yet to demonstrate that food plots established for bobwhites result in higher bird populations *62*
9. Supplemental feeding of bobwhite populations is practiced widely *65*
10. Prescribed burning improves bobwhite habitat in regions with more rainfall, but could have neutral or detrimental effects in regions with less rain *71*
11. Grazing by livestock may be the most economical way to increase bobwhite populations *76*
12. Ranch hands may burn the spines off prickly pear to provide forage for cattle *80*
13. Aldo Leopold recognized that more usable space for bobwhites could be created by rearranging available habitat types *90*
14. A flattened region often occurs in the relationship between something that matters and something that happens *95*
15. Quality habitat for bobwhites appears similar wherever the birds occur *101*
16. Biologists capture bobwhites for population analysis *104*
17. Leg-banding captured bobwhites provides information on harvest rates, survival rates, movements, and population abundance *107*
18a. Average mass of bobwhites *117*

18b. Average age ratio of bobwhites *117*

19. Bobwhite nests are vulnerable to predators, trampling, abandonment, flooding, and high temperatures *125*

20. Bobwhite hens may be responsible for raising up to three broods in one nesting season *133*

21. As the density of bobwhites increases, the average distance between coveys decreases rapidly and then flattens out. *140*

22. The extent (if any) to which harvest affects bobwhite populations remains a contentious issue in population management *153*

23. Individual bobwhites were more productive at lower breeding densities *158*

24. Under maximum sustained yield management of the harvest, bobwhite populations are harvested to a spring density *160*

25. Less than delicate treatments may be necessary to rejuvenate habitat *171*

26. Experiment on the effects of shade and soil moisture on the nesting environment *179*

27. Smoke plume from burning wheat stubble casts a pall over an agricultural landscape *196*

28. Cracks in clay soil may swallow a few bobwhite chicks *199*

ILLUSTRATIONS

Preface

THE PURPOSE OF MY RESEARCH IS TO GAIN RELIABLE
knowledge that will lead to an understanding of processes and the ability
to predict the outcomes of management activities. Since 1970 I have in-
vestigated the ecology and management of wildlife, with a large portion of
that effort devoted to bobwhites. The information in this book is based on
that research and on the research of many other biologists.

Biologists have been studying bobwhites since the 1920s and have
amassed an awesome—but little appreciated—knowledge base. As a result, many of the questions that arise during reflections after a hunt or in
discussions around a campfire already have answers. How many broods
do bobwhites raise? Will bobwhites hatched early nest in the same summer? What are best management plans for increasing abundance? Unfortunately, researchers (including this one) make mistakes. Scientists often
stumble along as if in a South Dakota blizzard. They prop themselves up
with a new theory now and then, only to have it blown away by a strong
gust of skepticism. The reader should bear in mind that all knowledge
is tentative. To foster this mind-set, *On Bobwhites* contains pretty essays
alongside those I know are ugly. In some cases, I comment on the original
thoughts from the perspective of time and new information.

The book is organized into four parts: Life and Times, Management,
Populations and Harvest, and Issues and Philosophies. To some extent,
On Bobwhites will have a southwestern flavor, because most of my work
was done in this region. The book, however, contains information from
the entire range of bobwhites, with references to Gambel's quail, blue
(= scaled) quail, and other species. The biology of quail and the principles of their management are basic and thus can be applied generally.
This is a compilation of essays on the biology and management of quail,
many written while I was a member of the Caesar Kleberg Wildlife Research Institute in Kingsville, Texas. I thank the faculty and staff of the institute for their generous support during this period.

Many of these pieces first appeared in *Quail Unlimited* magazine,
which has graciously released copyrights to permit their publication in

this book. I thank Quail Unlimited chapters and many private citizens (ca. 500) from the southern Midwest who made contributions to the research program I direct. These funds have helped take quail management deeper into the realm of technology and further from the realm of art. The writing of additional essays and the final preparation of the manuscript were supported by the Oklahoma Agricultural Experiment and the Bollenbach Endowment in Wildlife Ecology. I also thank Drs. Paul A. Johnsgard and R. J. Guttiérrez for their research on the types and relationships of bobwhites. The information in chapter 1 is a synopsis of their efforts.

Part One

LIFE AND TIMES

1 The Family Tree

NEW WORLD QUAIL CONSIST OF 31 SPECIES AND 128 – 45 subspecies (geographic races). Taxonomists generally recognize 4 distinct species of bobwhites and 46 subspecies. The most familiar species in the United States is the northern bobwhite, *Colinus virginianus*. CO-LINUS is a latinized form of the word COLIN, which means bobwhite in the language used by the Aztecs. Carolus Linnaeus (1707–78), a Swedish botanist, gave the bobwhite its scientific name in 1758. The specimen he examined apparently came from Virginia (hence, *virginianus*).

Few people in the United States are familiar with the other 3 *Colinus* species. The black-throated bobwhite (*C. nigrogularis*) occurs in Yucatan, Guatemala, and Belize. Except for the black throat, this species, which consists of 4 races, resembles northern bobwhites. Spot-bellied bobwhites (*C. leucopogon*) are found in Guatemala, El Salvador, Honduras, Nicaragua, and Costa Rica. White markings on the belly and a head crest (like blue [= scaled] quail [*Callipepla squamata*]) distinguish this species, which includes 6 races. The crested bobwhite (*C. cristatus*), comprised of 14 races, is found in Panama, Columbia, Venezuela, and extreme northern Brazil. Both sexes have distinct topknots resembling those of blue quail. *C. cristatus* is the most colorful of all bobwhites.

How did all these bobwhites come to be? Based on the fossil record, a quail-like bird first appeared about 40 million years ago in tropical America. These ancient ancestors resembled chachalacas (*Ortalis* sp.); they had long tails and spent much of their time in trees. The genus *Colinus* appeared between 7 and 12 million years B.P. Members of this genus that spread southward eventually became crested bobwhites, and those that moved northward evolved into northern bobwhites. In contrast, blue quail appeared about 2.8 million B.P. and Gambel's (*Callipepla Gambelii*) and California quail (*Callipepla Californica*) about 190 thousand years B.P.

Diversity in the northern bobwhite, which includes 21 races, is attributable to the normal processes of evolution. When birds occupy areas

Fig. 1. The bobwhite family tree consists of 4 distinct species and about 46 sub-species (geographic races) distributed from northern South America through the northern United States. PHOTOGRAPH BY R. D. WILBERFORCE

with different climates and vegetation, they will tend to be a size and coloration that best fit the conditions under which they live. For example, bobwhite subspecies in Wisconsin are heavier than those in Mexico. Higher body mass provides temperature maintenance benefits in colder climates, in which preservation of heat is a physiological priority. Conversely, lower body mass helps to get rid of body heat, an important requirement in warmer climates.

ON BOBWHITES

All bobwhites can interbreed with other species of quail. During the 1986–87 and 1987–88 hunting seasons, about 1 in 1000 bobwhites shot on a ranch in Zapata County, Texas, was a bob-blue hybrid, according to research by Tom Shupe, a research associate with the Caesar Kleberg Institute. Based on trapped samples, the hybridization rate was as high as 70 per 1000 bobwhites. Hybridization between bobwhites and blue quail occurs wherever the two species range together, and the plumage of hybrids shows traits of both species. Hybrids, however, have low fertility. Hence, the interbreeding is unlikely to result in "bluewhites" that run or "scaled bobs" that hold for dogs.

Bobwhites and other quail have several distinct features that make them unique among birds. Like all members of the order Galliformes (chicken-like birds that include grouse, pheasants, and partridges), bobwhites have 10 primary flight feathers and a crop (craw) for food storage. Bobwhites have three toes forward and one behind, which is elevated. The elevated rear toe is an adaptation for life on the ground; the toe is not elevated in perching birds.

While many birds use their calls to defend territories, quail are not territorial. Rather, they primarily call to communicate within and among social groups. Northern bobwhites (hereafter referred to as bobwhites) have a particularly rich vocabulary, and most people are familiar with the call that gave the bird its name. Other common calls that enrich its vocabulary include the following:

ASSEMBLY CALLS: *hoy, hoy-poo, hoy-ee, koi-lee.* Bobwhite coveys usually give this call at dawn and frequently at dusk. They also use this call to assemble members of a broken covey. If a male hears its mate giving the *hoy* call, the male will respond with the same call. If the male is not mated, it will respond with *bobwhite* (during breeding season). Research indicates that bobwhite populations have unique dialects for the assembly call; i.e., the assembly call of a Nebraska bobwhite sounds slightly different from that of an Oklahoma bobwhite.

The *hoy* call can be used to estimate bobwhite abundance. One arrives at a listening post shortly before dawn and tries to determine the number of different coveys heard calling. If the maximum distance at which calls can be heard is known, one can approximate density by determining the number of birds within hearing range (number of coveys times mean covey size) and dividing this number by the area of the circle over which coveys are heard.

Some biologists believe a *hoy* call can be heard from a distance of 0.25 mile (0.4 km), whereas others believe 0.50 mile (0.8 km). While the energy of a *hoy* call has not been measured, it would be reasonable to assume that it ranges between 60 (normal conversation) and 70 decibels (a noisy office). If bobwhites call at 65 decibels, they barely can be heard at a distance of 0.44 mile (0.7 km). This maximum range would be feasible only under ideal conditions: no wind, no competing noises, low humidity, and no brush between the bird and the observer. Conditions seldom would be ideal in the field. Therefore, 0.25 mile (0.4 km) may be the better estimate of average audibility range. A 0.25-mile (0.4 km) radius of audibility indicates that a person at a listening post could hear coveys from a circular area 126 acres (50 ha) in size.

FOOD CALL: Mated males give the food call, described as *tu-tu-tu* or *cu-cu-cu,* when they find a grasshopper or other morsel to give to the female. The male helps the hen find food at the time of laying because of the female's high nutritional demands.

ALARM CALLS: When a bobwhite encounters a strange object, it gives the *tip-tip* call—"Heads up, amigos." The *tee-wa* call is given when birds encounter a familiar object, but one out of place in their environment. Another alarm call is *tiree.* As danger increases, this call turns into *toil-ick-ick* or *toil-ick-toil-ick.* The latter expresses the most intense alarm.

FIGHT CALLS: The *squee* call is given when a male is in the presence of a rival, but is not overly agitated. CATERWAULING takes place during serious confrontations between two bobwhites. The bird giving this call will stand erect with feathers fluffed and tail fanned. Introducing a strange bird into a group or placing a female with two males will elicit caterwauling. Both males and females give the call, but males more frequently.

COPULATION CALLS: When a hen is mounted, it calls *tseep.* This leads to *ciew, squee,* and finally *tee-wa* (an alarm call) as copulation proceeds and finishes. Biologists have speculated that the series of calls indicates distress at the onset of copulation and antagonism at the end.

The recognized races of northern bobwhites and their geographic locations are:

1. black-breasted bobwhite (*C. v. pectoralis*) from Veracruz, Mexico
2. black-headed bobwhite (*C. v. atriceps*) from Oaxaca, Mexico
3. coyolcos bobwhite (*C. v. coyolcos*) from Oaxaca and Chiapas, Mexico

4. Cuban bobwhite (*C. v. cubanensis*) from Cuba
5. eastern bobwhite (*C. v. virginianus*) from Virginia to Florida
6. Florida bobwhite (*C. v. floridanus*) from Florida
7. Godman's bobwhite (*C. v. godmani*) from Veracruz, Mexico
8. Grayson's bobwhite (*C. v. graysoni*) from southern Jalisco, Mexico
9. Guatemalan bobwhite (*C. v. insignis*) from southern Chiapas, Mexico
10. Jaumave bobwhite (*C. v. aridis*) from Tamaulipas, Mexico
11. least bobwhite (*C. v. minor*) from northeastern Chiapas, Mexico
12. masked bobwhite (*C. v. ridgwayi*) from Sonora, Mexico
13. Nelson's bobwhite (*C. v. nelsoni*) from southern Chiapas, Mexico
14. plains bobwhite (*C. v. taylori*) from the Great Plains
15. Puebla bobwhite (*C. v. nigripectus*) from Puebla and Morelos, Mexico
16. Salvin's bobwhite (*C. v. salvini*) from the southern coast of Chiapas, Mexico
17. Thayer's bobwhite (*C. v. thayeri*) from northeastern Oaxaca, Mexico
18. interior bobwhite (*C. v. mexicanus*) from east of the Great Plains
19. New England bobwhite (*C. v. marilandicus*) from New England
20. Texas bobwhite (*C. v. texanus*) from south Texas and northern Mexico
21. mottled bobwhite (*C. v. maculatus*) from central Tamaulipas to northern Veracruz, Mexico

2 *Flight*

BOBWHITES AVOID DEATH FROM PREDATION BY FREEZING (holding perfectly still), running, or flying. The birds cannot survive in habitats that eliminate any of these options. Flight abilities and airspace, therefore, are habitat management considerations.

Until recently, information on bobwhite flight was limited. It was known only that the bobwhite was more like a crop duster than an F-16, its flight abilities paling in comparison to the aerial acrobats of birds such as mourning doves (*Zenaida macroura*), seagulls (*Larus* spp.), or peregrine falcons (*Falco peregrinus*). Anatomy constrains flight in bobwhites. The primary flight muscles in the breast are large, but poorly supplied with the nutrients that release energy for sustained flight. The heart is small relative to body mass, which reduces endurance. The aerodynamic

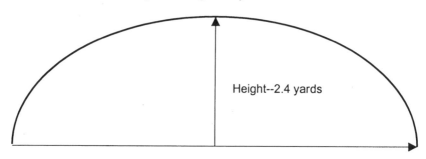

Flight arc length--49 yards

Height--2.4 yards

Take-off to landing distance--47 yards
Time in the air--5.1 seconds
Average speed--20 miles/hour

Fig. 2. Properties of the average bobwhite flight.

properties of the body are only slightly better than those of a brick. The short, broad wings limit maneuverability; quail have been known to batter themselves against buildings upon launching.

How do these constraints translate into flight behavior in the field? By necessity, the bobwhite is a short-distance flyer. When Nick Kassinis, a graduate student at Texas A&M University- Kingsville, measured 300 bobwhite flights in 1993–94, he found that the average distance from takeoff to landing was 47 yards (range: 4–148 yd.) (43 m, range: 3.6–134.7 m). Eighty-eight percent of flights were less than 75 yards (68.3 m).

Others, however, have seen longer flights. Herbert L. Stoddard, the father of bobwhite management, stated in 1931 that it was not uncommon for bobwhites to fly 350–450 yards (319–410 m) to a favorite thicket. A. W. Schorger, writing in the *Transactions of the Wisconsin Academy of Science, Arts and Letters* in 1946, reported flights of more than a mile (1.6 km) across the Mississippi River. While flights of this length may occur, they would be extremely rare.

The bobwhite is also a low altitude flyer. Kassinis observed a maximum height of about 13.0 yards (12 m), with the average maximum height being 2.4 yards (2.3 m). Bobwhites typically were back on the ground within 4 to 6 seconds after takeoff, although one flight lasted nearly 13 seconds.

Hunters are interested in the speed at which bobwhites fly. The data collected by Kassinis indicated an average flight speed of 20 mph (32 kph) with a high of 27 mph (43 kph). These values represent average speed over the duration of a flight. Maximum speed during the flight would have been greater, because a flight has three parts: acceleration, cruise, and deceleration. Flight speeds measured by odometer have reached nearly 40 mph (64 kph). Kassinis found evidence that female bobwhites were slightly slower flyers than males. Herbert L. Stoddard also reported this sex difference.

Because bobwhites are limited to short, low, relatively straight flights, they are restricted to habitats that permit flights having those properties. Kassinis analyzed airspace at takeoff and landing points to determine how this space affected habitat selection and use. The average takeoff point provided 272 degrees of flight opportunity; i.e., of the 360 degrees in a circle, 272 degrees provided unobstructed airspace at points from which bobwhites flushed. Obstructions were brush, trees, or other tall objects that prevented an escape flight. The take-home message is that bobwhites seldom occur where they cannot fly in nearly all directions to escape predators.

Landing points provided 250 degrees of flight opportunity, slightly less than takeoff points. Kassinis attributed this difference to selection of landing points having more woody cover, to hide from predators; i.e., predator avoidance was more important at landing points than at takeoff points. When bobwhites touched down after an escape flight, however, they preserved the option of a second escape flight; about 70% of airspace was unobstructed after a landing.

Why were flights not longer? Kassinis originally believed that flight distance was a compromise between security and energy expenditure, that bobwhites, in a robotic manner, would fly far enough to minimize the threat that precipitated the flight, but without draining energy reserves. When he calculated the energy cost of flights, however, he found them to be trivial. The average flight burned about 0.04 kilocalories, less than 1% of the energy a wild bobwhite would expend in a normal day without flying.

If acceptable escape cover is nearby, there is no need for bobwhites to push themselves to the limits of endurance, and energy expenditure becomes a moot point. If bobwhites have to execute long flights, muscle physiology probably limits distance. Their muscles are rich in fibers that permit bursts of activity but cannot sustain it. In human terms, bobwhites are more like Carl Lewis (a sprinter) than Roger Bannister (a miler).

Kassinis' findings are directly applicable to bobwhite management. Managers have reasoned that to improve bobwhite survival, it is beneficial to rotate hunting pressure among management units. It was assumed that flight drained energy reserves, and that rest periods of several days would permit replenishment of these reserves. Whereas allowing birds to rest in hunting areas may benefit bobwhite populations, this benefit clearly does not accrue from energy dynamics.

If airspace is obstructed by tall brush and trees, management must address the problem. Action would be needed only when the coverage of tall woody cover is high. For example, in a savanna habitat or in a pine forest with widely spaced trees, airspace obstruction would not be a management concern. Obstruction would become a concern in a dense, brush habitat or in a forest with closely spaced trees.

An area can provide all the requisites for quail survival, and yet support no quail if airspace is inhospitable. Quail may be programmed genetically to avoid areas in which they lose a predator-avoidance option such as flight. The management prescription in such cases is to remove obstructions in airspace using mechanical implements, burning, or a combination of these means.

The tendencies of bobwhites in terms of flight distance provide guidance on the arrangement of habitat types relative to each other. Herbert L. Stoddard suggested that escape cover should never be more than 200 yards (182 m) from any point in a management area. This number has been cited through the years and has become a standard recommendation. Yet Kassinis' study revealed that nearly 90% of flights were less than 75 yards (68.3 m); his recommendation is that escape cover should be within 75 yards (68.3 m) of feeding cover.

IT NOW IS KNOWN THAT TEMPERATURE PROBABLY AFFECTS the flight behavior of quail. The normal body temperature of bobwhites (108.7°F, 42.6°C) is perilously close to the body temperature (116.7°F, 47°C) that leads to death from heat overload. Flight, as a form of exercise, raises body temperature. Kassinis observed shorter flights in summer than during other periods, and short flights during hot periods make physiological sense. It also has been learned that bobwhites select cooler sites for landing, especially in warmer weather. Cooler sites help to rapidly dissipate the body heat gained during a flight.

3 Death Webs

TAKE AN ORDINARY SPIDER WEB, GLISTENING WITH DEW IN the garden. The web is anchored hither to cedar pickets, yon to live oak twigs, and thither to sago palm, Japanese yew, and blue plumbago. Clip a strand and the web stands firm. Keep clipping until only four strands remain — pointed north, south, east, and west. The web is now vulnerable to collapse.

The spider web serves as a homely analogy for the web of death that envelops quail populations. Consider some of the things that kill quail: rattlesnakes (*Crotalus* sp.), bullsnakes (*Pituophis catenifer*), coachwhips (*Masticophis flagellum*), other snakes, wild turkeys (*Meleagris gallopavo*), Cooper's hawks (*Accipiter cooperii*), red-tailed hawks (*Buteo jamaicensis*), grackles (*Quiscalus* spp.), crows (*Corvus* spp.), other birds, bobcats (*Lynx rufus*), coyotes (*Canis latrans*), striped skunks (*Mephitis mephitis*), gray foxes (*Urocyon cinereoargenteus*), house cats (*Felis* sp.), dogs (*Canis familiaris*), ground squirrels (*Spermophilus* sp.), other mammals, disease, accidents, blizzards, old age, and humans. The list goes on and on.

Some predators are more serious threats to bobwhites than others, and some minor threats have been unfairly chastised. The roadrunner (*Geococcyx Californianus*) provides an example of the latter. "Old myths and folklore die hard, and the roadrunner has both suffered and benefited from stories of its eating habits that have circulated throughout the century," wrote Wyman Meinzer in *The Roadrunner* (1993). "Early in the twentieth century, it was accepted as fact that chaparrals were predators on a few game bird species, notably quail. At one time, the federal government placed a bounty on the paisano in a misdirected attempt to save the struggling quail population."

Analyses of roadrunner foods did not support the belief that they preyed heavily on quail, according to studies reviewed by Meinzer. About 75% of the foods consumed by 84 roadrunners examined in California consisted of insects; these birds also ate lizards, mice, baby rabbits, and two unidentified birds (not quail). Meinzer reported insects made up 62%

Figs. 3. and 4. Bobcats and sharp-shinned hawks (*Accipiter striatus*) are among dozens of predators that take bobwhites. The effect of any one predator species on bobwhite populations decreases as the diversity of predators increases.
BOBCAT PHOTOGRAPH BY DALE ROLLINS; SHARP-SHINNED HAWK PHOTOGRAPH BY R. D. WILBERFORCE

of the diet in Arizona, even when quail were nesting and brooding. No quail remains were found in the stomachs of 100 roadrunners sampled.

Of course, the predators that kill quail operate on other prey: fruits and berries, insects, perching birds, rodents, rabbits, hares, and deer. In some cases, the taking of prey other than quail provides direct and indirect benefits to quail.

Jack M. Inglis, formerly with the Texas Parks and Wildlife Department and Texas A&M University, College Station, studied the competition for food between bobwhites and kangaroo rats (*Dipodomys* sp.) on the Gene Howe Wildlife Management Area in the Rolling Plains of north Texas. During the summer of 1956, kangaroo rats ate both themselves and bobwhites out of winter food supplies. Populations of both animals crashed in the ensuing winter. "Rats were aggressive in their response to available food—they stored seeds and reproductive activity was adjusted to supplies," Inglis reported. "Quail were passive—they simply used supplies available at any time; reproduction preceded highest availability of seeds."

Competition for food between rats and bobwhites was intense only during drought. During rainy periods, seed supplies were more than adequate for both species. Generally, Inglis concluded, kangaroo rats ate greater quantities of seeds that made up the winter diet of quail than quail did. The competitive significance of kangaroo rats, measured in terms of quail populations, varied from major importance to unimportance, depending on rainfall patterns and standing populations of rats and bobwhites.

The loss of quail to snakes could be considered a tax for the benefits snakes provide. Herbert L. Stoddard reported in 1931 that "the coachwhip is a serious enemy of quail." In the Southeast, Stoddard believed that coachwhips persistently hunted quail chicks. A study in Wilson and Gonzales Counties, Texas, in the late 1940s, however, indicated that coachwhips were not serious egg predators. A. J. Springs, formerly with the Texas Parks and Wildlife Department, found quail remains in 1 of 34 coachwhip stomachs he examined. Texas rat snakes (*Elaphe obsoleta*) were serious predators in Springs' study. Nearly half of 34 rat snakes examined had quail eggs, traces of quail eggs, or small quail in their stomachs. The full extent to which snakes prey on adult quail is largely unknown. Denise Sloan of Stephen F. Austin State University, Nacogdoches, Texas, lost two radio-tagged hens to snake predation on the Welder Wildlife Foundation Refuge near Sinton, Texas in the 1980s. One was eaten by a Texas rat snake and the other by a western diamondback rattlesnake (*Crotalus atrox*).

While snakes prey on quail, they also benefit the birds by preying on animals that compete for food. Some rodents, such as ground squirrels and cotton rats (*Sigmodon hispidus*), prey on quail nests. When snakes prey on those species, they are performing predator control for humans; i.e., the fox that ate the grapes saved the persimmon for the raccoon (*Procyon lotor*) that did not eat the snake that fed the bobcat that did not eat the turkey that fed the coyote that did not eat the grasshopper that fed the bobwhite.

Healthy predator-prey systems have multiple interconnections. One cannot predict how the system, or a component of the system (i.e., bobwhites), will respond if a strand is clipped. One can say the system will stand firm, like the spider web, if it has plenty of anchors. In fact, if one predator is clipped from a quail's death web, no matter how nefarious, only a small difference in the number of quail would result. The logic is not straightforward: death hinders death by leaving better-fit survivors, life fosters death by preserving less-fit individuals. This phenomenon is called density-dependent survival.

Old age, or senescence, hangs over quail populations like a pall. One should not discuss predation webs without first addressing senescence. It puts limits on the maximum possible responses of a quail population to management of predators. If all sources of loss except old age were removed, if a perfect environment could be created, annual death rates of 20 to 40% still would occur. Quail burn out like Roman candles, a characteristic of small animals with high metabolic rates.

Focus on the effects of a single predator, e.g., Cooper's hawks. Its removal from a predator-quail system could have only minor effects on total bobwhite mortality. Assuming these hawks take 5% of quail annually in a population that experiences an annual mortality of 80%, the elimination of hawks will decrease the annual mortality to 79%. When one source of loss is removed, other sources of loss will exert more influence. If a predator known to take 25% of a quail population is excluded, many — perhaps most — of the quail saved will be lost to other causes. More certainly will die from senescence, other predators, accidents, and perhaps, harvest.

The death web will stand firm when a strand is clipped in a healthy system. If the system is not healthy, meaning it has few species of both prey and predators, the web is not well anchored. A large number of quail might be saved by removing a major predator. The system, like a spider web guyed by four strands, however, is near collapse. The system will not be resilient to the normal quivers and shakes that characterize life in the hinterlands.

The arguments thus far have dealt with a single predator. What if all predators from a quail management area were removed? Total mortality perhaps could be reduced to 50% annually. Such management, clearly unacceptable from a social standpoint, also would be economically infeasible, given all the agents that kill quail.

The brush country of South Texas abounds with predators and quail. Research has been conducted in this region to determine if removal of a substantial portion of the predators increases bobwhite density. Sam L. Beasom, while a graduate student at the University of Wisconsin, Madison, removed coyotes, bobcats, and smaller predators from rangeland in

Kleberg County, Texas, during the late 1960s and early 1970s. He took out any ground predators that had, could or might have designs on quails. This intensive predator suppression caused a slight increase in bobwhite production.

Under Beasom's direction, I conducted experimental predator suppression in Zavala County, Texas, during the mid-1970s. Coyotes were the primary predator removed. There was no apparent difference in the densities of bobwhites and scaled quail in areas with and without predator control.

The Bomer Wildlife Research Area in Duval County, Texas, is managed primarily for bobwhites. This small area (120 ac. = 48 ha) typically provides headquarters for a bobcat; coyotes rest under tepee shelters constructed for quail; hawks of many species are common. Nothing is done to manage these predators, and yet the Bomer Area typically has bobwhite densities exceeding a bird per acre (2.5/ha).

A fascinating aspect of the relationship between quail and predators on a continental scale is that wherever quail populations persist, their population dynamics are fairly consistent. Although a slight variation in death and birth rates can be observed with changes in climate, on average, quail demography remains relatively constant. This constancy prevails in the face of huge differences in the species composition and abundance of predator populations in different areas and regions. If quail demography remains steady as predator populations change, what does this reveal about the effects of predators on quail?

Of course, bobwhites, blue quail, and other species are declining on modern landscapes. Demography is relatively constant only in populations that fluctuate around a fixed number of birds. The quail decline has prompted biologists to rethink the dynamics of predator-quail systems. Perhaps the balance has shifted in favor of predators.

The ecological web is neither well anchored nor resilient. Only time will tell, but one wonders whether a predator problem or a landscape problem would be responsible for a new predator-quail balance. The bottom line is that predation on quail is not a particularly salient management issue in diverse natural landscapes.

Accidents

Some accidents that befall quail, as catalogued by Aldo Leopold in *Game Management*, 1933.

- Burning of nests or young in fires.
- Drowning of nests in heavy rains or floods.
- Being hit by automobiles.
- Being encrusted while roosting on snow, or being imprisoned by sleet on vegetation.
- Drowning in steep ditches.
- Flying into white buildings and windows.
- Flying into woven wire fences, high wires, and backstops of tennis courts.
- Being impaled on splinters.
- Being killed by hailstones.
- Young falling into ditches, crevices, and plowed furrows.

 4 *Red Gopher Mounds*

RED GOPHER MOUNDS AND BUMPER CROPS OF BOBWHITES GO together like beans and tortillas. Gophers (*Geomys* spp.) live in the soil, where they mine for roots, tubers, and other foods. Occasionally, they come topside to gather and cache acorns or yaupon (*Ilex vomitoria*) berries.

Gophers are found only in certain types of soil; heavy clays carry few, if any. These soils usually occur in rainier areas, and many are saturated with water during some months. During dry periods, they cake and crack, often becoming hard as the playing field at the Astrodome. Gophers are not fit for such conditions, and bobwhites find them discouraging as well.

Clays give rise to conditions that depress bobwhite numbers in Texas. (In other states, clays may be prime candidates for management.) These soils support plant groups consisting largely of grasses (Poaceae). While some of the forbs on clays, notably western ragweed (*Ambrosia psilostachya*), crotons (*Croton* spp.), and snow-on-the-prairie (*Euphorbia marginata*), provide first-rate foods, food supplies generally are low. Buildups of grass and grass litter magnify the problem of food shortage by hiding seeds and hindering access. Periodic flooding can wipe out clutches, drown chicks, and impose hardships on adults.

Despite these shortcomings, clay soils can provide good hunting with proper management. The first requirement is good drainage, as occurs with rolling topography. This reduces problems connected with flooding. Then the countryside must be subjected to livestock, discs, or fire. In coastal Texas, fire is an incomplete measure, even if conducted every other year, because grasses quickly reappear after burning. Managers must take additional steps to promote the lower successional plants required by bobwhites. One phrase best summarizes habitat management on clay soils in rainy areas: Nuke it!

As in clays, gophers are scarce in shallow, rocky soils, such as those that occur on the Edwards Plateau or caliche outcrops in south Texas. Obviously, these animals cannot burrow through rock. Likewise, bobwhite populations do poorly on rocky soil. Some, however, is welcome because it increases habitat diversity.

Gophers are more abundant on loams than either clays or rocky soils. Likewise, quail do better on loams. In Zavala County, in the southwestern Rio Grande Plains, Texas, I estimated quail abundance on loamy soils in 1975 and 1976. The first year was a boomer as I flushed up to 70 quail— blue and bob—in a mile of walking. Density of bobwhites was about 1.5 birds per acre (3.8/ha) in autumn. The next year, however, drought struck the area. Quail numbers plummeted to about 25% of the previous levels. Still, the two-year average was noteworthy.

Loamy soils over limestone bedrock may support high densities of bobwhites in the Cross Timbers and Prairies of north-central Texas. This region provides some of the most scenic quail habitat anywhere. Mesquite (*Prosopis glandulosa*), Ashe juniper (*Juniperus ashei*), live oak (*Quercus virginiana*), Texas oak (*Quercus shumardii*), and flameleaf sumac (*Rhus copallina*) clothe the hilly uplands. Pecan (*Carya illinoensis*), bur oak (*Quercus macrocarpa*), and sycamore (*Platanus occidentalis*) watch over the narrow bottomlands. In such country, bobwhites prosper on deeper loams that accumulate along drainages. Likewise, flat ridgetops with a healthy complement of mesquite can support large numbers of quail.

The best gopher and quail soils, however, are sands. Gophers find their coarse texture ideal for burrowing. Quail find their plant communities wealthy in wild foods and premium cover. Four major outcroppings of wind-deposited sand occur on the Rio Grande Plains. Relatively small deposits occur in Zapata and Dimmit Counties. A large belt of sands (350 thousand ac. = 140 thousand ha) runs east-west from southeastern

Medina County through parts of Atascosa, Bexar, Wilson, and Guadalupe Counties. "Sands in these counties," wrote Val W. Lehmann, "have long produced some of the best quail hunting in Texas." The largest outcropping, known as the Wild Horse Desert, occupies most of Kenedy and Brooks Counties. This area totals 1.75 million acres (0.7 million ha).

White gopher mounds are evident in the Wild Horse Desert. They may crop up in mottes (isolated thickets) of mesquite, granjeno (*Celtis pallida*), and prickly pear (*Opuntia* spp.). Bobwhites loaf under the protective canopies of the mottes and snack on the ground-cherries (*Physalis* sp.) that grow on older gopher diggings. When the birds sally forth to feed, they enjoy a banquet of thin paspalum (*Paspalum setaceum*), croton (*Croton* spp.), dayflower (*Commelina* sp.), milkpea (*Galactia* sp.), snoutbean (*Rhynchosia* sp.), partridge pea (*Cassia* sp.), and sunflower (*Helianthus* sp.). The supply of native foods is extraordinary.

Besides rich food supplies, the sands offer other amenities. Sands favor bunchgrasses as opposed to sod-forming grasses. Interspaces of bare ground, essential for movement and finding seeds, occur between grass clumps. Seeds in the upper layer of soil are available to quail that scratch for them. (Seeds in clay would remain sealed in heavy dough, if wet, or in hardpan.) Indeed, the table-salt texture of sands facilitates banking of seeds for lean times, and rainfall percolates into sands with little loss to evaporation or runoff. The large soil particles readily yield groundwater to thirsty plants. As a result of these soil moisture relationships, plant communities are more stable than on other soils.

Plant stability leads to greater stability in quail populations. Although bobwhite numbers vary with rainfall on sands, the violent, feast-or-famine fluctuations found on other soil types are less common. Researchers have counted up to 0.5 bobwhite per acre (1.25/ha) during a drought year in Brooks County. During normal years, the soils may support 1.0 bird per acre (2.5/ha).

Red gopher mounds and even higher quail densities occur on sandy soils rich in iron. Unfortunately, the red sands have a limited distribution in south Texas. Red sandy loams are more widespread but less beneficial to bobwhites. Red sands and sandy loams in the lower Rio Grande Valley support a highly diverse brush community. Main species like mesquite and granjeno grow together with lime prickly ash (*Zanthoxylum fagara*), hog-plum (*Colubrina texensis*), anacahuita (*Cordia boissieri*), and brazil (*Condalia obovata*).

A 200-acre (80-ha) pasture may have 15 different species of brush. Such diversity begets stability in food and cover, which helps carry vigorous populations of quail. The red soils also support a wide assortment of herbaceous legumes, valuable sources of protein to wild and domestic animals. According to Ted B. Doerr, a graduate student at Texas A&M University during 1985–87, the red soils bear higher native food supplies than the white sands. The diversity and abundance of brush and foods lead to exceptional bobwhite densities. Enrique Guerra's San Vicente Ranch in Hidalgo County supported 3.1 bobwhites per acre (7.8/ha) in autumn of 1985, following a minor drought. The harvest that winter was about 1.0 bobwhite per acre (2.5/ha).

Nineteen eighty-seven was a boom year for quail in large portions of south Texas, especially at two sites with red sandy soils. On the Texas Parks and Wildlife Department's Chaparral Management Area near Cotulla, the harvest on opening weekend was 0.3 bird per acre (0.8/ha). On a nearby ranch with deeper sands, Harvey W. Smith, Jr., flushed a covey every 12 minutes during surveys prior to hunting. Estimated density exceeded 4.0 bobwhites per acre (10/ha), and the known kill was more than 1.0 bird per acre (2.5/ha). Yes, the Smith Ranch has red gopher mounds.

Gophers can aid in the search for hunting grounds in Texas. If one is not outside of quail range, red gopher mounds indicate that the soil texture is favorable for bobwhites and that a site has great potential, if it does not contain banner populations already.

THE STATEMENTS IN THIS ESSAY ABOUT THE RELATIONSHIPS among soil type, food supplies, and bobwhite abundance may be incorrect. Different soil types support different quantities of food as stated; however, a relationship between quantity of foods and abundance of bobwhites has never been demonstrated. Nevertheless, the relationships between soil type and bobwhite abundance remain acceptable, at least in the southern Midwest.

5   *Loafing Coverts*

BETWEEN MORNING AND EVENING FEEDING PERIODS, BOBWHITES rest in the shade of brush in areas called **LOAFING COVERTS**. They are an essential and easily managed habitat feature.

Dave Johnson of the Florida Game and Fresh Water Fish Commission spent two years (1985–86) measuring the characteristics of loafing coverts. He recognized that in order to manage brush or construct artificial coverts most effectively, the precise requirements of quail must be known. Surprisingly, little research had been done on loafing coverts until the mid-1980s. Most information merely listed plant species; details on height, structure, and preferences among species were lacking. Thus, much presumptive management was being applied, some of which was ineffective.

Johnson set about finding loafing bobwhites during midday in summer, autumn, and winter. He worked two areas: one had a poor brush community with 2 major species and the other had a rich community with about 15 species. In the brush-poor area, quail had little choice but to use Macartney rose (*Rosa bracteata*) or honey mesquite as loafing sites. Temperature affected the differential use of these species. During cooler days, birds loafed under or near Macartney rose; mesquite was the preferred species during warmer days.

Bobwhites avoided mesquite, however, in the brush-rich area. Bluewood, also known as brazil, received preferential use from bobwhites, especially in summer. (Brazil has a dense canopy protected by thorns.) Species such as granjeno, lime prickly ash, and hog-plum were used, but bobwhites showed no particular like or dislike for them. The birds, however, loafed under lime prickly ash and granjeno more often during cooler than on warmer days.

In both areas, Johnson found common themes in covert use. First, during hot days, bobwhites selected tall loafing coverts with dense, leafy canopies. The shaded loafing sites averaged more than 7°F (3.9°C) cooler than ambient air temperature. Quail simply were trying to stay comfortable and maintain body temperature at a normal level.

During cool days, on the other hand, bobwhites used low brush as loafing sites. The brush had no effect on temperature, and the birds did not always move under the canopy. Rather, some rested in shade along the sides of the covert. Coveys rarely loafed where there was no brush at all; this usually occurred on cool days with heavy overcast and low light intensity.

Second, the birds preferred low, evergreen brush species during winter. Macartney rose, granjeno, and lime prickly ash fit this category. In the brush-rich area, Johnson made another discovery that will be useful in covert management. Coveys sought out loafing sites in which the brush was relatively thick. For example, the canopy coverage of brush at loafing sites, on average, was twice as high as that generally available. (Canopy coverage refers to the percentage of soil surface shaded by brush canopies.)

At loafing sites, coverage averaged 23–33% within a 30-yard (27.3-m) radius. The average was 11–17% at other sites. Thirty percent coverage represents extremely dense brush to quail hunters. If cover is tall, it is difficult to walk through and nearly impossible to hunt; as many coveys will be heard as seen. Bobwhites, however, seem to prefer small amounts of this heavier brush.

Johnson's findings have direct relevance to brush management. His results may apply to most subtropical environments in which woody vegetation is managed in one way or another. The first pertinent finding is that, given a choice, bobwhites utilized two types of coverts. Older and taller shrubs with thicker canopies received use on hot days, and shorter, evergreen shrubs on cool days. The birds, however, showed great flexibility in covert use during cool days.

Therefore, ranchers or hunters who remove mature brush to improve hunting opportunities—and increase bobwhite density—must preserve some strips or small blocks of mature brush. Hot-day coverts are a more important management concern than cool-day coverts because quail requirements are more specific on hot days and more general on cool days. Furthermore, covert preservation should take into account the birds' preference for high canopy coverage at loafing sites. In application, this preference means preservation of strips or mottes rather than singletons.

Throughout the Southern Plains, brush management programs preserve mature, isolated mesquite. While this is certainly better than no preservation at all, mesquite is not used if other species are available. It has a sparse canopy and is therefore less effective in shading. A better

Fig. 5. Tepee shelters and brush piles may increase the amount of habitat available to bobwhites; research indicates that clusters of artificial structures are better than singletons. These structures, however, cannot replace widely dispersed, native brush as the key component of bobwhite habitat.

practice would be to preserve mottes consisting of a mature mesquite and, if possible, two or three additional brush species. Usually, this is practical because mesquite will serve as a NURSE PLANT for other brush. As a pioneer of new habitats, it is one of the first species to establish. Later, the shade and soil enrichment it provides will create suitable conditions for granjeno and other species.

The mottes need not be large. A diameter of 10 to 20 yards (9.1 to 18.2 m) probably would be adequate. This will leave 300–1300 square yards (248–1077 m²) of older brush. Whitetails (*Odocoileus virginianus*) and wild turkeys will also use mottes, especially larger ones, and are less likely to use singletons. Often, the problem is too little, rather than too much, woody cover. In such cases, construction of loafing coverts may rejuvenate habitat. Here, too, Johnson's results are important. Managers must keep hot days in mind. At least some of the shelters erected should provide dense shade and cooler temperatures during summer. This will necessitate an elevated, dense canopy. Hot-day coverts have been constructed using cinder blocks for legs, with scrap lumber or limbs piled on metal or wood panels. The tepee shelter, popular throughout south

Texas, also provides hot-day coverts. On Joe Coleman's ranch near Rami-
rez, Texas, one sees many coveys using tepees, even if older mesquites are
available.

Artificial cool-day coverts can be much less elaborate. If larger junipers
(*Juniperus* sp.) are available, simply cut them down and tow them to
brush-deficient areas. These bushy shrubs provide suitable cool-day
coverts even after leaves drop. An alternative would be to erect simple
brush piles (i.e., stacks of trunks and limbs). The canopy need not be
elevated for cool-day coverts.

Based on Johnson's research, managers will be more successful if they
erect clusters of coverts instead of singletons. Coveys, as pointed out earlier, seem to select sites with relatively high canopy coverage of brush. A
cluster of shelters would simulate this condition best. For example, one
might construct a rather elaborate hot-day covert with four to six cool-day
coverts within a 10- to 20-yard (9.1- to 18.2-m) radius. This design has not
been tested, but if the above statements on bobwhite behavior are correct,
the plan makes sense.

WHEN DAVE JOHNSON'S RESEARCH WAS CONDUCTED, IT WAS
not known that temperatures lethal to bobwhites occur on semiarid
rangeland. Their use of taller loafing coverts on hotter days probably is a
matter of survival. See the next three essays.

6 *Thermal Brinkmanship*

A BOBWHITE WILL DIE: IF IT IS CONTINUOUSLY EXPOSED TO
an air temperature of 104°F (40°C); if its body temperature rises about
8°F (4.4°C) above normal; or if it leaves its loafing covert and begins feeding on a hot summer afternoon—possibly within minutes. Bobwhites live
perilously close to death from overheating. This little known fact helps to
understand where the bird occurs, why it does not occur in some areas,
and why it behaves as it does.

To understand the thermal perils faced by bobwhites, imagine being in
a car with the heater on full blast. The heater represents the fire of life in
a bobwhite. These birds generate heat through the metabolic processes of

living. The car's windows absorb rays from the sun, and the car emits heat called long-wave radiation. Likewise, a bobwhite absorbs and emits radiation. Wherever the car is parked, the temperature inside will eventually stabilize. This occurs when heat input from the heater and heat absorbed from sun rays equal heat emitted through long-wave radiation. If parked in full sun on a hot summer day, the temperature in the car will exceed 160°F (71.1°C), the approximate core temperature of a medium-rare crown roast.

Birds in general, and bobwhites in particular, will die if core body temperatures reach 116.7°F (47°C). Because normal body temperature is about 108.7°F (42.6°C) for bobwhites, these birds have at most 8.0°F (4.4°C) leeway. Eight degrees represents little heat. The bobwhite's body consists of tissue and water and its weight is such that about 0.13 kilocalories of net heat gain will cause body temperature to rise 1.8°F (1°C). About 0.57 kilocalories of net heat gain will result in death. If the human calories in an old-fashioned diet soft drink were converted to heat and transferred into the body of a bobwhite, the bird would die.

Although all this may sound alarmist and academic, heat kills wildlife. Gulls nesting on islands in California have died en masse during heat waves. Heat can kill chicks directly (documented for California quail by E. Lowell Sumner, Jr., in 1935). A bobwhite chick exposed to full sunlight could die within 122 seconds. Chicks are especially vulnerable because they have smaller bodies; a small amount of solar energy can kill them.

Quail living in desert environments must stay in the shade and remain quiet if they are to survive hot days. David L. Goldstein estimated in 1984 that if a Gambel's quail started walking on a hot summer day in Arizona, it would die after little more than a minute. Bobwhite hens have died in the nest during hot, droughty summers in the Great Plains. Biologists assumed they had starved, but heat overload is an equally plausible cause of death. Roger Wells of Quail Unlimited, Inc., has observed that chick production in the Midwest was lower during hotter summers than during milder ones. Heat also can stress adult birds and inhibit the laying effort.

My research showed in 1988 that the breeding season for bobwhites is about two months shorter in the western than in the eastern Rio Grande Plains. The thermal environment of the western Rio Grande Plains is more rigorous, lacking the cooling influence of the Gulf of Mexico. The air has lower humidity, which permits more of the sun's rays to reach the ground. Clouds block solar energy less frequently in the western plains. Perhaps these circumstances render the western Rio Grande Plains too

hot for nesting and brood-rearing during July and August, when reproduction effectively ends in most years. In contrast, reproduction declines
but remains strong during these months in the eastern plains.

It has been observed that flights of bobwhites are shorter during summer than in other seasons. This was assumed to have occurred because
the birds had forgotten hunting season, or because bountiful escape cover
permitted short summer flights. Now it is realized that long flights during
summer can be lethal. What does the threat of heat overload mean to
those concerned about quail conservation and management? That quail
maintain body temperatures putting them on the brink of death and that
the sun emits death rays in summer must be acknowledged. By recogniz-
ing these two facts, habitat is seen in a new perspective.

In those portions of quail range subject to intense summer heat, woody
and herbaceous cover is perhaps more important as a thermal shield than
as a predator shield. One could remove all predators and, lacking cover,
bobwhite populations would perish from overheating; one hot, clear day
would be sufficient to eliminate hundreds of birds.

Research by my student, Dave Johnson, in 1985–86 has shown that
loafing coverts used during cooler seasons lack distinguishing features.
Those used during summer, however, are tall and dense, providing a
thick thermal shield and a cool site for resting between feeding bouts.
Without the tall coverts, quail will not persist. See chapter 5, Loafing
Coverts.

Although the management literature states that bobwhites need woody
cover, a thermal perspective on habitat suggests that woody cover may
be unnecessary in cooler environments. Regions with lower air temperatures and robust ground cover may be able to support bobwhites in the
absence of shrubs. Perhaps this explains why barrier islands off the coast
of Texas sustain bobwhite populations with little brush; the cooling effects of the Gulf of Mexico and its breezes perhaps make woody cover
thermally unnecessary. In early Wisconsin, bobwhites apparently were
abundant on the open prairie.

Plant cover also keeps ground temperatures lower by blocking sunlight. The soil absorbs and emits radiation and may reach temperatures of
130 to 160°F (54.4 to 71.1°C) in full sun. The shade provided by ground
cover keeps soil surfaces at a temperature acceptable to quail.

THE OPENING SENTENCE IN THIS ESSAY IS SOMEWHAT
misleading. Bobwhites can endure temperatures above 104°F (40°C) if

the time of exposure is short. A bobwhite exposed continuously to 104°F (40°C) might die within 24 hours according to research by Professor Robert J. Robel of Kansas State University, Manhattan. Of course, wild bobwhites would not be exposed to such high temperatures for 24-hour periods.

Landmark Temperatures for Bobwhites

- 32°F (0°C)—a wild bobwhite needs about 50 kilocalories per day, the energy equivalent of 550 milo seeds.
- 68°F (36.7°C)—a wild bobwhite needs 30 kilocalories per day (350 milo seeds).
- 76–78°F (24.4-25.6°C)—embryo development begins in an egg held at this temperature.
- 80–85°F (26.7-29.4°C)—somewhere in this range, bobwhites must begin to actively dissipate body heat.
- 86°F (30°C)—a wild bobwhite needs 20 kilocalories per day (250 milo seeds).
- 99–100°F (37.2-37.8°C)—temperature for incubation.
- 102.2°F (39°C)—a bobwhite's ability to dissipate heat cannot keep pace with heat gain, and body temperature will begin to rise above normal.
- 104°F (40°C)—a bobwhite experiencing prolonged exposure to temperatures at or about this temperature will die of hyperthermia.
- 108°F (42.2°C)—normal core body temperature for bobwhites (some small variation among individuals and seasons).
- 116–17°F (46.7-47.2°C)—body temperature resulting in death of most vertebrates, including bobwhites.

 7 *Gular Flutter*

WHY DOES A MARCHING BAND BREAK STEP WHEN IT CROSSES a bridge, and what does this have to do with quail biology? The answer begins with a hot summer day somewhere in quaildom.

If the air temperature is above about 95°F (35°C), bobwhites face a dilemma. They must cool their bodies and reduce the rate of heat gain via evaporation; however, these processes require expenditure of energy, which in turn increases body temperature. This dilemma can be resolved if the rate of heat gain due to increased activity is less than the rate of heat loss from evaporation. Evaporation of water is the physical process by which many animals control body temperature. Horses and humans sweat; dogs pant. For each gram of water evaporated, a body dissipates 0.54 kilocalories of heat.

A bobwhite under heat stress will have its beak open. If observed closely, the gular or throat region can be seen vibrating rapidly. This is called gular flutter, a common method of body temperature control in birds. The basic physics models for the process quail use to dissipate heat were established by Robert Hooke and Sir Isaac Newton more than 200 years ago. Hooke studied the properties of springs and Newton provided laws that define and reconcile conflicting forces.

The gular pouch is an elastic membrane that behaves like a spring. If the pouch were tweaked, it would vibrate like a rubber band stretched between two fixed objects. As a vibrating membrane, the gular region has a small set of opposing forces acting upon it. These forces include its resistance to stretching, which can be modeled using Hooke's Law. This law states that the force exerted by a stretched spring is proportional to the distance it is stretched.

Another force to consider is the damping force exerted by air pressure. Air pressure offers resistance to a vibrating membrane and eventually will cause it to stop vibrating. Finally, if a bobwhite is actively cooling, it exerts muscular force on the membrane. Newton provided the means and mechanisms of describing and understanding the conflicting forces present in gular flutter. Gular flutter represents what is called a periodic or cycling mechanical system. These types of systems have some remarkable properties with respect to external forces, such as the muscular force applied by a hot bobwhite.

Imagine pushing somebody in a swing. The force being exerted is similar to that a bobwhite administers in gular flutter. If the force is applied at random, both parties would become bruised and battered and the swing will stop. If, however, the force is applied in phase with the motion of the swinging person, little energy is required to keep the pendulum in motion. In a similar manner, if bobwhites exert force on the gular membrane in phase with its natural vibrating tendencies, the amplitude of membrane displacement increases; i.e., it moves farther to the right and left of equilibrium, illustrating the physical phenomenon of resonance.

Forces applied in phase with a periodic or cycling system have magnified effects. Airplanes have crashed when engine vibrations came into phase with body vibrations. An unbalanced tire vibrates violently at certain speeds but runs smoothly at slower or faster speeds. This has to do with in-phase and out-of-phase circumstances.

Evaporation from gular membranes and the rate of cooling increase with larger displacement and faster average velocities of the membrane. This is the same effect a human feels when moving from a still to a breezy area. By taking advantage of the properties of periodic mechanical systems, the rate of body heat loss by evaporation exceeds the rate of body heat gain by muscle exertion in bobwhites. The net effect is a reduction in body temperature, or at least a reduction in the rate of body heat gain. At high air temperatures, however, gular flutter cannot prevent elevated body temperatures. These birds can dissipate heat at a maximum rate of 0.3 to 0.5 watts (the same unit as in a light bulb). When the rate of heat gain exceeds this value, bobwhites are in danger of death from heat overload.

That bobwhites use the properties of periodic mechanical systems to survive represents a remarkable blend of physics and biology.

Now the question that opened this essay can be answered. A band marching across a bridge in lockstep might be marching in phase with the bridge's natural tendency to vibrate. This could invoke resonance, in which case the bridge might collapse. Resonance took the Tacoma Narrows Bridge on November 7, 1940.

8 *Postmortem of a Dead Season*

THE BOBWHITE CROP WAS GENERALLY POOR IN THE SOUTHERN Plains during the 1994–95 hunting season. The low autumn populations were remarkable, having gone against all expectations. Many portions of Texas, for example, received ample, widespread rainfall in the spring and summer of 1994. This was supposed to cause a population boom. Although the reasons for the low population numbers are not known, some ideas have been advanced.

Was it an illusion? It has been suggested that the season was not as bad as it seemed. Hunting season opened with warm weather and luxuriant habitat conditions. Bobwhites were awash in quality foods and did not have to spend much time foraging or forage far from loafing and roosting headquarters. Moreover, the November to mid-December period was abnormally warm, reducing the effectiveness of dogs in finding coveys. Poor scenting conditions and few scent trails (due to limited movements) may have resulted in low hunting success. If this hypothesis has merit, then hunting should have improved with cooler weather after the first of the year. However, it did not.

Although the "illusion" hypothesis has a firm biological and physical basis, it appears flawed based on convincing data that populations were in fact low in 1994–95. My students and I documented average production and a lower than expected spring-to-fall population increase on a ranch in Duval County. Based on extensive surveys in Brooks County, Ronnie Howard, manager of the San Tomas Hunting Camp in south Texas, saw a 47% population decline from the fall of 1993 to the fall of 1994. Statewide surveys by the Texas Parks and Wildlife Department also revealed weak populations.

The vitamin A hypothesis, like the mythical phoenix, rises from the ashes with each poor quail year. This hypothesis relies on a "magic bullet," a singular, chemical explanation of variation in quail production (e.g., plant hormones, dietary phosphorus, dietary water, or vitamin A). The hypothesis first arose in the 1940s based on laboratory feeding trials with bobwhites. These trials showed that egg production declined as dietary vitamin A decreased. Biologists reasoned that variation in dietary intake in the field might explain boom-bust fluctuations in quail productivity. Rainy years with copious greens would yield high levels of vitamin A in the diet, whereas droughty years with sparse greens would produce low levels.

Two field tests of the vitamin A hypothesis have been conducted. The results of a 1964 study in Arizona on Gambel's quail supported the hypothesis, albeit weakly. The number of birds examined was too low to draw a firm conclusion. A 1953 study on south Texas bobwhites by Val W. Lehmann failed to support the hypothesis. There was no relation between vitamin A levels and population productivity. Moreover, rainfall was relatively heavy in 1994 and ample quantities of greens were present. Therefore, the vitamin A hypothesis must be rejected as an explanation for poor production in 1994. Bobwhites in the laboratory trials of the 1940s laid with low levels of vitamin A in the diet, a fact often overlooked by proponents of this hypothesis. Since Lehmann's results refuted this hypothesis in 1953, the phoenix analogy is apt. Indeed, no magic boom-bust bullet has ever withstood testing as an explanation of reproductive failure in the wild.

The skinny hen hypothesis holds that bobwhites entered the breeding season in poor condition and that this was reflected in poor reproductive effort. When a biologist refers to POOR CONDITION, low levels of body fat is what is usually meant. Bobwhites in subtropical environments average about 10% body fat. A bobwhite dead from starvation has about 3 to 4% body fat, most of which is in the brain. The difference between starvation and average condition is a only about 11 grams (0.4 ounces) of fat.

When a hen begins to form eggs, hormones mobilize the stored energy in the body and convert this energy into eggs. Low quantities of body fat might delay the onset of laying. Examining this possibility, consider that a bobwhite egg contains about 18 kilocalories of energy. Eleven grams of fat provide about 99 kilocalories of energy, enough for 5.5 eggs. The average first nest contains 12.0–15.0 eggs. Therefore, a bobwhite hen cannot rely on body fat alone, and must obtain energy from foods to lay a first clutch.

The skinny hen hypothesis cannot be rejected because it has a demonstrated physiological basis; however, it must be regarded as an incomplete explanation of low bobwhite populations in 1994. There is every reason to believe food supplies were ample. It is known that bobwhites can recover rapidly from low body fat levels and that game bird hens with low fat levels will lay normally if provided sufficient food.

The ticking clock provides yet another hypothesis. To accept that rainfall guarantees quail numbers conceals certain population realities. If the countryside is green during spring and summer, great expectations for fall hunting ensue. Bobwhite populations, however, have distinct and absolute limits on increase during any time period; at best, a population can double from one year to the next. Therefore, any region with low populations in 1993 was likely to have low populations in 1994.

This is called the tick-tock hypothesis, implying that it takes time for populations to recover from lows. This hypothesis is inarguable and accepted without reservation. Recalling 1985 and 1986, years in which populations generally were low despite ample rainfall, the problem in these two years was the population crash in 1984. The year 1987 saw unprecedented quail abundance; the clock had been ticking three years since the 1984 bust. The tick-tock hypothesis, however, is not complete. It does not explain those areas with good populations in 1993 and poor ones in 1994. Mediocre production in excellent habitat, as researchers observed in Duval County, needs examination. A powerful yet subtle explanation of production failure in 1994 is needed, and it would be delightful if the explanation is found to be consistent with long-term observations of quail production.

Another explanation is presented by the hot-kitchen hypothesis. The chicken literature provides solid data that heat is a powerful mediator of egg production. The summer of 1994 was hot. M. O. North, author of *Commercial Chicken Production Manual,* (1978) observed, "At temperatures above 80°F (27°C) laying pullets begin to suffer, and the cost of producing market eggs increases. At 100°F (38°C) things become serious. Egg production drops drastically, and many birds die from heat exhaustion." Rising temperatures have several effects on laying pullets. Water consumption, respiration rate, and body temperature increase. At the same time, oxygen consumption, pulse rate, feed intake, bird weight, egg production, egg weight, eggshell quality, and interior egg quality decrease.

Is there evidence that quail in the wild are similarly sensitive to heat? "In drought years, high prevailing ground temperatures and much-below-normal moisture prior to and throughout the production period affected quail behavior in various ways and at important stages of the production cycle," reported Jack Stanford of the Missouri Department of Conservation in the First National Bobwhite Quail Symposium (1972). Stanford observed the following problems in Missouri bobwhites:

- Pairing, covey breakup, and nesting are delayed.
- Limited nesting occurs during May, June, and July.
- Many nests containing full clutches are abandoned.
- Hens become emaciated and die in the nests.
- Eggs are prematurely incubated by high ground temperatures prior to incubation by the hen. Much egg spoilage occurs.
- Unhatched chicks pip and partially ring their eggshells, but rapid desiccation traps them in half-opened eggs.
- Uneven hatching, with a few eggs hatching early, causes hens to leave nests with fewer young (often as few as two to four chicks).

Unfortunately, Stanford did not quantify what he meant by drought. He said droughts were characterized by "rainfall much below average, prolonged high temperatures above 100°F [37.8°C]."

Fig. 6. When drought and heat cause reproductive failure in bobwhite populations, rewards of the hunt are limited largely to companionship. PHOTOGRAPH BY WILLIAM P. KUVLESKY, JR.

The timing of peak production in different geographic areas provides striking testimony to the power of heat. Peak production of Gambel's quail in Arizona is during April and May. In south Texas, with the cooling influence of the Gulf of Mexico, peak production of bobwhites occurs in May and June. In southern Illinois, peak production is in July. Earlier production is observed in hotter environments and later production in cooler environments. This could be a response to heat. There also is evidence that the power of heat is subtle.

Research by John L. Roseberry and Willard D. Klimstra in southern Illinois, published in 1975, has shown that the length of the laying season declines as summer temperatures rise. For every 1°F (0.6°C) increase in late summer maximum temperatures, the laying season declines by one week. This means that in hot summers, the last egg is laid in mid-July, whereas in cool summers, the date is in early September. Air temperature alone can shorten the laying season in Illinois by 45 to 60 days.

The laying season of bobwhites in the western Rio Grande Plains (near Laredo) is about two months shorter than for birds in the eastern plains (near Corpus Christi). Temperatures and heat loads are higher in the western plains, because they are farther from the Gulf of Mexico and because they receive less rainfall. Roseberry's and Klimstra's research showed that temperature differences could explain the difference in length of laying seasons.

An interesting outcome of the hot-kitchen hypothesis is its full compatibility with the general observation that quail production correlates with rainfall. This correlation holds in semiarid environments for bobwhites, blue quail, California quail, Mearns quail (*Cyrtonyx montezumae*), and Gambel's quail. It does not hold well in humid environments for bobwhites, and does not guarantee good production in semiarid environments.

In general, rainy years would foster a cooler environment at the quail level. Plant growth would shade the soil surface. Green plants also would cool by transpiring and evaporating water. More water in the air (humidity) would block the heating effects of sunlight. M. O. North had some interesting recommendations for management of laying chickens during heat waves: insulate the ceiling, use foggers, sprinkle the roof, run sprinklers intermittently, and wet the area outside and around the house (conditions not unlike a rainy summer).

Conversely, a lack of plant growth (analogous to ceiling insulation), transpiration, evaporation, and humidity during drought years would foster a hotter environment at the quail level. There is now the possibility that previous thinking on boom-bust fluctuations and the role of rainfall have been wrong for all these decades. Perhaps less heat in rainier years and more heat in drier years were being observed. The search for a cause and effect process may have been like Don Quixote's tilting at windmills.

The hot-kitchen hypothesis remains speculative but intriguing. For the skeptical reader, the hypothesis makes some definite predictions that can be tested:

- In bust years, peak chick production should occur early in the breeding season when heat loads are more compatible with bobwhite physiology. The approximate hatching date of juveniles can be determined based on the molt sequence of the flight feathers. (Some hunting camp managers will have data for the 1994–95 season.)
- In years generally characterized by poor production, sites with certain thermal properties should have above average production for the year. These sites will have cooler microenvironments. Examples might include coastal areas in which the ocean moderates the environment, or ungrazed sites in which more standing vegetation moderates heat at ground level.

 ## 9 *Fat Bobwhites*

BODY FAT IS TO A BIRD AS BLUBBER IS TO A WHALE. FAT provides high-octane energy that keeps the body heaters running during extreme cold. With enough fat, quail and other birds can survive short periods of fasting during times that seeds are unavailable (e.g., freezing rain or snow). Thus, a bobwhite manager needs to be concerned about fat levels in birds. The fatter they are, the better they are able to withstand the rigors of nature.

My students and I collected 671 bobwhites in South Texas during a 1982–83 sampling period to determine body fat levels. Extraction of body fat is a tedious laboratory process. Samples are frozen and then are coarsely ground, dried, and finely reground. Fat is extracted from small samples of the resulting "quailburger" with a solvent such as ether. The procedure takes about eight hours per bird.

Whole body fat levels were high during winter, averaging 10.4%. This number represents the percentage of fat in dry tissue. Winter bobwhites had fat equivalent to that of a 160-pound (72.7-kg) man with a 28-inch (71.1-cm) waist. In other words, south Texas bobwhites were lean, even during winter. In contrast, winter bobwhites in Kansas averaged 22.0% body fat—similar to a 160-pound (72.7-kg) man with a 34-inch (86.4-cm) waist. Average fat levels in South Texas declined to 8.7% in spring, increased to 10.5% in summer, and decreased to 9.8% in autumn.

The seasonal changes reflect different needs and behaviors of bobwhites. In winter, average coveys of 11 to 12 birds may lay on extra fat in case of weather emergencies. In spring, the demands of reproduction depress fat levels. Body fat in males drops markedly, perhaps because they are more interested in securing and holding mates than in maintaining body condition. Fat levels of females also drop in spring, but not to the extent as those of males; indeed, laying females have high levels of body fat.

Females require a lot of energy during egg laying. Research by Ronald M. Case of Kansas State University, published in 1972, has shown that the requirement of laying hens rises from 35 to 70 kilocalories per day during egg production. These extra calories go into eggs, particularly the yolk. The yolk has a rich store of energy that fuels chicks for up to three days after they hatch. Fat and skinny bobwhites were found during all seasons in south Texas. Whole body fat levels never dropped below 4%—virtually the point of starvation. The highest level recorded was 23% for a laying female.

What can the manager do to maintain high body fat levels in a population of bobwhites? The most obvious answer is to maintain a high availability of food. This can be accomplished with traditional methods of food management, such as discing, seeding, and feeding. Food rich in carbohydrates, such as millet (*Panicum* sp.), sorghum (*Sorghum vulgare*), croton, and many fruits and berries, will elevate fat levels if the foods are readily available. A second answer is to foster those foods that have high levels of fats. Most plant foods are low in fats (ca. 3–5% fat), but there are exceptions. Seeds of the sunflower family (*Compositae*)—golden crownbeard (*Verbesina* sp.), western ragweed, annual sunflower, and many others—range from 15 to 20% fat.

A less obvious way of ensuring high body fat levels is to minimize energy losses. Bobwhites lose energy continually from the time of hatching until death—that is the cost of living. The cost rises with increasing foraging effort, increasing disturbance, and decreasing quality of the cover that protects them from cold. The manager can ensure that energy loss is kept low by maintaining a habitat of the proper structure and making certain that cover requirements of the birds are well dispersed throughout an area.

WILDLIFE BIOLOGISTS HAVE OPERATED UNDER THE ASSUMPTION that the level of body fat in wild animals reflects the quality of their habitat. The assumption may hold for big game (e.g., deer and elk), but is questionable for game birds. The fat levels of quail are an adaptation to prevailing climate; fat levels seem to hold steady as food supplies vary within a climatic province.

The energy costs of movement (i.e., walking, running, and flying) are trivial for bobwhites relative to the energy costs of thermoregulation. Thermoregulation requires the maintenance of body temperature within a narrow range. Therefore, the above recommendations on habitat are valid, but the basis for the recommendation does not lie in energetics.

Finally, the fat levels of bobwhites are a weak hedge against cold temperatures and fasting conditions. These birds starve to death in one to three days if they fast at freezing temperatures.

 10　*Food Choices*

IF GIVEN A CHOICE OF FOODS, WHICH ONES WILL BOBWHITES select? Do their selections make sense in terms of nutrition?

Victor C. Michael and Stephen L. Beckwith of the University of Georgia, Athens, studied quail preferences for seeds from farm crops in the 1950s. The most highly preferred food of 53 tested was sorghum seeds (milo). This food was number 1 in 94% of 600 trials and number 2 in the remaining 6%. Other preferred foods included wheat (*Triticum aestivum*), cattail millet (*Pennisetum glaucum*), German millet (*Setaria ital-*

ica), switchgrass (*Panicum virgatum*), hegari (*Sorghum* sp.), sesame (*Sesamum indicum*), rape (*Brassica* sp.), and Thunberg lespedeza (*Lespedeza thunburgii*). Cracked corn (*Zea mays*) ranked number 15 in preference and whole corn ranked number 33.

The bobwhites in Michael and Beckwith's experiment had other surprises for quail managers. These birds did not like seeds from partridge pea (*Cassia fasciculata*) and kobe lespedeza (*Lespedeza* sp.), two widely touted food plants. These species ranked numbers 24 and 25 in preference, respectively. The worst food of all was showy crotalaria (*Crotalaria spectabilis*), which is poisonous to bobwhites. Bobwhites do not eat crotalaria seeds. Bermuda grass seeds (*Cynodon dactylon*), likewise, ranked near the bottom.

Generally, these bobwhites selected foods that were high in metabolizable energy and avoided foods that were low in metabolizable energy or poisonous. METABOLIZABLE ENERGY is that portion of the total energy in seeds that bobwhites can extract during digestion. Sorghum has up to 3.7 kilocalories per gram of metabolizable energy. Partridge pea has as little as 2.4 kilocalories per gram. The total diet of bobwhites should have at least 2.8 kilocalories per gram of metabolizable energy. Crickets are the best known food, contributing up to 4.9 kilocalories per gram. Corn is also highly metabolizable. (Quail in the Michael and Beckwith study must have avoided corn for reasons other than nutrition.)

Why do bobwhites eat partridge pea if it is a poor food? Partridge pea and other less nutritious seeds may show up in the diet during late winter and early spring. At this time, the preferred and more nutritious foods are not available. The birds are eating low quality foods because the alternative is starvation.

Does the availability of grit affect the metabolizability of foods? Grit serves a food grinding purpose similar to the teeth of mammals. "Grit as a grinding agent in the gizzards of bobwhite quail is not essential for growth, welfare, or reproduction," reported R. B. Nestler, a wildlife nutritionist, in the 1940s. He compared the performance of birds with and without grit in the laboratory and concluded that seeds in the diet serve the same grinding function as small rocks. Research in the 1970s confirmed Nestler's observation. Robert J. Robel at Kansas State University concluded that supplemental grit had no effect on digestion of hard seeds, such as partridge pea and lespedeza, or on digestion of soft foods, such as commercial poultry mash.

Of course, energy is not the only major nutrient that varies among quail foods. "Survival and reproduction of game birds is dependent on protein quality in their diet . . . ," according to Alan D. Peoples and Robert L. Lochmiller of Oklahoma State University, Stillwater. "Northern bobwhites require 23–28% crude protein for optimum growth and reproduction. . . . Dietary proteins comprise 20 amino acids that constitute the true protein value of forage. Ten are [essential amino acids] for birds because they cannot be synthesized in sufficient quantities to meet cellular requirements and must be acquired from the diet. . . ."

Peoples, Lochmiller, and associates evaluated the protein quality of 21 bobwhite foods in 1994. "Forb seeds did not provide sufficient crude protein to meet growth requirements of quail, and only queensdelight stillingia [*Stillingia sylvatica*] met requirements for reproduction," they reported. Forb seeds tested included dayflower (*Commelina erecta*), woolly croton (*Croton capitatus*), redroot amaranth (*Amaranthus retroflexus*), giant ragweed (*Ambrosia trifida*), and western ragweed (*A. psilostachya*), among others.

"Grass seeds contained low levels of essential amino acids. None of the grasses provided sufficient protein to meet growth, reproduction, or maintenance requirements." Cattail millet (*Pennisetum glaucum*), grain sorghum (milo), Johnson grass (*Sorghum halepense*), and sorghum almum (*S. almum*) were evaluated.

Seeds of herbaceous legumes, including trailing wild bean (*Strophostyles helvola*), partridge pea, perennial wild bean (*S. umbellata*), and Illinois bundleflower (*Desmanthus illinvensis*) were of higher protein quality than other seeds tested. "Overall, forbs, grasses, and woody plants were deficient in 74, 98, and 67% of [essential amino acids], respectively, for maintenance. Legumes were deficient in 13% of [essential amino acids] and best met [essential amino acid] requirements for growth, reproduction, and maintenance," reported Peoples and Lochmiller.

Bobwhites and other quail have built-in hedges against variation in the quality of foods they eat. W. M. Giuliano and co-workers at Texas Tech University, Lubbock, conducted a study in 1994 to determine the effects of protein and energy deficiencies on reproduction by bobwhites and blue quail. "We found that energy deficient diets led to increased food consumption by bobwhites and scaled quail, suggesting that both species can respond to low dietary energy by increasing food consumption."

The practical ramification of this finding is that reproducing quail in the wild have some flexibility in diet selection. From a quail's standpoint, the major concern with respect to energy and protein is the absolute quantity taken in, not the relative amount. Thus an individual can eat more of a low energy food or less of a high energy food to get the same total energy. When energy becomes too low, quail face problems. The time available for foraging and the capacity of the digestive tract limit the amount of food that can be processed in a day. In other words, with food too low in energy, quail would have neither the time nor the capacity to get the required amount.

Quail seem able to detect the energy content of foods and adjust intake accordingly. They do not seem able to detect protein content, and therefore cannot make adjustments for this nutrient. "We found that low protein and/or energy in the diet negatively affected egg production and ovary mass in both northern bobwhite and scaled quail," stated Giuliano. "Egg mass is a good measure of egg quality; large eggs have a higher fertility rate and produce chicks with higher survival rates. Egg mass of northern bobwhite and scaled quail in our study was unaffected by any dietary treatment."

This finding means that quail in the wild can deal with a range of diet qualities and still produce eggs of good quality. Furthermore, this means that food management to increase the quality of the diet would not necessarily have any impact on egg quality or production of young; i.e., once a certain level of diet quality is reached, better quality diets would have no effect.

Perhaps the most interesting outcome of the Giuliano studies was the finding that quail can detect energy but apparently cannot detect protein in their diets. In the grand sweep of natural selection, these birds seem to have evolved to live first and reproduce second.

Food plot managers must recognize that bobwhite foods are not created equal if they want their expenditures to be most effective. They should consider the nutritional value of the seeds from plants selected for establishment. Lochmiller and Peoples recommended management strategies resulting in a diverse seed base (several species) and high insect densities to ensure that bobwhites have adequate nutrients.

11 The Question of Water

IN THE 1980S, NO MANAGEMENT PRACTICE ELICITED MORE campfire discussions in the arid Southwest than the provision of water for bobwhites. Landowners built water systems ranging in design from basic to complex and in all price ranges. More systems are in planning or development stages.

What does the basic biology of bobwhites reveal about making these programs most effective? First, it must be recognized that water is the most vital nutrient. Life as we know it cannot go on without water, and bobwhites are no exception.

Bobwhites derive water from three sources. The first is produced from the burning of foods. This is called OXIDATIVE or METABOLIC water because it is a by-product of metabolism, the chemical and physical processes that sustain life. Foods differ in the amount of metabolic water they provide. The carbohydrates in milo seeds or the protein in insects generate about 0.50 gram of water for each gram eaten (1.00 g = 0.035 oz). Fats, on the other hand, yield a gram of water for each gram consumed. Metabolic water alone is insufficient for bobwhites in semiarid environments, but can fulfill 25% of their needs.

The second source is PREFORMED water—the water in foods. Dry seeds contain up to 3% water by weight, depending on humidity. Insects hold 60%, fleshy fruits 70%, and leafy greens contain up to 90%.

Bobwhites can and do thrive on metabolic and preformed water alone. On sandy soils near the Gulf Coast of Texas, as in portions of Jim Hogg, Brooks, and Duval Counties, the typical summer diet of chicks and adults is about 55 to 65% preformed water. For an adult male, the diet yields about 13.6 grams (0.5 oz) of water each day. Add to this 3.6 grams (0.13 oz) of metabolic water. This totals 17.2 grams (0.6 oz), or about 11% of body weight. In short, metabolism and the diet provide enough water for comfort and survival.

A potential danger becomes apparent upon examining the foods that provide the dietary water. Only about 10 to 15% comes from invertebrates (e.g., insects, spiders, and snails), and 85 to 90% is derived from moisture-laden greens and berries. Moist plant foods are crucial to the water balance of bobwhites in semiarid environments. Without such foods, the birds must turn to the third source—FREE or SURFACE water—to survive.

There are conflicting opinions as to whether bobwhites require standing water. Bobwhites may not visit free water if moist foods are broadly available, temperatures are cool, or if their needs can be fulfilled with dew. Thus, someone in a cool, rainy environment could watch water holes till the third millennium without seeing bobwhites come to drink; however, a person in Zapata County, Texas—quail hell—could observe bobwhites drinking each July and August, if not for more extended periods.

Zapata County is the hottest, driest bobwhite habitat north of the Rio Grande. High annual evaporation rates (85 in., 216 cm) and low summer rainfall (5 in., 12.7 cm) result in a scarcity of the green plant matter so essential to water balance; high temperatures increase water loss from quail, because they cool their bodies via evaporation (see chapter 7, Gular Flutter).

What happens to bobwhites denied sufficient water? The birds probably can lower their normal intake somewhat without serious damage being done. If necessary, Gambel's quail, a desert species, can reduce daily consumption during tough times with no negative effects. These quail somehow condition their bodies and modify their behavior to survive with less than optimum amounts. More severe denial, however, will cause a series of predictable physiological events: levels of stress hormone will rise in the bloodstream, appetite will wane, and weight will decline. If the birds are in breeding condition, the reproductive organs will shrivel and become inactive. Death, of course, will be the outcome of extreme water denial.

The biology discussed above can be translated into management practices. Obviously, there are vast reaches of bobwhite range in North America where, because of cooler temperatures and heavier rainfall, provision of water would serve no purpose in management. Likewise, there are regions in which the birds will use surface water readily, if it is available and accessible.

It is now believed that bobwhites could benefit from water in those portions of the Rio Grande Plain in which mean annual pan evaporation exceeds 65 inches (165 cm). The 65-inch zone roughly follows a line drawn between McAllen and San Antonio. West of the line, evaporation increases, while it decreases to the east. Where evaporation exceeds

75 inches (191 cm), it is a certainty that watering facilities will reduce stress on bobwhite populations during summer and drought.

Within the torrid, arid zone, watering can be made more efficient due to knowledge of quail biology. Watering can be discontinued with the onset of fall rains and cooler temperatures. The birds will need less water for body cooling, and moisture-rich, sprouting greens will be widely available. In all but drought years, the water holes will not require maintenance until the critical months of June through September, when temperatures peak.

If watering seems to be a reasonable option in a given area, do not expect miracles. Watering is never higher than third on a list of management priorities. First, the proper habitat structure must be created. Second, if necessary, the food supply has to be managed. In the hotter and drier environments, water may have a place after structure and food.

In the event that water systems are installed, many species will benefit, including nongame species, whitetails, wild turkeys, mourning doves, and white-winged doves (*Zenaida asiatica*). Regardless of the effect on quail populations, providing water will surely enrich the habitat for many species of wildlife.

THE BIOLOGY PRESENTED IN THE ABOVE ESSAY IS SOUND, but the management recommendations concerning water are wrong. I wrote this essay after my research crew at Texas A&M University- Kingsville had discovered exceptional bobwhite densities on the San Vicente Ranch in south Texas, which has waterers. Subsequent research has refuted the value of water provisioning in bobwhite management. See the next essay.

12 Another Shot of Water

IF BENEFITS ACCRUE TO BOBWHITE POPULATIONS THROUGH provision of supplemental water, there have to be biological reasons. The most obvious reason would be that bobwhites will die of thirst without any water. Is this likely to happen in the field?

Availability of greens, which may provide 80% or more of the water in quail foods, can become extremely low; still, bobwhites would have enough to meet their water needs. Laboratory studies done by Nancy E. Koerth and me in the 1980s have indicated that birds can survive during summer with a water intake of 5.6% of body weight per day. For the typical bobwhite in the Rio Grande Plains, this amounts to ⅙ jigger (9 g). Requirements are higher in the field than in the lab. Wild birds have to eat more, because they move about more and burn more energy. Free-ranging bobwhites may require at least 8% of body weight per day, roughly ¼ jigger.

If a wild covey of 15 bobwhites obtains water by eating greens and the greens are 90% water, this covey would need six ounces (170 g) of succulent foliage each day. This amount yields 3⅓ jiggers or 11 tablespoons of water. If the covey foraged along a path 6.0 feet (1.8 m) wide and 0.25 (0.4 km) mile long, the standing crop of available and accessible greens needs to be only 0.0008 ounce per square foot (0.2 g per square meter). This level of availability would be like finely chopping a head of lettuce and scattering the cuttings over an acre (0.4 ha).

The water requirements of laying hens increase by 40 to 60% over non-laying birds. Daily intake will increase to about ⅓ jigger. Available and accessible greens for 15 laying females would have to increase to 0.0011 ounce per square foot (0.3 g per square meter) to meet the additional water requirement. Again, this level (ca. 1.5 heads of lettuce/ac.) would be extremely low.

Will bobwhite hens lay without drinking water? That is, will they lay if their sole source of outside water is that obtained from foods? Nancy E. Koerth, a research associate at the Caesar Kleberg Institute, addressed this question in the laboratory in the 1980s. Koerth divided birds into three groups, all of which received high protein laying ration: free water, free water plus dry lettuce, and fresh lettuce only.

The average rate of laying in the two groups receiving free water was one egg per two days. Birds on fresh lettuce laid one egg per three days. In this case, the absence of free water reduced the rate of egg production. The birds obtaining water from fresh lettuce, however, took in more water than those with free water available. The lettuce birds had to adjust to a high fiber diet, which may have been associated with the lower laying rate.

Results of this study demonstrated that bobwhites lay successfully when plant water is their sole source of water. Because population busts have occurred when ample plant water was available, water stress probably was not the cause of reproductive failure in drought. Suppose, however, for the sake of argument, that free water allows hens to lay during drought. This would not necessarily prevent a bust in production. Chicks must have insect foods to grow, develop, and survive during the first few weeks of life. Insects need succulent plants, without which, few or no insects would be available as chick foods; many chicks would perish.

Perhaps it is not surprising that quail populations have crashed during dry times despite ample free water. T. S. Robinson studied bobwhites in Kansas during the 1950s. One area (640 ac., 256 ha) he worked had eight ponds, or one pond per 80 acres (32 ha). In a year with normal rainfall, this area carried 462 bobwhites. After two years when summer rainfall was seven to eight inches below normal, the population declined to 165 birds. It cannot be concluded from Robinson's work that water had no effect. Perhaps the population would have dropped below 165 birds without the eight ponds. It can be said only that quail numbers declined severely (64%) despite a high availability of water.

I directed research in the 1980s to determine the value of supplemental water on a ranch in Jim Hogg County, Texas, for five consecutive years. The study included rainy and droughty years. We saw quail at waterers (1.0 waterer/20 ac.) (1 waterer/8 ha) on numerous occasions. Bobwhite abundance, however, was the same on study sites with and without supplemental water. Given the current state of knowledge, providing water to bobwhites is a luxury that sits near the bottom of a management priorities list, even in areas prone to drought.

THE MYTH REMAINS THAT BOBWHITE HENS DIP THEIR BELLIES in water to increase humidity at the nest, thereby fostering hatching success. See chapter 54, Falling into Cracks.

13   *Fire Ants*

ONE OF THE MORE INTERESTING CONTROVERSIES IN THE
annals of bobwhite biology involves the red imported fire ant, *Solenopsis
invicta*. Limited data, evolutionary surprises, and sheer speculation have
fueled the controversy. Recent developments, however, have given a measure of hope for a solution to the fire ant problem.

"Red imported fire ants . . . are native to areas along the Paraguay and
Parana Rivers of South America," reported to Craig R. Allen and associates of Texas Tech University, Lubbock in 1995. "[The species] was accidentally introduced to the United States around 1930, at the port of Mobile, Alabama. . . ." By the early 1980s, it occupied most of Mississippi,
Louisiana, Florida, Georgia, and South Carolina, and parts of North Carolina, Tennessee, Arkansas, Oklahoma, and Texas.

Gary Valentine, a U.S. Soil Conservation Service biologist in Temple,
Texas, compiled available information on fire ant–quail interactions in
the early 1980s. The following are capsule summaries of his findings and
other reports.

- In Georgia and southern Florida, Herbert L. Stoddard found that 34 of
  278 nests were taken over by fire ants in 1928. This 12% loss probably
  was caused by a native species, the tropical fire ant.
- In Alabama, A. S. Johnson, working in 1961 with penned quail forced to
  nest near mounds of black imported fire ants (*Solenopsis sp.*), recorded
  an 8% loss of 242 eggs to ants. He could not determine whether ants
  killed the chicks or fed on them after they had died from other causes.
  Quail counts showed no abnormal decrease in fall populations of bobwhites following fire ant invasion of an area in east-central Alabama; instead, a slight upward trend was observed.
- In Georgia, Oscar Dewberry reported in 1962 that 9% of 248 eggs were
  destroyed by ants. Losses to other causes totaled 24%. Incubating birds
  were not molested by the ants. The ants ate cracked quail eggs placed on
  their mounds.

- In the Southeast, Walter Rosene pipped Asiatic quail eggs near active imported fire ant mounds. He reported in 1969 that chicks hatched without damage.
- In southwestern Georgia, Ron Simpson found only 5 of 1092 nests destroyed by ants. Imported fire ants destroyed only 1 of the 5. Fall quail densities averaged about two birds per acre (5.0/ha) despite the presence of imported fire ants, he reported in 1976.
- In Jim Hogg County, Texas, Val W. Lehmann reported in 1984 fire ant damage to 1.5% of the eggs in 194 nests. The ants were probably native.
- In Brooks County, Texas, in the 1970s Ruben Cantu observed a possible loss of 3 of 40 eggs to fire ants. It could not be determined whether the ants killed emerging chicks or fed on them after they died from other causes.
- In Victoria County, Texas, in the fall of 1986, my research crew at the Ceasar Kleberg Institute estimated bobwhite density at 0.3 per acre (0.8/ha) on a pasture with 3.5 imported fire ant mounds per acre (8.8/ha). Quail density was 0.6 per acre (1.5/ha) on a pasture with 18.0 mounds per acre (45/ha). In other words, quail density was higher in the presence of more fire ant mounds.

These results did not condemn imported fire ants, but were not reassuring. Herbert L. Stoddard's vivid descriptions of fire ant damage (in this case, a native species) remained in the psyche of biologist and hunter alike. Then more observations on fire ant–bobwhite interactions were reported.

Biologists with the Texas Parks and Wildlife Department built pens on a site infested with red imported fire ants and observed nesting activity. Wild-trapped birds refused to nest in captivity, but one pen-reared hen laid and incubated. The biologist watching the nest saw that two eggs had pipped when the hen left to feed at 0850 h on September 8, 1987. When the hen returned at 0902 h, it pecked and ate ants until leaving the nest at 1028 h for five minutes. No ants were present when the hen returned. At 1245 h, the hen left the nest for a few minutes; another hen stole an egg during its absence. A hole in the stolen egg allowed the chick to struggle from its shell, but fire ants quickly killed the hatchling. Later, other birds ate ants from the dead chick. As eggs continued hatching, the hen pecked and ate ants more frequently. "It seemed like they knew what was happening and were doing their best to help chicks hatch," a M. R. Mitchell reported. At about 1700 h, the hen left the nest to feed and stretch and did not return until 1811 h. Fire ants swarmed the nest in its absence. The hen frantically ate ants for about one minute, then abandoned the nest. None of the 12 eggs hatched and survived. The pen-reared birds staved off fire ants for 10 hours.

Concern has been expressed over the possible effects of imported fire ants on the food supplies of bobwhite chicks. "It can be roughly estimated that there is over one to two and a half million tons of fire ant biomass in infested areas," observed Awinash Bhatkar, an entomologist with the Texas Agricultural Experiment Station, College Station in 1988. These incredible numbers could eat a lot of quail food.

"The invertebrates most susceptible to a fire ant invasion are probably those used as prey and those in direct competition for food or nesting space," Sanford D. Porter, an entomologist at the University of Texas, Austin reported in 1988. "Native species living on the ground, in leaf litter, or on stems and trunks would generally be the most susceptible because each of these areas is intensely scouted by foraging workers.

"Species living on vegetation would be at less risk because foraging pressure is less on leaves."

Little is known about fire ant effects on insect populations. Porter has stated that fire ants are known to control sugarcane borers (*Lepidoptera*) and reduce damage from boll weevils (*Anthonomus grandis*) in cotton. They also reduce tick (*Acarina*) populations. "Generally, the invasion of imported fire ants has resulted in a marked decline in the number and diversity of native ants," Porter reported. "We found many fewer pill bugs (*Isopoda*) in fire ant areas and fewer spiders in the summer." Porter, however, found a cricket (*Orthoptera*), a beetle (*Coleoptera*), and a roach species (*Orthoptera*) (all good quail foods) that were more common in areas with fire ants.

Around 1970, the imported fire ant problem took a turn for the worse when multiple queen (polygyne) colonies developed. Before then, single queen (monogyne) colonies had prevailed and the territoriality associated with them kept mound densities below 40 per acre (100/ha). Territoriality broke down with the advent of polygyne colonies; these colonies generally occurred at mound densities above 80 per acre (200/ha), with maximums exceeding 2000 per acre (5000/ha).

A research team at Texas Tech University directed by Scott Lutz began the first formal studies of fire ant–bobwhite interactions during the early 1990s, analyzing trends in bobwhite abundance of 15 Texas counties. They reported stable populations before the introduction of fire ants and declining populations thereafter. Bobwhites were stable in Texas counties lacking fire ants. The county trends were questionable, because the counties with fire ants included metropolitan areas: Dallas, Fort Worth, San Antonio, Corpus Christi, Denton, and College Station. Bobwhites would have declined in these areas with or without fire ants because of urbanization and human population growth.

Results of Texas Tech research in the Coastal Bend Region of Texas have provided further information on the fire ant–bobwhite interface. The researchers established five paired treatment and control areas. Fire ants were killed with chemicals in the treatment areas and left alone in the control areas. Bobwhite densities were measured to determine if the birds increased when the ants were removed. During the two years of study, autumn densities of bobwhites averaged about 0.8 per acre (2.0/ha) in the fire ant treatment areas versus about 0.4 per acre (1.0/ha) in the control areas. In other words, estimated bobwhite density was twice as high, on average, in areas without fire ants.

The density estimates provided other interesting information. One area without fire ant removal averaged more than 1.0 bobwhite per acre (2.5/ha) during the two autumns, and another with fire ant removal averaged only 0.2 bobwhite per acre (0.5/ha). Thus, it is possible to have high bobwhite densities in the presence of unmanaged fire ant populations. Likewise, it is possible to have low bobwhite densities even with fire ant control. The researchers concluded that polygyne red imported fire ants were negatively impacting bobwhites in the Coastal Bend Region of Texas. This conclusion supported management to suppress red imported fire ants.

"In its native range in Brazil, the red imported fire ant is just another ant," according to Lawrence E. Gilbert, Chairman of the Department of Zoology at the University of Texas, Austin. "Its densities are low, less than 10% of its mound densities in Texas, and it is patchy across the landscape rather than continuous as in Texas."

Gilbert concluded that imported fire ants were here to stay, and stated that standard approaches to fire ant control using pesticides have been a costly failure. "Pesticides used to control fire ants are not specific to it and kill competing native ant species as well. Since these native ants provide resistance against the invasion, pesticides work to soften that resistance and speed the takeover by *Solenopsis invicta*."

Gilbert's research crew at the Brackenridge Field Laboratory has discovered the fire ant's nemesis in South America. An obscure fly of the family Phoridae and genus *Pseudacteon* consists of about 40 species that parasitize and kill fire ants. These fly species are host-specific; i.e., a species of fly will attack only a particular species of fire ant.

The consequences of importing the fire ant parasites, however, must be carefully researched. Thus far, Gilbert has imported flies and conducted preliminary tests, and has gained permission for field releases. He has stated that ultimately, a combination of specific pesticides, native ants, and several phorid fly species that attack imported fire ants may be necessary to break up the solid carpet of fire ants in Texas. Once established, however, the native ants and phorid flies would not require further maintenance or expensive chemical fixes.

Part Two

MANAGEMENT

14 *The Value of a Seed*

CONSIDER KLEINGRASS (*PANICUM COLORATUM*), WIDELY recommended as beneficial to bobwhites on southern rangeland. This perennial bunchgrass provides palatable forage for livestock and good ground cover for bobwhites. Quail eat its seeds; however, the seeds are nearly worthless as quail food. The average Kleingrass seed weighs 0.000032 ounce (0.0009 g) and provides about 57 kilocalories of usable energy per ounce (28.35 g), which is roughly the amount a wild bird would need on a cold day. This wild bobwhite, if it lived on Kleingrass, would have to eat 32,870 seeds per day to balance energy demands with energy intake. If the bird foraged 10 hours a day (unlikely), it would have to eat a Kleingrass seed every second.

Consider common lespedeza (*Lespedeza striata*), widely recommended for quail food plots in humid environments. The average weight of one seed is 0.000052 ounce (0.001 g) and the amount of usable kilocalories in an ounce is 62. Assuming a bobwhite needs 60 kilocalories per day, it would have to eat 18,639 common lespedeza seeds to maintain body weight. This translates to 1 seed every 2 seconds in a 10-hour feeding period.

Consider grain sorghum (*Sorghum vulgare*), popularly known as milo. One seed weighs 0.0008 ounce (0.02 g), and an ounce provides 107 kilocalories of usable energy. A bobwhite requiring 60 kilocalories would have to eat 666 seeds, or 1 seed every 54 seconds in 10 hours.

Some seeds, obviously, are better than others. Many are too small and poor in nutritional quality to provide anything more than filler. Bobwhites will starve slowly on these types of seeds unless high quality foods also are eaten. The point about low quality seeds seldom receives attention in quail management; the traditional approach to food management has been based on foods found in craws. It was assumed that seeds eaten in large numbers were good, and those species were planted. Large numbers of seeds in the diet do not necessarily indicate high quality. In fact, large numbers sometimes indicate low quality. Now, however, if a bobwhite is shot and has 10,000 Kleingrass seeds in its craw, it would be known that the bird was starving.

Quail enthusiasts owe a debt of gratitude to Dr. Robert J. Robel and his students at Kansas State University, Manhattan. Thanks to their foundation research, the value of seeds and other quail foods is better understood and management can proceed on a more scientific basis. The value of a seed varies first with the amount of usable energy it provides. Animals cannot extract all the energy from foods they eat; that portion of total energy they can extract is called usable energy. Robel's research showed that seeds differ greatly in amounts of usable energy (see table).

Corn, soybeans (*Glycine max*), sorghum, common sunflower (*Helianthus annuus*), and western ragweed (*Ambrosia psilostachya*) provide more than 100 kilocalories per dry ounce. Examples of poorer seeds, from the standpoint of usable energy, are black locust (*Robinia pseudo-acacia*), hemp (marijuana) (*Cannabis sativa*), smartweed (*Polygonum* sp.), and common lespedeza; these foods yield less than 80 kilocalories per ounce.

The value of a seed also varies with its size. Wheat (*Triticum aestivum*) and Korean lespedeza (*L. stipulacea*), for example, each provide about 90 kilocalories of usable energy per ounce. A wheat seed, however, weighs 15 times more than a Korean lespedeza seed, and therefore provides 15 times more usable energy. A bobwhite could eat 650 wheat seeds or 9500 Korean lespedeza seeds to obtain sufficient energy on a cold day. Conceivably, a bird eating wheat would reduce its exposure to predation by limiting the time required for feeding. If it ate a wheat kernel every 15 seconds, it would spend 2.7 hours obtaining a daily energy fix. At the same feeding rate, the time required with Korean lespedeza is 39.6 hours; energy requirements could not be met during 10 hours of daylight. Seeds with relatively low amounts of usable energy can counteract this deficiency if they are relatively large.

To address skeptics who planted a food of marginal value, like lespedeza, and saw a positive response from bobwhites, there are plausible reasons for this to have happened. Food plots that are established where plant succession has advanced too far (i.e., too much grass is present) benefit quail by breaking the sod and allowing native weeds to move into the disturbed site. Under such conditions, benefits may accrue whether or not a quality seed producer is planted. Also, foods planted for seed could provide quality habitat for insects. As a group, these animals grow and develop best on plants with considerable water and high levels of

Seed type	No./lb.	Usable energy (kcal./oz.)	Seeds needed each day[a]
Corn	1200	109	41
Soybean	3000	109	103
Wheat	15,000	87	648
Grain sorghum	19,000	107	666
Common sunflower	32,000	103	1160
Black locust	24,000	72	1257
Hemp	27,500	71	1448
Partridge pea (*Cassia fasciculata*)	65,300	68	3605
Western ragweed	115,000	110	3923
Smooth sumac (*Rhus glabra*)	68,600	42	6152
German millet (*Setaria italica*)	220,000	98	8396
Korean lespedeza	225,000	89	9490
Thistle (*Cirsium* sp.)	288,000	77	14,057
Smartweed (*Polygonum* sp.)	260,000	65	14,952
Common lespedeza	310,000	62	18,639
Switchgrass (*Panicum virgatum*)	389,000	53	27,693
Kleingrass	497,000	57	32,870

[a] Number of seeds required to provide 60 kilocalories of usable energy, about enough for a wild bobwhite on a cold winter day.

nitrogen in leaves. A legume, such as lespedeza, offers these chemicals more abundantly than many other types of plant.

Based on Professor Robel's research, insects are the best bobwhite food available. The common cricket (*Gryllus* sp.) yields 139 kilocalories of usable energy per ounce, more than 30% greater than corn or sorghum.

What does this information mean to the food plot manager? To make food plots more effective, consider usable energy and size of seeds. Generally, seeds rich in oils are rich in usable calories. Seeds with less foliaceous material, like the husks of corn, provide more usable energy than seeds having more of that material. A larger seed often will contain more calories than a smaller seed. Corn and sorghum, for example, have similar amounts of energy per unit weight, but one corn seed provides more total energy than one sorghum seed because the corn seed is larger.

THIS ESSAY CAUSED A MILD STIR IN QUAIL CIRCLES WHEN IT first appeared. Upon completing the calculations, I was surprised at the number of seeds required for daily energy maintenance. The numbers seem shocking, and in fact, need to be put into perspective.

The estimates are based on a daily requirement of 60 kilocalories which is a large amount. A bobwhite living in the wild at freezing temperatures would require about 60 kilocalories based on Professor Robel's work. The figures were based on a cold day, and the number and quantity of seeds required will decline as air temperature increases.

Another consideration regarding the value of seeds is time. Bobwhites might spend more time eating low quality seeds than those of high quality. With reasonable amounts of time spent foraging, the quality of seeds becomes somewhat irrelevant and the increased exposure to predation is not all that serious.

15   *Food Management for Bobwhite Chicks*

WHEN A BOBWHITE CHICK HATCHES, IT HAS A THREE-DAY supply of energy remaining in the yolk sac. Soon, however, it must obtain a diet that provides nutrients for growth and survival. All growing animals require high levels of protein in their diet to build body tissues.

Bobwhite managers can take steps to ensure that chicks eat well. Ideally, their foods should average 28% crude protein during the first three weeks of life. Adult quail do well with 10 to 12% protein if not breeding; laying hens need foods averaging 23% protein. For a human perspective, a 20-year-old man needs only 7 to 10% in his diet.

Fig. 7. Bobwhite chicks require high levels of protein in their diet during the first three to four weeks of life. Insects and other invertebrates are essential at this time.
PHOTOGRAPH BY R. D. WILBERFORCE

People go to the meat counter for high protein foods. Likewise, bobwhite chicks seek insects and other meaty invertebrates. The bodies of insects are about 40 to 50% protein. Insects are also rich sources of methionine and cysteine, amino acids crucial for growth and feather development.

Management of foods for young chicks is largely a matter of managing grasshoppers (Orthoptera), beetles (Coleoptera), leafhoppers (Homoptera), and other invertebrates. It involves two considerations: abundance and availability. To increase insect abundance, preferred habitat must be provided; insect populations wax and wane with the diversity and succulence of forbs. Increases in diversity and succulence (referring to the amount of water in plants) will lead to higher insect abundance.

In arid and semiarid areas, rainfall plays a key role in insect abundance. Diverse groups of succulent weeds do not occur without rain. Rainfall, of course, is beyond the control of managers, but managers can create conditions to take advantage of the rain that does fall by giving weeds the opportunity to grow. Weeds are products of soil disturbance; grazing and discing are two practical methods of disturbing the soil to create plant communities that harbor insects. Both methods will reduce the abundance of grasses and prevent buildups of grass litter. This, in turn, will favor weeds, insects, and bobwhites.

As chicks age, plant foods become more important in their diet. Sprouting forbs (greens) are rich sources of vitamins and minerals, but their main contribution is water (see chapter 11, The Question of Water). Greens will occur in the habitat that was created for insects. Smaller grass seeds are also important. Laura Weaver, a graduate student at Texas A&I University, Kingsville, found in 1984 that grass seeds made up nearly 25% of the diet of younger bobwhite chicks. Ben Koerth, a researcher with the Texas Agricultural Experiment Station, reported similar results in 1986.

What types of grass seeds are eaten by bobwhite chicks? Botanists call them panicoid grasses, referring to a group with fairly large seeds (for grasses) wrapped in a material similar to human fingernails. The millets in wild bird seed at the grocery store are an example. Species important to quail include the panic grasses (*Panicum* spp.), bristle grasses (*Setaria* spp.), and paspalums (*Paspalum* spp.). Many of the grasses eaten by bobwhite chicks occur naturally on rangeland; thin paspalum (*Paspalum setaceum*) is common on deep sands and bristle grasses occur on a variety of soils.

Panicoid seeds can be purchased for planting; dealers sell millets (*Panicum* sp.), foxtails (*Setaria* spp.), and other species. If grasses are planted for chick cover management, bear in mind that dense stands of the grasses will inhibit the succulent weeds necessary to maintain insect populations. Plant the grasses at light seeding rates or in limited areas.

When their digestive tracts have matured, older chicks will eat the larger and more nutrient-rich seeds of forbs. Legume seeds, such as partridge pea, snoutbean, and milkpea, contain up to 30% crude protein. Seeds of croton, a food used heavily by older chicks and adults everywhere this plant occurs, consist of 20 to 25% protein. Many of these plants grow on disturbed soil.

Availability of foods is the second consideration in brood cover management. Chicks must be able to use the insect habitat created for them. The feeding grounds must be near suitable loafing cover. In the Southwest, broods need cool resting places for protection from the midday heat. Taller, older brush species, like brazil (*Candalia obovata*), granjeno (*Celtis pallida*), and lotebush (*Condalia obtusifolia*), provide dense shade and security from hawks (see chapter 5, Loafing Coverts).

Chicks will not use insect habitat created too far from loafing cover. Disc strips so they touch the edges of loafing coverts; strips disced along the edge between old and young brush provide many benefits. These include vegetation diversity and proximity to feeding and resting sites. If hot-day loafing coverts are lacking, build them. At least one elaborate loafing shelter surrounded by four or five simple brush piles is recommended (see chapter 5, Loafing Coverts). Space shelters at 100-yard (91-m) intervals or less in areas that have few natural loafing sites.

Keep in mind the physical attributes of bobwhite chicks when managing for food availability. Newly hatched chicks weigh a fraction of an ounce. They cannot plow through dense vegetation or travel long distances to obtain food and cover. To feed, they need ample amounts of bare ground shaded by the protective canopies of plants.

16 *The Thanksgiving Syndrome*

When goods increase, they are increased that eat them.
—ECCLESIASTES *5:11*

MODERN QUAIL MANAGERS SEEM TO HAVE DERIVED THEIR management philosophy from the *Old Testament,* operating under the assumption that more food for quail will result in greater quail numbers. This philosophy of striving to make everyday Thanksgiving Day for quail does not always solve problems for bird populations.

Quail managers are similar to other game managers on the question of food. Whether the target of management is ducks, geese, deer, or doves, FOOD PLOT is a major topic of discussion for outdoor writers and professional biologists alike. The fixation on food arises from a variety of sources. First, it is logical to provide food, because animals have to eat. Second, food management is a traditional approach to wildlife management. It has been going on since the days of Genghis Khan. Third, television and magazines carry graphic images of wildlife, particularly big game, starving during severe winters. The images are strong—a malnourished doe that can barely raise its head and is too weak to eat. When these images are seen, they elicit the sentiment: If only there had been more food.

What concerned conservationists do not see are images of healthy wildlife that survive hard winters with little loss. Game animals may do quite well, even if the nearest food plot is in the next state. Under some circumstances, it seems, food plots and similar management activities are unnecessary.

What are these circumstances? Before answering the question, the work of Margaret Nice will be examined. She was an amateur ornithologist with keen powers of observation. In 1910 Mrs. Nice wrote that a bobwhite needs about 12 pounds (5.5 kg) of seeds to live for one year. Subsequent research has shown her estimate to be remarkably accurate, if the seeds are of good quality and the winters not too severe. As a rule of thumb, multiplying the number of bobwhites desired by 12 will indicate the annual amount of seed (in pounds) that must be made available EXCLUSIVELY FOR THE BIRDS. Some multiple of 12 will be needed because not all food will go to quail. Nongame birds, rodents, and invertebrates eat some of the same seeds preferred by bobwhites. Natural weathering and decay also take seeds. Thus, for each bobwhite that is to be carried, more than 12 pounds of seeds must be supplied annually.

Assuming the desired average density from one spring to the next is 50 quail on a 100-acre area (40-ha), 600 pounds (273 kg) of seed will be needed each year (6 lb./ac. = 6.8 kg/ha). (This would be excellent habitat based on density.) What type of habitat might produce six pounds per acre (6.8 kg/ha) on an annual basis? Most agricultural crops would be too productive; irrigated corn yields roughly 4500 pounds per acre (5114 kg/ha), enough food for 375 bobwhites per acre (938/ha). Grain sorghum (dryland milo) yields 2000 pounds per acre (2273 kg/ha), enough to feed 160 bobwhites per acre (400/ha). Grasses such as foxtail, browntop (*Panicum ramosum*), and proso millet (*Panicum miliaceum*) produce 750–1500 pounds per acre (852–1705 kg/ha)—a year's supply of food for 60 to 120 bobwhites.

To put food requirements in another perspective, suppose just enough food plot is provided on each acre to produce six pounds (2.7 kg) of seed. Recall that an acre is about 70 square yards (58 m²). The corn plot would be roughly 60 square feet (5.5 m²), similar to the floor space of a bathroom; sorghum would require 121 square feet (11.2 m²), the size of a small office or bedroom. When food requirements are considered in terms of physical space, it becomes clear that bobwhites can be oversupplied.

One intensively managed quail operation in Duval County, Texas, in the 1990s had 20 acres (8 ha) of food plots that produced at least 1000 pounds per acre (1136 kg/ha) of good to high quality seed. This operation also provided supplemental feeding—one feeder per 6 acres (2.4 ha); each feeder dispensed 50 pounds (22.7 kg) of milo for five months each year. Enough energy was being produced and dispensed on this operation to support 25 bobwhites per acre (63/ha) year-around. This does not count unmanaged food sources, such as insects, wild fruits, and wild seeds, which may have added another 25 bobwhites per acre (63/ha) to the carrying capacity. Based on food supplies, this operation theoretically could have supported 50 bobwhites per acre (125/ha).

If food requirements are extremely low, food plots can be irrelevant—from the standpoint of food provisioning—in many situations. In other words, higher numbers of bobwhites would not be expected if food plots were provided, because food is not limiting in the first place. Research has not demonstrated increased quail densities with food plots, although the technical literature provides limited support for this management technique.

Professor Robert J. Robel determined that bobwhites living within 600 yards (546 m) of food plots had more body fat than those living more than 600 yards (546 m) from the plots. This would have a positive effect in areas subject to snowfall. The more body fat a quail has, the longer it can survive when food supplies are unavailable because of snow (see chapter 9, Fat Bobwhites).

Other biologists have not been impressed by food plots. Mike Porter with the Noble Foundation in Ardmore, Oklahoma, compared food plots and burning as management tools in tallgrass prairie in the 1980s. He observed net increases in quail abundance with burning, but food plots had little, if any, effect. Ronnie Howard, who manages bobwhites on the San Tomas Hunting Camp in the eastern Rio Grande Plains of Texas, points out that in semiarid environments subject to variable rainfall, managers must contend with the "irony of food plots": they are unnecessary in rainy years and will not grow in droughty years. In this context, there would be no point in planting foods.

It is one thing to question food plots as a management measure, and another to offer sound alternatives. In some settings, management may be unnecessary. Portions of the eastern Rio Grande Plains come to mind. Here, brush is well dispersed for loafing and escape cover, but not too dense. Native foods are abundant and, with some grazing, ground cover is ideal. Nothing can be added to this type of situation; the habitat is as good as it can be. A hallmark of prime quail habitat is that bobwhites can use each and every square inch of countryside, a condition termed 100% habitability (see chapter 27, Space, Time, and Relativity).

If areas are less than fully habitable, providing more usable space—not

Fig. 8. Research has yet to demonstrate that food plots established for bobwhites result in higher bird populations. PHOTOGRAPH BY DALE ROLLINS

more food—should be the key management concern. Space can be provided by establishing windbreaks or other types of permanent cover, especially in intensively farmed areas. Openings in mature forests, dense brush communities, or sod-bound prairies also can create usable space. If these openings are planted with food, one wonders if food or space would have the greater impact on bobwhite numbers.

The Thanksgiving syndrome, the attempt to oversupply populations with food, undoubtedly is hindering quail conservation. The syndrome is forestalling a full appreciation of bobwhite biology; one habitat deficiency is presumed and faith is being placed in a single management remedy. If food supplies are adequate, or if other habitat features are deficient, food management will not be rewarding.

FOOD PERMEATES THE HUMAN PSYCHE TO SOME LARGE (BUT subconscious) degree. The human system of socialization is based on food. Perhaps people have a food instinct, borne of trying times in the hinterlands of antiquity. Managers must be careful about separating human evolutionary longings from practical wildlife management.

17 *Thoughts on Supplementation*

PERHAPS NO BOBWHITE MANAGEMENT PRACTICE IS APPLIED with more vigor than supplemental feeding. Feeding makes sense, at least on the surface, but the practice may not benefit bobwhites.

Research biologists have tested feeding programs throughout the range of bobwhites by comparing populations on "fed" and "not fed" sites. The value of feeding cannot be evaluated without making this comparison. The experimental programs each had a high density of feeders and long feeding periods.

Roy Frye, working in Florida during the 1950s, fed year-round. Supplemental feeders, one per 63 acres (25.2 ha), were associated with a doubling in abundance; however, quail numbers in the fed area were less than impressive (0.18/ac. = 0.45/ha) and the program was inefficient.

James E. Keeler, in Alabama during the 1950s, fed cracked corn and wheat year-round, with a feeder every 40 acres (16 ha). At the end of four years, average autumn bobwhite densities on a fed and not fed area were identical.

Brad Gruver, in the Rolling Plains of northwest Texas during the 1970s, set out feeders at the density of one per 63 acres (25.2 ha). He fed a 2:1:1 mixture of high protein laying ration, corn, and grain sorghum year-round. There was no difference in average autumn density between a fed and not fed site.

Ted B. Doerr, performing research in the Gulf Prairies and Rio Grande Plains of Texas during the 1980s, fed milo from September through March. Feeder density was one per 25 acres (10 ha). On certain sites, supplementation improved winter survival, but had no effects on reproductive vigor or hunting season abundance of bobwhites.

Arlo H. Kane, working in the Texas Gulf Coast Prairies during the 1980s, fed milo during winter. Every 34 acres (13.6 ha) had a feeder. Average autumn bobwhite densities were similar at a fed and not fed site.

No one knows precisely why supplementing has failed as a population management tool. The reasons probably differ from area to area and from time to time; however, there are several potential causes of ineffectiveness. Perhaps other habitat problems were and are more serious than food deficiencies. Bobwhites have a suite of habitat needs. Supplementing cannot counteract a deficiency in cover quality or critical habitat availability.

Could feeders cause more problems than they solve? Some people believe feeding might increase predation, because it concentrates those animals using feeders into a small area. Rattlesnakes (*Crotalus* sp.) are known to form dens beneath feeders. Hawks have been observed perching in trees near feeders. Some predators, such as raccoons (*Procyon lotor*), eat feed put out for quail.

What about diseases and parasites? Mourning doves (*Zenaida macroura*), according to some reports, contract trichomoniasis, a protozoan disease, at feeders. Wild turkeys (*Meleagris gallopavo*) contract blackhead, another disease caused by protozoans. Perhaps bobwhites also become infected with diseases and parasites. The feed itself may be hazardous. Moldy feed can lead to aspergillosis, a fungal disease that results in pneumonia-like symptoms. Corn grown during drought carries aflatoxins, which kill poultry (including quail) raised in captivity. Turkey producers in the British Isles lost more than 100 thousand poults to aflatoxin poisoning in 1961.

Fig. 9. Supplemental feeding of bobwhite populations is practiced widely. Supplementation changes the distribution of coveys but appears to have neutral effects on populations.

Aflatoxins are colorless, odorless, and tasteless compounds produced by certain molds that contaminate feedstuff. (The molds are similar to the dark green mold that grows on bread or citrus fruits.) These mycotoxins reduce egg production, growth rates, and resistance to disease. They are among the most potent carcinogens. Quail biologists have recommended that aflatoxin contamination be kept below 20 ppb (parts per billion) in grains provided to wild quail, a level considered safe for domestic poultry. Recent research suggests higher levels would be safe in field supplement programs.

Based on studies in 1978 at the University of Florida, Gainesville, the mortality rate of bobwhite chicks up to four weeks old was similar between groups fed 400 ppb and groups receiving no aflatoxin. A short-term mortality rate, however, is not a good criterion upon which to base management decisions. Aflatoxins have insidious effects that may not appear until later in life. The recommendation that foods provided to wild chicks should contain less than 400 ppb, however, appears reasonable and safe.

Older bobwhites are more resistant than chicks to aflatoxins. Four-month-old birds can withstand 1000 ppb in the diet with few ill effects, based on 1985 research by Robert Gregory Stewart at the University of Georgia, Athens. The guarded management conclusion is that bobwhite managers should provide foods with less than 1000 ppb aflatoxins.

Why are quail more resistant to aflatoxins than domestic chickens and turkeys? Perhaps natural selection in quail has produced a genetic resistance to aflatoxin poisoning. Through time, those individuals vulnerable to aflatoxin would have been removed from populations by predators and other mortality agents. Genetically resistant strains of Japanese quail (*Coturnix coturnix*) have been produced in captivity.

Besides possible genetic resistance, diversity in the bobwhite diet may help cushion the effects of aflatoxins in supplemental feed. Wild quail do not (and cannot) survive solely on food supplements such as corn and milo. By maintaining this diversity in diet, toxin intake is lessened because the diet includes uncontaminated foods. University of Georgia researchers showed that when field corn was contaminated at 1200 ppb, well above the management guideline, the foods eaten by wild quail contained only 70 ppb. About 92% of the diet, by weight, consisted of uncontaminated food. In Florida, some bobwhites in areas with high aflatoxin contamination in corn were found to have no aflatoxins in the foods they had eaten, based on Robert Gregory Stewart's research.

Aflatoxin contamination of supplemental feed seems to be a relatively minor concern for wild quail. Nevertheless, managers should not ignore the danger posed by this mycotoxin. Managers should purchase supplemental feed with low levels of aflatoxin and store it under dry conditions to prevent growth of mold.

While it is hard to deny the potential health problems to bobwhites using feeders, the danger does not seem to be severe. In fact, on eight study sites in Texas, bobwhite density averaged 0.6 bird per acre on not fed areas and 0.7 per acre on fed areas. The odds are extremely high that the difference in density occurred because of chance factors associated with sampling bobwhite numbers; i.e., for all intents and purposes, densities were equal between areas. The point is that densities were not affected by feeding. Either the benefits of feeding were counteracted by disease and predation, resulting in no net response, or the problems were minor and feeding simply had no average effect.

If quail do not use feeders, feeders obviously would not be beneficial.

These birds, however, have been observed using feeders and feed scattered along roads. Perhaps bobwhites use supplemental feed less frequently than is believed. My research crew at Texas A&M University-Kingsville, radio-tagged bobwhites on a south Texas study area during the 1988–89 winter. The area had feeders at a density of one per 20 acres (8 ha). Grain sorghum was provided, a popular food with quail. Of 18 radio-tagged birds in which movements and habitat use were followed, one-third ranged over areas without feeders. About two-thirds lacked feeders in their core use areas, where they spent 75% of their time. These birds did not concentrate at feeders, which makes sense from a quail's perspective.

Sorghum or any other single food item is not nutritionally balanced. This imbalance would force birds to seek natural foods. Also, bobwhites may benefit from haphazard use of habitats. Irregular feeding patterns might help them discover alternative food supplies and render them less vulnerable to predation. Camping at a feeder would void these benefits.

Feeding programs are invariably inefficient. Little of the food put out gets into the craws of bobwhites. Consider the Florida study mentioned earlier. This experiment had eight feeders on 10 square miles (25.6 km^2) of land. From October through January, wildlife in the study area ate between 3000 and 7000 pounds (1364 and 3182 kg) of corn and hegari (a type of sorghum) (*Sorghum* sp.) each month.

Assuming the average was 4000 pounds (1818 kg) per month, this represents enough energy to carry about 4000 bobwhites for one month. Yet the area carried, on average, about 1150 quail. At a minimum, 71% of the energy put out for bobwhites went to songbirds, insects, rodents, and other nontarget animals.

The net gain associated with feeding was 510 bobwhites (ca. 1 covey/ 188 ac. = 1/75.2 ha). Despite the fact that density was two times higher in the fed area than in the not fed area, density was low in the fed area — about one covey per 85 acres (34 ha). Hunting begins to get good at about one covey per 30 acres (12 ha).

Yet another reason for failure of supplemental feeding is that the practice may be redundant; natural foods may be in adequate supply. Astonishingly low food supplies can carry high densities of bobwhites through southern winters.

Assume 100 acres (40 ha) support 80 birds on October 1, a high density. Assume further that 50% of the birds die by April 1, a reasonable expectation. If natural foods are of high quality, less than six ounces per acre (425 g/ha) dedicated exclusively to bobwhites, must be available at the start of October to carry the population to April.

How much seed might be available naturally in October? A fallow garden in Michigan had 457 pounds (208 kg) of weed seed per acre based on research by P. S. Baumgras in 1943. Assuming the seeds were of average nutritional quality and bobwhites could use the entire supply, there was enough energy on the acre to carry 60 bobwhites through winter. By the end of winter, this garden still had 13 pounds per acre (14.8 kg/ha) of weed seed. Bobwhite range in Kansas had 3,206,016 quality seeds (ragweed and sunflower) per acre (8,015,040/ha) in early October based on 1965 research by Professor Robert J. Robel. The supply dwindled to 714,385 per acre (1,785,962/ha) in late January. One study area in Texas had 1,080,000 quality seeds per acre (2,700,000/ha) in October; by March, 270,000 per acre (675,000/ha) remained.

In southern climes, insects and other invertebrate foods are available during most of the year. These rich foods would add to the energy supply provided by seeds. Thus, vast food supplies may be available to bobwhites entering winter. Remember that many other animals will be using these foods, that some foods will deteriorate, and that some will be unavailable to bobwhites. Despite these reductions, it is easy to see that supplementing quail in suitable habitat could be like supplementing weevils in a grain elevator.

18 *Prescribed Burning*

HERBERT L. STODDARD HAD ONE OF THE GREATEST INSIGHTS in the history of bobwhite management. He recognized that prescribed burning was a powerful method of managing bobwhite cover in the rain forests of the southeastern United States. In retrospect, he saw the obvious, but seeing the obvious is often quite difficult.

Certain questions remain about the value of fire in bobwhite ranges. One has to do with the danger fire might pose to individuals and coveys. "Bobwhites don't necessarily fly over or away from fire when their home range is burning," according to Carol Feather of the Texas Parks and Wildlife Department. From November 1993 to April 1994, Feather and other TPWD employees radio-tracked 50 wild-trapped bobwhites (wild birds trapped and fitted with radio transmitters) on the La Paloma Ranch in Kleberg County, Texas.

Three radio-tagged birds, in separate coveys, were monitored either during or after a prescribed burn on February 17, 1994. The signal from one female was monitored during the fire. This bird remained in the same area, even after being surrounded by fire; it did not flush, despite both the fire and the presence of 30 to 40 hawks hunting immediately following the burn.

The other two radio-tagged birds were checked the morning after the fire. One male flushed with about eight bobwhites from under a vine-covered mound of soil. One by one, they emerged from a hole in the ground. The area surrounding this hideaway was completely burned. A second male flushed with seven other quail from a woodrat (*Neotoma* sp.) hole in a clump of prickly pear cactus (*Opuntia* sp.). Both males had responded to the burned habitat by hiding in burrows created by small mammals.

Whereas fire per se does not seem to endanger bobwhites, the paucity of ground cover shortly after a burn could increase their vulnerability to predation. Bobwhites appear extremely sensitive of the degree to which they allow themselves to become exposed to hawks. Imagine a gigantic cone (upside-down dunce cap) emerging from the head of a bobwhite. The imaginary cone represents a volume of airspace; if a hawk is inside the cone, it has a direct line of attack to the bird. If the hawk is outside the cone, either it cannot see the bird or it would have to fly through obstructions to attack the bird.

The cone will be large—up to a hemisphere—when woody and herbaceous cover is sparse, and small when cover is abundant. Indeed, the cone will shrink to zero volume when a covey hides under the canopies of herbs or brush. Clearly, the survival advantage will go to those bobwhites that minimize the volume of their "head cones" by using cover as shields from raptors.

Ongoing research by my colleagues and I has demonstrated that bobwhites prefer a cone with zero volume, and rarely let the cone grow to more than 20% of the airspace they would be exposed to while standing in a plowed field. Burning, by removing cover, creates larger head cones for bobwhites. Therefore, patchy or small burns interspersed with unburned plots, probably would be best for bobwhites, if burning is desirable at all.

Loren M. Smith and Anthony P. Leif of Texas Tech University, Lubbock, reported in 1993 the response of bobwhites to prescribed burning on pastures dominated by redberry juniper (*Juniperus pinchoti*) (the "cedar" of the Rolling Plains). These pastures had been chained to take out large cedar 12 years prior to the experiment. The burn was done to remove woody debris and top-kill sprouting cedar. Improvement of quail habitat was not a consideration.

Common broomweed (*Xanthocephalum dracunculoides*) was more abundant on four-year-old burns than on sites without burning or on eight-year-old burns. Seeds of this broomweed, which are 25% fat, were a major food of blue quail and bobwhites in the area. Broomweed also created good ground cover. Despite the response of broomweed, bobwhites were more numerous on unburned pastures than on burned pastures. Densities were 17 birds per 100 acres (40 ha) on four-year-old burns, 22 per 100 acres (40 ha) on eight-year-old burns, and 24 per 100 acres (40 ha) on unburned pastures. Differences in density among pastures, however, were so low as to be meaningless from a management standpoint.

Smith and Leif recognized that this operational ranch management burning was planned poorly with respect to wildlife cover. No loafing coverts or travel lanes had been preserved. The researchers recommended burning 150- to 200-yard (137- to 182-m) strips alternating with preserved strips of the same width. Such a plan should increase forage production for livestock while improving habitat diversity for wildlife. Moreover, the preserved strips would provide desirable cover for quail.

Results of the Texas Tech research has shown that prescribed burning could fail as a management practice. Fire is most useful in high rainfall areas, especially forested areas, in which vegetation moves rapidly to junglelike conditions. Some quail plantations in the Southeast burn up to 75% of the land each year to foster livable conditions for bobwhites. Ron Masters of Oklahoma State University, Stillwater, says that annual and semiannual burning in the pine forests of eastern Oklahoma and western Arkansas best promote habitat and populations of bobwhites in this region.

Fire, however, is not a panacea for quail. In drought prone areas, fire

Fig. 10. Prescribed burning improves bobwhite habitat in regions with more rainfall, but could have neutral or detrimental effects in regions with less rain. PHOTO-GRAPH BY DALE ROLLINS

is not necessary to maintain excellent habitat, although it may be useful if applied infrequently. People have come to expect too much from prescribed burning because of the successful use of this practice in rainy environments.

SEVERAL YEARS AGO, I SPOKE AT A FIELD DAY ON THE RANCH where Texas Tech scientists conducted the research reported in this essay. We found cattle resting in the shade under a narrow line of mature juniper (cedar) that was preserved from brush control and burning. Cattle need shade during the heat of the day, just like wildlife. Research has shown that cattle gain weight more rapidly in the presence of shade.

Brush control programs that result in the clearing of large areas not only sacrifice cattle performance, but also affect populations of game. The end result is lost opportunities for hunters and lost revenue for landowners.

Finally, this brief essay in no way does justice to the technology associated with prescribed burning. The literature on the ecological effects of fire is vast. My main purpose in writing the essay was to point out that fire can fail as a management practice for bobwhites.

19 *The QUAILity of CRP Fields*

"PLANT KLEINGRASS AT A RATE OF *ONE SEED PER ACRE* AND disc the entire stand every two or three years," was my tongue-in-cheek recommendation on proper management of Conservation Reserve Program (CRP) fields when the program started. Prescriptions for management of CRP fields, as legally constrained (no brush, no weeds), are similar to prescriptions for ridding an area of bobwhites. Brushless, weedless, undisturbed grasslands are bankrupt quail habitat.

The CRP was established as part of the Food Security Act of 1985. Although the program was intended to reduce soil erosion and grain surpluses, wildlife benefits were expected. The program involved planting cropland with grasses that largely would be left undisturbed, thereby providing cover for quail and other wildlife.

"We examined three indexes of northern bobwhite abundance in Illinois at various geographic scales to determine possible relationships with the Conservation Reserve Program," reported John L. Roseberry of Southern Illinois University, Carbondale, in 1994. "There was no strong evidence that autumn population densities increased as a result of the program."

Roseberry and co-workers gauged the abundance of bobwhites in areas with total harvest (number of birds) in the area, estimated harvest per hunter trip, and counts of whistling males. These abundance indexes were expected to increase as the population increased. Roseberry identified three possible reasons why the CRP program had little, if any, effect on bobwhite abundance: (1) only a small percentage of the land was enrolled in CRP; (2) the CRP fields were arranged poorly relative to other permanent cover; and (3) most CRP fields were planted with cool-season grasses (e.g., tall fescue [*Festuca arundinacea*]) that provided inferior cover for bobwhites.

"Tall fescue is the dominant grass seeded in Conservation Reserve Program plantings in the central and southcentral United States," reported Thomas G. Barnes of the University of Kentucky, Lexington. "It has excellent agronomic properties as a pasture grass." Barnes and co-workers analyzed tall fescue plantings relative to habitat quality and food availability for northern bobwhites and reported their results in 1995. "Tall fescue fields studied in Kentucky during 1990–1991 had dense vegetation with little bare ground and low plant species diversity," according to Barnes. Low diversity means there were few different species of plants. "Thus, northern bobwhites did not have an opportunity to select high quality, preferred foods. Available food did not meet basic requirements for growing and breeding quail."

"Invertebrate populations appeared diverse and abundant, but were likely inaccessible to bobwhite chicks." The dense vegetation structure prevented bobwhites from occurring where these important foods (i.e., insects and spiders) were available. Barnes and co-workers concluded that tall fescue plantings provided unacceptable habitat for bobwhites because of improper vegetation structure and composition and low food supplies.

"In retrospect," Roseberry reported, "we believe CRP value for bobwhite in Illinois would have been enhanced had there been: (1) less mowing, especially mid-summer mowing, (2) more weedy vegetation via strip discing and controlled burning, (3) [more planting of warm-season grasses and less cool-season grasses], especially tall fescue, and (4) more provision of food in the form of food plots or Korean lespedeza seedings."

The legal constraints on management of CRP fields (no brush, no weeds) impose hardships on bobwhite populations, which probably will keep them from reaching their full potential under most circumstances. Nevertheless, certain acceptable practices should benefit quail:

1. Plant a warm-season bunchgrass as opposed to a cool-season grass or a sod-forming grass. Bunchgrass communities have bare interspaces between clumps in which quail can move and find seeds easily. Conversely, sod-forming grasses create continuous turf that impedes movement and hides seeds. In southern latitudes, Kleingrass, a manageable bunchgrass, would be preferable to Bermuda grass (*Cynodon dactylon*). Avoid buffel grass (*Cenchrus ciliaris*) (a bunchgrass) in most situations, because this aggressive foreign grass seems to inhibit native plants that are more valuable to wildlife.
2. Plant large-seeded as opposed to small-seeded bunchgrasses. With the exceptions of corn and sorghum, grass seeds are of minor nutritional value to bobwhites, but larger seeds are better than smaller seeds (see chapter 14, The Value of a Seed). The bristle grasses have larger seeds

than Kleingrass (*Panicum coloratum*), blue panic (*Panicum antidotale*), or switchgrass.

3. Plant perennial forbs to the maximum extent permissible. Forbs provide better habitat for insects than grasses, and insects are the number one quail food.

4. Take full advantage of allowable soil disturbance programs such as food strips. If a strong response from native forbs can be foreseen, simply disc strips throughout the CRP field and seed some acceptable food plant at a low rate. Select a food plant that has large, energy-rich seeds, such as annual sunflower, sesame (*Sesamum indicum*), cowpeas (*Vigna unguiculata*), or sorghum.

5. Make sure quail can use all of the CRP field at all times. Generally, ground cover will be more than sufficient. Woody cover for protection during rest periods may be insufficient.

On the Bomer Wildlife Research Area in southern Duval County, Texas, five clusters of six tepee shelters were established to create woody loafing cover in a CRP field (see chapter 5, Loafing Coverts). The six shelters in a cluster were set on a 10- by 15-yard grid (9.1- by 13.7-m). With one natural motte, the clusters provided a loafing covert for each 10 acres (4 ha).

On the Bomer CRP field, huisache (*Acacia farnesiana*), mesquite, retama (*Parkinsonia aculeata*), and willow baccharis (*Baccharis salicina*) were invading and had to be controlled in accordance with the contract. The invasion, however, points out that woody cover will move into CRP fields. As far as local regulations permit, limited amounts of this brush perhaps could be preserved as woody cover for bobwhites. If planting is permitted, a low, evergreen shrub with a dense canopy would be desirable. Candidates for south Texas include brazil and granjeno; skunkbush sumac (*Rhus aromatica*) and wild plum (*Prunus* sp.), although deciduous, would provide good cover in north Texas and Oklahoma.

THE MAJOR DEFICIENCY OF CRP FIELDS IS WOODY COVER. Clusters of tepees receive use from bobwhites, but this use seems to occur largely during spring and summer. The ideal density of clusters is probably around 25 per acre (62.5/ha), which would be a huge investment in materials and effort. Bobwhite populations, however, cannot be expected to fare well at cluster densities of 1 per 5–10 acres (12.5–25.0 ha).

Also, the image of buffel grass in the range of bobwhites has improved since the above essay was written. Buffel grass may provide the only herbaceous cover in some areas inhabited by bobwhites, and respectable densities of birds have been measured where buffel grass was the dominant herb.

Recent changes in federal law permit stronger wildlife considerations in the management of CRP fields. The planting of woody cover in such fields is permitted, and in some cases, encouraged.

 ## 20 *The Economics of Bobwhite Management*

A PERSON IN THE COMMERCIAL HUNTING BUSINESS HAS TO view dollars spent on management as an investment. If a practice is cost-effective, it will return the money invested plus profit. In planning an investment, the commercial operator must estimate the revenue that will be gained by improving the program. In Texas, each bird per 100 acres (40 ha) is worth at least U.S.$0.05 in terms of the fair lease price. If a program increases the density of bobwhites by 10 birds per 100 acres (40 ha), it has increased the lease value of the property by about $0.50 per acre ($1.25/ha).

A recreational hunter – manager, on the other hand, is not interested in profit. This person spends money simply for the entertainment value (fun) of successfully managing and hunting quail; the primary financial concern is the cost of each quail produced — the lower, the better.

Grazing provides the most cost-effective management tool in this day and age. Consider a sandy prairie in the eastern Rio Grande Plains that lacks grazing. Bobwhite density would probably hover around 20 birds per 100 acres (40 ha), giving a fair lease price of $1.00 per acre ($2.50/ha). By simply introducing the proper number of cattle, density could climb to 80 birds per 100 acres (40 ha) and the fair lease price rise to $4.00 per acre ($10/ha). If the cattle can be maintained without further cost, the quail would be free. The lease value of the property would increase by $3.00 per acre ($7.50/ha) with no investment. (Admittedly, the accounting methods used here are somewhat creative.)

Fig. 11. Grazing by livestock may be the most economical way to increase bobwhite populations in a given area. This photograph illustrates how cattle reduce the amount of cover, churning the soil with their hooves. Here, too much ground cover has been taken, and the stocking rate of cattle should be reduced.

Mechanical brush control (e.g., roller chopping or discing) is a practice that can cause bobwhite populations to boom; however, the economics are not as good as those of grazing. During the 1980s, my students and I measured the response of bobwhites to brush management on a ranch in south Texas. A pasture was disced in a strip pattern to remove about 70% of the mature brush. The discing not only improved habitat structure by lowering the age of brush but also created extensive soil disturbance. Food plants bloomed and quail thrived. Average bobwhite density exceeded 100 birds per 100 acres (40 ha) on the treated plot versus about half as many on an untreated plot. Respective fair lease prices were $5.30 and $2.75 per acre ($13.25 and 6.88/ha).

While this was a substantial increase, the management was not cost-effective. The annual cost of the discing, expected to last five years, was $9.23 per acre ($23.08/ha), with an annual loss of about $4.00 per acre ($10.00/ha). In a recreational sense, discing was also expensive. Cost per each additional bird averaged about $18.00 each year; quail bought from a commercial breeder cost about $3.00 per bird.

Other brush treatments have proven cost-effective for commercial operators. Quail responded well to roller chopping in one Texas experiment done by Sam L. Beasom in the 1980s. (A roller chopper is a heavy drum with blades; it chops brush stems into football-length pieces when pulled behind a tractor.) The response was so strong that the increase in bobwhite numbers paid for the treatment. A concomitant increase in income from the livestock operation and a positive deer response represented almost pure profit.

Supplemental feeding (see chapter 17, Thoughts on Supplementation) and supplemental watering (see chapter 12, Another Shot of Water) are practices of questionable economic merit, because populations do not increase with supplementation. The cost per bird of bobwhites produced from feed or water supplementation is roughly equal to that of a stealth bomber.

Food plots also fail to make economic sense. The cost of fencing, fertilizing, and seeding a one-acre (0.4-ha) food plot for quail could reach $430.00, according to Alan D. Peoples of Oklahoma State University, Stillwater. Peoples calculated costs at $300.00 per acre ($750.00/ha) for fencing, $20.00 ($50.00/ha) for seedbed preparation, $50.00 ($125.00/ha) for seed, $10.00 ($25.00/ha) for drilling, $5.60 ($14.00/ha) for burning, and $50.00 ($125.00/ha) for fertilizing. The cost of food production was found to be the least expensive using the most expensive treatment. The costs per pound (0.45 kg) of food produced were $0.42 using fence–plant–fertilize, $0.69 using burning, $0.76 using fence–disc, $1.02 using fence–plant, and $1.76 using fence–disc–fertilize. Note that "plant" involves seedbed preparation, seed, and drilling.

"In common, everyday . . . English," Peoples wrote, "what does this research tell us about quail management? This is where scientists get nervous; we all get cold feet when pushed to make conclusions based on preliminary research results.

"But let me cautiously suggest that the management of native plant species may be a more cost-effective means to producing quail foods than the planting of domestic varieties in our study area."

GRAZING IS COST-EFFECTIVE ONLY IF IT CAN BE APPLIED under preexisting habitat conditions. In the more arid portions of bobwhite range, grazing does not benefit populations.

The cost estimates given above held for 1990.

21 *Weird-year Management*

THE 1996 PRODUCTION YEAR IN THE RIO GRANDE PLAINS OF Texas was one of the strangest on record. The region endured a blistering drought from January through mid-August. Even buffel grass, an aggressive alien from South Africa, withered and crumbled. The soil baked like pottery. Prickly pear wilted. Temperatures on the ground were hot enough to kill bobwhites and blue quail.

Then, about mid-August, rain squalls appeared and hell turned into paradise. Butterflies hatched in huge numbers, stock tanks overflowed, buffel grass reemerged, and quail populations responded with one of the strongest late-season hatches of the last decade. Hens were flushed from nests even in November.

The year was weird because an apparent bust turned into a reasonable production year. Drought, rain, and a glut of very young quail during hunting season raised several questions about management: Is hunting an additive mortality factor such that one should reduce pressure during droughty times? One cannot simply ask if harvest is an additive mortality factor, meaning it adds to rather than compensates with total mortality (see chapter 43, A Trilogy on Quail Harvest Management, Fuzzy Logic).

There is no single answer. The killing of a quail with a shotgun is always additive to some degree and compensatory to some degree. This statement will hold unless all the quail are going to die, in which case harvest would be fully compensatory; the same population number — zero — would result whether or not harvest occurs.

Harvest mortality might be additive to a greater degree in low populations than in high populations. When low populations result from weak production, the population will consist primarily of adults. These adults are survivors in a Darwinian sense, meaning they are better fit to deal with the hardships in nature than a bird in a normal or high population. Survivors also have experience, and this learning makes them even better survivors. The more survivors there are in a given population, the more hunting mortality becomes an additive factor.

Computer simulations suggest that the optimum harvest with low populations is no harvest, i.e., no harvest of low populations maximizes long-term yield. Under this scheme, the manager can maximize the total number of quail taken during a series of years. Light harvest (ca. 5%) of low populations, however, would have little effect in the long term; i.e., populations will be about the same whether they are unharvested or lightly harvested during bust years.

Acknowledging that quail cannot be stockpiled, would a more conservative harvest in poor years carry some breeding adults over in years of low population numbers? This is basically the same question as above, but with a twist. The often repeated notion that quail cannot be stockpiled began at least 50 years ago. The notion is acceptable over a time frame of several years. For example, suppose a state has a good, strong quail population and a group of uninformed but politically persuasive hunters convinces the state legislature to close the hunting season for five years to build up the quail population. It will not work. If the population is strong to begin with and normal weather patterns ensue, the population number will be about the same after five years.

On the other hand, quail can be stockpiled in specific areas at specific times. During the late 1980s, my research group at Texas A&M University-Kingsville, analyzed bobwhite populations on two ranches in South Texas. On one ranch, which was hunted, the total winter loss was attributable to harvest. The second ranch had no harvest and virtually no loss of quail. "We decided to save them for breeders," the rancher said. So he stockpiled his quail, successfully.

If quail populations cannot be stockpiled, it is difficult to imagine how populations could ever increase from the lowest level ever reached. Since populations do not remain at the lowest level, it must be possible to stockpile quail, at least within a reasonable time frame.

What about situations involving a late hatch like this year? How would that change the way quail are to be harvested? Will winter mortality be higher on these young birds and necessitate reduction of harvest? This question raises an issue of hunter preference: Are full-sized birds desired? If so, hunting should be delayed until most birds reach adult size.

Research biologists have convincing evidence that survival of younger birds is lower than that of older birds. Younger birds die at a faster rate. By virtue of age-dependent survival and a strong late hatch, managers might expect higher than average winter mortality. This, however, is not necessarily a sound reason for reducing the harvest. Harvest mortality becomes more compensatory as natural mortality increases.

Fig. 12. When drought strikes southwestern rangeland, ranch hands may burn the spines off prickly pear to provide forage for cattle. When the rains return, areas like that pictured will bloom with grasses and forbs. Deluges that follow short, stiff droughts raise questions about population management.

What about predator control in drought years? Is it something a landowner should consider? This is a difficult question and will be addressed from the standpoint of nesting success.

Birds are classified as determinate or indeterminate layers. Determinate layers produce only one nest. Indeterminate layers produce two or more nests; they renest and have multiple broods. As a rule of thumb (although subject to several exceptions), predator control benefits determinate layers but has neutral effects, if any, on indeterminate layers. The difference arises because the probability of at least one successful attempt increases with the number of attempts.

Because quail are indeterminate layers, one would question the benefits of predator control. Quail, however, may become determinate layers in drought years. They may have only one chance for nesting success, early in the nesting season when air temperatures are acceptable. Later in the season during drought years, many quail quit laying because of high temperatures. In principle, it would seem possible that predator control could elevate production. My dissertation research in South Texas, however, revealed that predator control (coyotes, foxes, raccoons, bobcats, opossums) had no effect on populations of blue and bobwhite quail in either drought or rainy years.

22   *Management Makes a Difference*

"BARBERSHOP BIOLOGISTS" IN SEMIARID QUAIL RANGE SAY that habitat management is pointless. "If it rains," they say, "we'll have lots of quail. If it don't, we won't."

While this defeatist attitude has elements of truth, it paints with too broad a brush. Many details get lost in the generalization. Rain on southwestern quail range can be good, bad, or indifferent. Regardless of rain, management does make a difference.

Rain, however, is also important. Water of any kind is sparse in semiarid regions, particularly during late summer and early fall. Rain during the growing season usually benefits quail and other wildlife in several ways. Fall rains stimulate cool-season weeds that are primary sources of water, vitamins, and minerals during late fall, winter, and spring.

Some people believe that spring and summer rains trigger the breeding instinct. This belief, however, makes little sense. The length of day is the primary determinant of breeding urges, and it does not vary from year to year. Warm-season rains set the stage for high chick survival and persistent renesting if early clutches fail. The rains cause germination of the succulent grasses and weeds that support the insects needed in large quantities by laying hens and young chicks. Rains and associated effects cool the quail house; cooler quail houses lengthen the laying season. Nonbreeding adults also benefit from warm-season rains. Research by Nancy E. Koerth and me, published in 1988, has shown that downpours during the growing season are associated with more body fat. Birds fatten within two months and the effects last up to six months.

Winter rains, on the other hand, may be associated with lowered body condition. Birds may be unable to eat enough to maintain fat reserves during cold, rainy winters. Gully washers during peak laying and hatching periods can flood nests and drown chicks. In many areas, the problem for bobwhites is too much rain, not too little. Too much rain leads to rapid plant succession, dense stands of tall grasses, and low quail numbers. Rain, for certain, has a downside for bobwhites.

In wet or dry climates, however, habitat management can lessen the negative effects of too much or too little rain. In dry climates, it is easy to show, in a management sense, flaws in the wait-till-it-rains logic. One needs only to consider the concept of habitability: TO MAXIMIZE QUAIL NUMBERS, 100% OF THE AREA MUST BE HABITABLE. If less than 100% of the area is habitable, then the area must be managed to maximize population sizes.

Suppose, for example, a 1000-acre (400-ha) pasture consists of dense, tall brush that provides marginal habitat. Seismograph lines and ranch roads crisscross the area, giving about 200 acres (80 ha) of suitable cover. During poor years, density averages 20 birds per 100 acres (40 ha) on suitable habitat, giving a total population of 40 quail.

With brush management, the population can be increased fivefold, even during poor years. If the age of the brush is reduced with a roller chopper or rangeland disc, 100% of the pasture can be made habitable. Evenly distributed stands of old brush will need to remain. Then at 20 birds per 100 acres (40 ha) during drought, 200 quail instead of 40 will be carried.

The positive response of bobwhites to brush management has been well documented. Rangeland discing, for example, can improve habitat structure by reducing the age and height of woody cover. On Rancho El Carrizo in Sonora, Mexico, discing has been used to increase livestock forage as well as to improve habitat for the endangered masked bobwhite (*Colinus virginianus ridgwayi*) (see chapter 49, La Perdiz Mascarita). Bobwhites persist in this area despite average annual rainfall of only 14 inches (35.6 cm).

Double chaining of mature brush improves habitat and increases numbers of bobwhites in south Texas, according to W. P. Kuvlesky, Jr., and W. G. Swank, who conducted research at Texas A&M University's La Copita Research Area near Alice in the late 1980s. Chaining is a mechanical method of brush control in which a large ship's anchor chain is pulled between two crawler tractors. The practice flattens trees and older brush plants, and may uproot them on the second pass in the opposite direction (double chaining). Young brush plants with supple stems are not affected for the most part.

"Our data indicate that quail are not particularly fond of mature South Texas brush," the researchers reported, "and hunters are even less enthusiastic about hunting them there. Essentially, quail like areas that are characterized by sparse, low-growing shrubs, a high forb species diversity, a relatively large amount of bare ground, high forb coverage, and less grass coverage and plant litter. They seek and use the areas that are more open . . . than the norm."

Bobwhite harvest on a chained pasture ranged between 30 and 60 birds per 100 acres (40 ha) during 1983 and 1984. In an unchained area, harvest averaged less than one bird per 100 acres (40 ha). The chained area made up less than 15% of the research area, but contributed 52% of the bobwhite harvest.

Bobwhite populations in Jim Hogg County, Texas, responded better to brush management than to food and water supplementation during the 1988–89 drought. Brush discing in strip patterns resulted in a net gain of 29 birds per 100 acres (40 ha) compared to an unmanaged site, whereas supplementation had little, if any, effect. Why?

"Many rangelands and pastures with undesirable soil and vegetation characteristics have such low water storage capacities that plant stress is inevitable when rains do not occur frequently," according to C. Wayne Hanselka of the Texas Agricultural Extension Service. These undesirable characteristics not only lower forage production for livestock, but also lower habitat quality for bobwhites. "Water must enter the soil before it can be stored for later use by plants," Hanselka stated. If soil compaction becomes a problem, rain will run off or puddle and evaporate.

Rangeland renovation involves breaking up soils that have been compacted or breaking up hardpans that prevent infiltration of water into the soil. Plows, chisels, discs, and aerators are implements used for this purpose.

Research has indicated that management also can raise the carrying capacity of habitable land during poor years (i.e., drought). I first became aware of this principle based on research I directed in the High Plains of Texas, where we established managed plots on the Pitchfork Ranch in the 1970s. Management consisted of strip discing, half-cutting, and erecting brush shelters. On a sandy loam pasture garbed in mesquite and pencil cactus (*Opuntia leptocaulis*), bobwhite density was six times higher on the managed plot than on the unmanaged plot during a drought year. Density was twice as high with management during a wet year.

The beneficial effects of habitat management became apparent in south Texas during 1984. This year saw millions of acres denuded of weeds and grasses as spring and summer rains failed. Cattle and deer died; termites fed on plant skeletons. Bobwhite populations also suffered throughout the region. High densities, however, were found on a ranch using intensive habitat management in Hidalgo County. Density was five times higher on the managed ranch than on a check ranch that lacked intensive management. Subsequent counts showed that density averaged about two times higher on the managed ranch.

Counts after the 1984 drought further validated the positive effects of management. Population trends on several ranches have been monitored since then. Birds on managed ranches reached normal to high densities within one or two years after the drought; it took three years for populations to rebuild on unmanaged ranches.

The naysayers who trust only rainfall serve neither themselves nor the quail resource. While reasonable management practices cannot fully reverse the negative impact of low rainfall, the practices can lessen the severity of the population decline. It is fair to say that, with management, lows will be higher and highs will be higher as populations fluctuate. The moral of the story is to not wait for rain before beginning habitat management.

THE OPENING SENTENCE OF THIS ESSAY WAS NOT MEANT TO offend barbers, although I know it offended one because he told me so. By using the term barbershop biologist, I was trying to describe the mind-set that arises when something is talked about over and over without considering exceptions to generalizations and understanding the underlying processes.

Rainfall is a powerful influence on quail populations in semiarid environments. Rainfall may explain 40–80% of the variation in quail production and populations in dry environments. This leaves 20–60% of the variation left for management to address.

Readers should keep in mind that the management that is applied should make biological sense, and that certain management activities are neutral. Also, when bobwhites occur in habitat that is operationally perfect, no management practice can influence their abundance.

23 Effective Management

YOU HAVE PROBABLY HEARD ABOUT THE ZEALOUS YOUNG research assistant who studied cockroaches. One day, in a dither, he called in his major professor to demonstrate an experiment. He selected a cockroach and set it on a table.

"Forward march!" he yelled, and the cockroach walked away.

He selected another, repeated the command, and again the insect marched off.

He removed the legs from the third subject. When he yelled "Forward march!" the cockroach just sat there.

"I've proven," said the young researcher, "that cockroaches hear with their legs."

Whether one is a naive scientist or a quail manager, observations can be misinterpreted. Misinterpretations lead to faulty management policy, wasted effort, and sloppy expenditures. In short, they lead to bad quail management. To gauge the effectiveness of specific management practices, one can follow certain principles to ensure sound interpretations of what is being observed.

First, beware of CONFOUNDING. This occurs when the effects of one practice are hopelessly entwined with the effects of other practices. Imagine starting a management program consisting of strip discing, food plots, and brush shelters. Better hunting is observed after the program has been running a couple of years than before it was running. The food plots, however, are expensive: U.S.$50.00 per acre ($125.00/ha) for seedbed preparation and seeding, and additionally, fencing the plots at $1.10 per foot ($3.62/m) becomes necessary because of cattle.

If one asks the extent to which the food plots are contributing to management success, there is no way of answering the question. The management effects of food plots are confounded with the effects of disced strips and brush shelters. Which practice is to be credited with the better hunting? If all practices are beneficial, what is the relative importance of each?

To determine the benefits of a specific management practice (i.e., to avoid confounding), that practice must be applied with other practices being controlled. For example, in the 1980s we studied the effects of brush management, food management, and supplemental watering in Jim Hogg County, Texas. We had one area with no management, one with brush management alone, one with brush management plus food, and one with brush management plus food and water. With this approach, we were able to isolate the effectiveness of each practice. The area with no management is called an experimental control. Controls are crucial to measure the effectiveness of a program. Lack of an experimental control can — and often does — lead to misinterpretations.

In 1987, I spoke to a group on the economics of quail management practices. I argued that feeding and watering were extremely expensive in terms of their beneficial effects on population density (see chapter 20, The Economics of Bobwhite Management). During the lunch break, an individual cornered me and said that I was wrong. "I put in feeders and waterers this year," he said, "and my place is crawling with quail."

The year 1987 was a boom year. Counts by the Texas Parks and Wildlife Department were the highest on record. Almost everywhere was "crawling with quail," whether grazed or not grazed, managed or not managed, fed or not fed. If the individual had an experimental control, a portion of his area without food and water supplementation, he most likely would have found similar populations in each area. Because he lacked an experimental control, he almost certainly misinterpreted the effects of supplementation.

After an experimental control has been established to guard against confounding, how can a quail response be measured? Research biologists frequently use one of two fairly technical methods of analyzing quail density (see chapter 28, Counting Bobwhites). One method consists of capturing and leg-banding birds and maintaining records on the number of banded and unbanded quail in the harvest. The other method entails walking straight lines through pastures and recording the number of birds in coveys and the right-angle distance from the line at which coveys flushed.

A rough idea of breeding response can be obtained by analyzing age ratios of birds in the harvest. Keep track of the number of adults and immatures in the kill. Adults lack white tips on the primary covert feathers of the wing. Immatures (birds hatched in the immediate past breeding season) have white tips on these feathers. If the age ratio (immatures/

adults) is higher on the managed area than on the experimental control, this is circumstantial evidence that the management increased breeding success. Age ratios, however, can be misleading as they reflect relative survival of adults as well as their productivity. Two populations theoretically can have the same age ratio while one is plummeting to extinction and the other is increasing at a high rate.

Thus, some idea of population density is needed. A simple and effective index of density is hunting success rates. Maintain records of hours spent hunting and number of coveys flushed. Calculate coveys flushed per hour on managed and control areas. If the success rate is higher on the managed area, this again is evidence that the management was effective.

To have confidence in the analysis, fairly large samples are required in terms of the number of birds harvested for age ratios or the number of hours hunted. This is because a good deal of chance is involved in determining age ratios and hunting success. Larger samples reduce, but do not eliminate, possible misinterpretations arising from chance processes. To gain a sound idea of management success, information from three or more years or from three or more management areas (each with an experimental control) should be obtained. People who want to measure the results of management activities can get help from extension biologists or consultants.

INCIDENTALLY, SOME TYPES OF INSECTS HAVE HEARING organs in their legs.

24 Aldo Leopold (1887–1948) on Bobwhites

"MAN THINKS OF HIMSELF AS NOT SUBJECT TO ANY DENSITY limit. Industrialism, imperialism, and that whole array of population behaviors associated with the 'bigger and better' ideology are direct ramifications of the Mosaic injunction for the species to go the limit of its potential, *i.e.,* to go and replenish the earth.

"But slums, wars, birth-controls, and depressions may be construed as ecological symptoms that our assumption about human density limits is unwarranted; that we may yet learn a lesson from the lowly bobwhite, which . . . 'refuses' to live in slums, and concentrates his racial effort on quality, not ciphers. Where his racial exuberance gets the upper hand and causes him to depart occasionally from the rule, he suffers economic cycles and social unrest, and his civilization relapses to near-zero for a new start." Aldo Leopold penned these words in *Game Management,* a classic book that outlines wildlife management principles as understood in 1933. Some of the principles remain potent to this day.

Born in 1887, Leopold grew up on the banks of the Mississippi River in Burlington, Iowa. His father Carl, an avid hunter and rigid adherent of hunting regulations, introduced Leopold to gunning on marshes and lakes of the Missouri Flint Hills. These early experiences generated a deep respect for and an abiding curiosity in the workings of nature.

Leopold received his professional training at the Yale School of Forestry, where he graduated with a master's degree in 1909. His first job took him to the territories of Arizona and New Mexico as an employee of the U.S. Forest Service. At his urging, the service created the Gila Wilderness Area in 1924, its first.

Leopold's career in game management began in 1929, when the University of Wisconsin, Madison, asked him to deliver a series of lectures on the topic. The university soon invited him to become America's first Chair of Game Management, and he published his classic book.

"Bobwhite quail," he wrote, "probably reached maximum abundance during that stage of settlement when the composition of their range accidentally reached an equal proportion of brush, woodland, and crude cultivation."

By "stage of settlement," he was referring to that period of American history when pioneers had advanced to the western fringe of bobwhite range. These pioneers changed the face of the landscape. In the Southeast, virgin forests were cleared to plant cotton. In the Midwest, virgin prairie was broken to plant corn and wheat. Fields were small, because a farmer with a mule was less aspiring than one with an air-conditioned tractor. This patchwork agriculture created ideal conditions for quail and the "good ol' days" were born.

Leopold argued that densities (number of bobwhites per acre) were no higher in the good ol' days than would be possible at the time of his writing. Based on conversations with old-timers, he speculated that, even in the time of patchwork agriculture, a bird per acre (2.5/ha) was an excellent density. The key difference between then and now, according to Leopold, was the percentage of the land surface suitable to quail.

Virtually 100% of the land was habitable in the heyday of patchwork agriculture. As air-conditioned tractors replaced mules and fields grew in size, large chunks of countryside became inhospitable and quail disappeared.

Leopold realized that reverting to patchwork agriculture and restoring the proper mix of brush, woodland, and cropland was socially and economically unacceptable. Therefore, he advised that quail managers focus on habitat quality rather than quantity.

"A covey of quail may originally have found its requirements for brush satisfied by ten acres of hazel. The reason it was satisfied, however, did not lie in the acreage, but in the accidental existence of a few grapevine tangles, brush piles, or fallen treetops occurring in the hazel, but aggregating only half an acre in total area.

"In short, the function of the ten acres of hazel brush was concentrated on a twentieth of its total area. By restoring either the particular things formerly discharging this function, or their equivalents in plants or structures having the same properties, a satisfactory quail population might be restored by management without the 'expenditure' of more than a fraction of the acreage formerly used.

"In short, restoration is a matter of simulating the quality, rather than the quantity, of the original coverts."

One of Leopold's most enduring contributions to wildlife management is his law of dispersion, better known as the principle of edge. From countless hours afield, packing a shotgun or a bow, or simply absorbing nature's offerings, he came to suspect that "game is a phenomenon of edges. It occurs where the types of food and cover which it needs come together, *i.e.,* where their edges meet."

He stated that the law of dispersion applies to species of low mobility that require two or more habitat types. "I know of few convincing instances where edges attract mobile, one-type game like geese, or buffalo, or antelope, or plover, or sea-ducks."

Species like bobwhites, however, that spend their lives in small areas and need at least one type of cover for refuge and another for resources, are going to occur where the edges of these types meet. Further, according to Leopold, their abundance will increase as edge increases: "The potential density of game of low radius [restricted movement patterns] requiring two or more types is, within ordinary limits, proportional to the sum of the type peripheries."

What did Leopold mean by "ordinary limits"? Mathematicians have

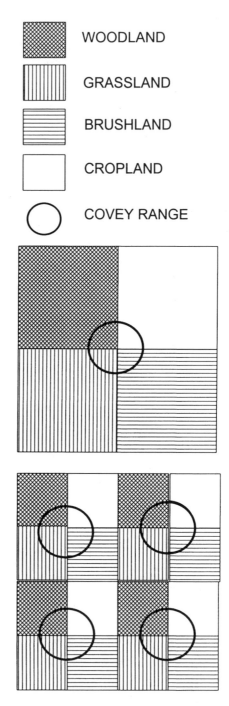

Fig. 13. Aldo Leopold was among the first biologists to recognize that more usable space for bobwhites could be created simply by rearranging available habitat types.

shown that it is possible to put an infinite amount of edge in a fixed space. Obviously, at some point, additional edge becomes redundant because an infinite bobwhite population cannot be placed in a fixed space. Managers need only to provide adequate amounts of edge for a decent quail population.

The edge must be meaningful for the principle to apply. Do not expect to find a covey where an interstate highway abuts a Bermuda grass pasture. Edge between a dirt road and bunchgrass prairie, however, could be useful to nesting and brooding hens. Often, edge valuable to bobwhites occurs where habitats that provide refuge from harsh temperatures and predators meet habitats that provide roosting cover, nesting cover, and food.

THE ABOVE ESSAY CONTAINS SUBSTANTIAL REVISION COMPARED to the original that appeared in *Quail Unlimited* magazine. The principle of edge, as formulated by Leopold, has taken an empirical and theoretical beating in the last few years. The principle holds for certain species under specified conditions, but it is not a general principle. Leopold did not recognize the limitations of edge. A quail manager should not assume that quail populations will increase if more habitat edge is created.

Also, Leopold's reminiscences on the value of patchwork agriculture may be incomplete and somewhat misleading. Southwestern rangeland has bobwhite densities of up to three birds per acre (7.5/ha) without agriculture. Impressive bobwhite irruptions occurred in the northern plains states before patchwork agriculture had much impact on the countryside (see chapter 35, The Great Wisconsin Quail Irruption).

Leopold's argument that management may improve habitat quality and thereby increase bobwhite density does not seem to hold. Management may create more space for bobwhites to live in, as he reported, and increase populations. More interspersion may create more usable space; however, management has not yet been able to increase populations by increasing habitat quality on fully usable areas. The concept of habitat quality is a human invention, and does not appear to be a concern of bobwhites.

25 *Slack Zones*

habitat in Kansas bears little resemblance to quality habitat in Florida. Rangeland and farmland habitat may look as different as horses and tractors, and yet be equally productive for quail.

Because bobwhites occur naturally from Minnesota to Guatemala, and from eastern Colorado to Virginia, it is obvious that they live under a diverse array of conditions. Their range includes tropical and temperate climates. They occur in rainy and droughty areas. Depending upon subspecies, bobwhites occupy habitat from sea level to 5000 feet (1,520 m) in elevation. The bobwhite is a remarkably adaptable species.

Throughout its broad range, however, the bobwhite itself is more or less a constant. It is about the size of a beer can. It is a poor flier that prefers walking to flying. Accordingly, nature has endowed its walking muscles (legs) with rich supplies of blood and fats, and has left its flight muscles (breast) relatively bereft of these items. Nature designed the bird for a diet of seeds and insects that occur on or near the ground, no matter where it lives.

Given this constancy in the bird, one would expect certain habitat features to be similar on good bobwhite range, whether that range is in Mississippi or Mexico. Given its broad geographic range, however, one also would expect any key property of habitat to have a range of acceptable values. One would therefore expect similar, but not identical, habitat features in all good bobwhite country.

Hunters know that better quail habitat has a certain "look." They may not be able to say precisely why habitat looks appealing, but they hold a mental picture, based on many days afield, of areas they would expect to produce and hold bobwhites. To paraphrase Supreme Court Justice William O. Douglas, "Good quail habitat is like pornography: you can't define it, but you know it when you see it."

Species–habitat models, a concept first developed by the U.S. Fish and Wildlife Service in the 1970s, are used to put precise descriptions on that "look." A model is simply a verbal or mathematical narrative that identifies key habitat features, acceptable variation in these features, and costs to a wildlife population (if key features are not acceptable).

Richard L. Schroeder of the National Ecology Research Center in Denver, Colorado, developed a species–habitat model for bobwhites in the 1980s. This model, considered applicable throughout bobwhite range in the United States, identifies the following key habitat features:

- Canopy cover of herbaceous food plants should range from 25 to 75%. This means that between 25 and 75% of the ground should be shaded at midday by the grasses and forbs providing food.
- At quail level (below 8 in. = 20.3 cm), 30–60% of the soil surface should be bare or have only a light covering of plant litter (e.g., dead or dormant leaves, twigs). This does not mean that between 30 and 60% of the soil should be free of vegetation. Rather, it means that quail will feed where the vegetation is relatively open. Above this level, the canopies of brush and herbaceous plants provide more cover.
- Crops planted in the area should include those that provide seeds of value to quail. These crops include corn, soybeans, sorghum (milo), cowpeas, small grains, and others. The ideal (but impractical) solution would be to leave crops unharvested. Schroeder's model indicates that the second best alternative is to leave stubble standing until spring.
- Low woody cover with dense canopies should be dispersed throughout the area. Woody cover provides refuge from predators and inclement weather, and serves as a focus from which coveys go about daily activities.
- The height of herbaceous cover where quail forage should range from 10 to 20 inches (25 to 50 cm). Cover lower than 10 inches (25 cm) might increase risks of predation and prevent birds from using areas. Cover higher than 20 inches (50 cm) might impede escape flights, particularly takeoffs, and also prevent use of areas.
- More than 10% of an area should provide suitable nesting cover. Biologists generally hold that perennial grasses 12–18 inches (30–45 cm) tall provide the best nesting cover.
- No required cover type should be farther than about 100 yards (91 m) from another required cover type. In other words, required cover types should be well interspersed. Bobwhites, if possible, will walk from type to type. Because of short legs, however, they cannot walk very far in a day. Therefore, each necessary habitat type must be close to other necessary types.

The above descriptions provide only the highlights of Schroeder's quail habitat model. The salient point the model makes for bobwhite managers is that A RANGE OF CONDITIONS PROVIDES SUITABLE HABITAT. Seventy-five percent coverage by food plants is no better than 25% coverage. Thirty percent bare ground is just as good as 40, 50, or 60%. Ground cover is acceptable as long as it ranges between 10 and 20 inches (25 and 50 cm) tall. Cover can be dispersed in any imaginable pattern if no two required types are farther than 100 yards (91 m) apart.

Acceptable arrangements of woody cover on southwestern rangeland illustrate the flexibility in Schroeder's model. Our research and observations in the 1990s indicate that canopy coverage of brush should range between 5 and 15% for bobwhites. Within this range of coverage values, we have observed densities above a bird per acre (2.5/ha) where the woody cover was distributed in: (1) large, circular mottes; (2) small, scattered individual brush plants; (3) long, narrow strips of mature brush with no brush between strips; and (4) long, narrow strips of mature brush with small, scattered brush plants between strips. These patterns held in common the coverage values mentioned above and the condition that a covey was never more than 100 yards (91 m) from brush. The options for arranging woody cover appear limitless within these constraints.

In a similar vein, bobwhite individuals and populations have slack zones, or ranges of acceptability, built into the biological processes that sustain them. To define these slack zones in words and pictures, imagine building a bench on the patio. The goal is to maximize the comfort of all possible guests who might settle on the bench. Then a question arises of how high to build the bench. A bench 2 inches (5 cm) high, or one 5 feet (1.5 m) high, would not provide a maximum level of comfort; at some height, say 16 inches (40 cm), comfort level would peak.

The height, 16 inches (40 cm), has slack on either side. A bench 12 or 20 inches (30 or 50 cm) high would have about the same comfort level as one 16 inches (40 cm) high. A slack zone arises whenever a relationship between something that matters (a dependent variable) and something that happens (an independent variable) has flat areas. The relationship between comfort and bench height is flat from about 12 to 20 inches (30 to 50 cm). Comfort is stable in this slack zone. Many relationships between something that matters and something that happens in the world of quail are mound-shaped. The mound may be warped compared to the one graphed. Warped or not, however, all such relationships have slack zones.

Suppose one asks what the best possible temperature is for laying hens.

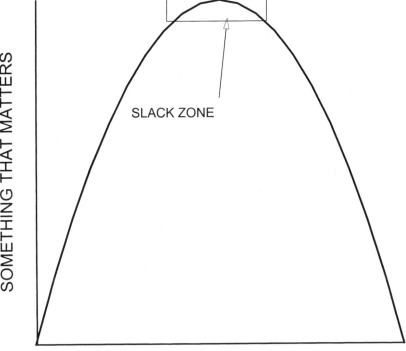

SOMETHING THAT HAPPENS

Fig. 14. In nature, a flattened region often occurs in the relationship between something that matters (a dependent variable) and something that happens (an independent variable). Bobwhite managers can take advantage of these flat parts, as the quail response will change little in response to large environmental or management activity changes within these areas.

By best possible, I mean the temperature associated with the highest rate of egg laying in the field or propagation facility. The ideal temperature could be estimated with experiments. In fact, it is known to be about 70°F (21.1°C). The relationship between eggs laid per day (what matters) and temperature (what happens) is mound-shaped for bobwhites. The slack zone ranges between 59 and 77°F (15 and 25°C). At temperatures within the slack zone, the rate of laying is steady at 0.5 to 1.0 egg per day. Outside the slack zone, the rate declines to between 0.1 and 0.2 egg per day. If temperatures are far outside the slack zone, hens quit laying.

Quail populations also have slack zones. A zone of particular interest to the harvest manager is the one that appears in the mound-shaped relationship between the number of breeders and total production from spring to fall. A goal of harvest management might be to maximize production, thereby maximizing the potential harvest. Total production will maximize at some breeding density between low and high. The exact maximizing density is of major concern but difficult to identify; fortunately, a range of breeding densities will lead to similar total production. The relationship between breeding density and total production has a flat part. This slack zone cushions the effects of inaccurate counts and erroneous harvest decisions.

Nature is replete with mound-shaped relationships of the form discussed in this essay. Such relationships are the ecological analogs of air bags, guy wires, and shock absorbers. The relationships provide support to wildlife individuals and populations, and soften the effects of disasters. Quail managers owe thanks to slack zones, because without such zones, quail probably could not persist.

WHEN ALL OF THIS FLEXIBILITY IS PUT INTO A MANAGEMENT context, one concludes that many, many habitat situations are acceptable. One can look at a habitat setting and say, to paraphrase the beer commercial, "It doesn't get any better than this." When this condition prevails, the quail manager has done all that is humanly possible.

26 Robots and Quail Management

CONSIDER BACKING AN 18-WHEELER UP TO A LOADING DOCK. Really, this feat is a remarkable human accomplishment. Now consider developing a robot that can do the same thing. It can be done, and Keith R. Crawford, a quail hunter and robotics engineer from Dallas, has discovered that the underlying technology has applications in quail management.

"The ability to measure the impact of a wild quail management program," according to Crawford, "has always been reduced due to the inability to compensate for the impact of precipitation—a key component in the life cycle of a wild bobwhite quail. The dilemma facing the manager of a wild quail population is that he cannot determine the impact of any particular management technique on a quail population independent of the one variable he cannot control—precipitation.

"Because a quail manager cannot isolate the impact of precipitation, he cannot accurately determine the value of his management program. More importantly, the quail manager cannot alter management techniques according to those techniques that yield the best results. Also, the inability to quantify the value of quail management makes the cost of quail management more difficult to justify.

"While there are factors other than precipitation that impact a quail population—predation, habitat destruction, hunting pressure—all these can be controlled to some degree. The idea is to understand the population Mother Nature will produce against which you can measure the impact of a quail management program.

"Furthermore, absent of a quail management program, being able to benchmark the quail population will serve as an early warning to habitat destruction. Being able to understand that a quail population is in decline will enable one to take corrective action before it is too late."

When teaching a robot to back up 18-wheelers, one would want the robot to learn from its mistakes. This is made possible through the use of neural networks. "Neural networks were designed by mathematicians to approximate the thought process of the human mind," Crawford stated. "By attempting to mimic the neural connections of the brain, mathematicians reasoned that large, complex problems too cumbersome for traditional statistical methods could be more efficiently and effectively solved."

Before proceeding further, a model is just a way of viewing how the world works. Aldo Leopold's principle of edge is a model. It says that the more useful habitat edge there is available to a quail population in a given area, the more quail there will be in the area, within limits of course. Everyday life is full of models of one form or another; models provide a way of anticipating the future and making appropriate plans. Neural networks may be used as models of how the world works.

"A neural network seems to address the primary problems with modeling the response of a wild quail population to precipitation," according to Crawford. "The key advantage the neural network has over more conventional approaches is the ability to train on historical data. Learning by example gives the neural net the ability to adapt to the nuances of ecological regions and weight precipitation around the life cycle of quail."

Crawford constructed his neural net by using monthly precipitation values for specific counties, plus the previous year's count of bobwhites, to predict how many bobwhites will be counted in the current year. The count data are from 20-mile (32-km) routes run annually by biologists from the Texas Parks and Wildlife Department.

Here is how Crawford's model performed in 1995:

County	Prediction range	Actual count
Collingsworth	11–19	16
Jim Hogg	7–19	24
Jim Wells	29–54	23
Shackelford	16–29	24
Stephens	13–39	30
Stonewall	65–100	28

The prediction range is a neural net prediction of the number of bobwhites expected on a 20-mile (32-km) route based on rainfall in each month of 1994 and the 1994 count on the route. The actual count is the number of bobwhites observed by TPWD biologists in 1995.

The neural net models missed badly in Stonewall County and missed but were closer in Jim Hogg and Jim Wells Counties. Model predictions were remarkably accurate in Collingsworth, Shackelford, and Stephens Counties.

Crawford points out that the neural net models perform better if they are based on complete historical records of rainfall and populations. To a certain extent, the inaccurate predictions may have arisen from an incomplete record. Nevertheless, from the standpoint of a bobwhite management technology, the overall performance of the neural net models was quite impressive. A persistent problem in the management of all species of wildlife is that of predicting population responses to management and environmental variables. This problem must be solved to take wildlife management into the realm of science.

"I think the greatest potential for this tool lies in the hands of the individual manager interested in managing a wild quail population," Crawford stated. "The quail manager has the ability to overcome the data problems I encountered. For instance, by consistently gathering rainfall and quail population data from a localized area, the model will be able to more accurately predict quail populations. Furthermore, using more proactive methods to count quail—such as counting birds moved during selected days of hunting—will result in a better quail census.

"No longer do years need to go by without the knowledge that something outside of weather is destroying a quail population. This is the value of the model—a benchmark to monitor a quail population and measure the impact of a quail management program."

27 *Space, Time, and Relativity*

WHAT IF ALBERT EINSTEIN HAD BEEN A QUAIL MANAGER instead of a physicist? Perhaps quail conservationists would be thinking now in terms of space, time, and relativity instead of brush piles, feeders, and food plots. Perhaps better management decisions would be made.

Einstein's space, the boundless heavens filled with stars and galaxies, has little to do with earthbound game birds. The concept of space, however, is quite relevant to game bird management. Quail must have space or there would be no quail. Here, space is defined as area (e.g., 1000 ac. = 400 ha). All of the space must be fully usable. Such space would have the right mix of herbaceous and woody cover in the right pattern. Required cover types would be interspersed so that birds could obtain life needs with little movement.

Many principles and practices of quail management are applied to create usable space. Aldo Leopold's principle of edge is an example (see chapter 24, Aldo Leopold on Bobwhites). Leopold observed that wild animals like cottontails (*Sylvilagus* sp.) and quail spend their lives in small areas. These animals will be more abundant, he said, as the edge between required cover types increases. In some, but not all cases, more edge creates more usable space.

Burning creates usable space under some circumstances. In areas with high rainfall and long growing seasons, a problem in bobwhite management is a buildup of herbaceous and woody plants. These buildups prevent quail from using space, because these birds cannot walk through heavy cover. While burning may alter the composition of vegetation and favor food plants, its primary function is the creation of usable space.

If an area lacks woody cover, management could establish artificial loafing shelters (see chapter 5, Loafing Coverts) or plant shrubs. Because quail require woody cover under most circumstances, these practices increase usable space. Space, however, cannot stand alone in either astrophysics or quail habitat management. Time must be considered.

Space-time is the product of usable space and time. For example, if every square inch of a 1000-acre (400-ha) area was fully usable every day of the year, then there would be 365,000 acre-days (146,000 ha-days) of space-time for quail. The concept of space-time leads to a principle of quail management as simple, powerful, and true as 2 + 2 = 4: TO MAXIMIZE QUAIL ABUNDANCE, MAXIMIZE USABLE SPACE IN TIME (or more briefly, maximize space-time). In general, more space-time will result in more quail, but there are exceptions.

Areas must be space-time saturated for the principle to hold. Consider what happens on farmland with large fields and little natural cover. Just before crops are ready to be harvested, all of this farmland would be fully usable. Cover would be everywhere. After harvest, stubble would be turned under, and space would not be usable for lengthy periods. Such farmland settings lack space-time saturation, meaning that a low percentage of potential space-time is available. The net result is few or no quail relative to the size of the area.

It also is possible to have fully usable space (quality habitat) available all the time (space-time saturated) and no quail. This outcome could occur if the usable area were too small to support a self-sustaining population. Quail populations cannot persist on small, isolated areas (see chapter 39, When 2 + 2 = 0).

Space-time cannot be maximized without an appreciation of relativity. Einstein realized that our perceptions depend on our circumstance. For example, if one stands in front of a clock, time will move endlessly forward. Time will stand still if one moves away from the clock at the speed of light. The perception of time depends on one's velocity.

Relativity in quail habitat management means that the value of any practice depends on the circumstance within which the practice is applied. In other words, the value of a practice depends on the habitat conditions in which the practice is applied. For example, an artificial brush shelter has no value in a thicket, but serves a purpose in a prairie. A disced strip has no value on properly grazed rangeland, but serves a purpose in undergrazed rangeland. A prescribed fire has little value in an area prone to drought, but serves a purpose in a rainy area.

Fig. 15. Quality habitat for bobwhites appears similar wherever the birds occur. This habitat for masked bobwhites in Sonora, Mexico, shows ground cover of the proper structure, with plenty of low, woody cover nearby. The key principle of habitat management for bobwhites is to ensure that their habitats resemble that shown, on a consistent basis through time.

The above observations may seem obvious, but relativity often is ignored or unappreciated in quail habitat management. As a result, practices are applied that have no effect on space-time and thus, no effect on quail abundance.

Habitat management on the Bomer Wildlife Research Area, Duval County, Texas, demonstrates the practical application of space-time, space-time saturation, and relativity in management of bobwhite habitat. The Bomer Area consists of 120 acres (48 ha), 60 (24) of which are in a Conservation Reserve Program field planted with Kleingrass. The CRP contract requires brush (loafing and escape cover) to be kept out of the field. To provide woody cover, five clusters of six tepee shelters were erected on the field (see chapter 5, Loafing Coverts). The shelters were needed RELATIVE TO conditions in the Kleingrass field. This practice gave the bobwhite population 21,900 acre-days (8760 ha-days) of space-time on an annual basis.

The second 60 acres (24 ha) originally consisted of dense, mixed brush largely unusable to bobwhites (no space-time). This situation was corrected by rootplowing in a strip pattern. Ten-yard-wide (9.1-m-wide) strips of brush were preserved and 75-yard-wide (68.3-m-wide) strips were cleared; this pattern was repeated throughout the 60 acres (24 ha). Brush management clearly was needed relative to existing habitat conditions; it also added 21,900 acre-days (8760 ha-days) of space-time.

Because the Bomer Area is not grazed, buildups of herbaceous vegetation on the cleared areas could reduce space-time. This problem is addressed by discing one-half of the cleared strips every other year to maintain usable space in time and promote plants that produce and harbor bobwhite foods. No other management is practiced on the Bomer Area. No food or water is provisioned; no predators are controlled. None of these practices has merit relative to conditions in the Bomer Area.

The management goal has been to maximize space-time. Of 43,800 acre-days (17,520 ha-days) of potential space-time, management has provided about 41,800 of them. This is 95.4% saturation. Some space-time is lost because of wetland areas unsuitable for bobwhites and because disced areas are unusable for brief periods. The abundance of bobwhites on the Bomer Area has matched or exceeded populations in the Rio Grande Plains for several years, illustrating the power of space-time maximization.

THE SIMPLE CONCEPTS PRESENTED IN THIS ESSAY ARE QUITE powerful. A more technical exposition of these ideas can be found in my paper "A Philosophy of Habitat Management for Northern Bobwhites," which appeared in *The Journal of Wildlife Management* in 1997.

Although it is perhaps fair to say that the overriding importance of space-time maximization was recognized only recently, the notion has been around for a long time. Witness these quotations.

*"In short, development of all types of quail preserves . . . consists in diversifying the vegetation as much as possible and providing a balance of open woodlands, weedy fields, cultivated and fallow ground, thickets, and scattered grass or broomsedge areas of proper density and small extent, for this is the most favorable environment for bobwhites. It provides the essentials in each range and the **maximum number of covey ranges.** " (bold added)* —HERBERT L. STODDARD, *1931*

"The highest quail populations recollected by the old-timers on their home farms in the early days of settlement fail to show any former

*populations in excess of a bird per acre. This indication, if substantiated by fuller data, means that the period of great abundance in quail, which is known to have occurred during the early days of settlement in the cornbelt regions, consisted of a higher proportion of populated acres, **rather than a higher maximum population per acre than now obtains.**" (Leopold's bold)* —ALDO LEOPOLD, 1933

"Experience on game management areas has shown that efforts to raise carrying capacity are more likely to be fruitful if emphasis is placed upon the creation of new covey territories."
—PAUL L. ERRINGTON AND F. N. HAMERSTROM, JR., 1936

"To supply most of the needs of high populations of quail, they must be assured continuous use of virtually every square foot of ground."
—VAL W. LEHMANN, 1984

28 *Counting Bobwhites*

"CENSUS IS THE YARDSTICK OF SUCCESS OR FAILURE IN conservation," wrote Aldo Leopold, the father of game management in North America. State and federal biologists spend untold hours driving the back roads and hiking the hinterlands to count wildlife. These counts provide a basis for management decisions.

Private quail managers, likewise, can use counts to follow populations under their charge. The counts might show that a management program is effective or ineffective, and could be the basis for planning a liberal or restricted harvest in the next hunting season. The quickest and cheapest way to count quail is to use an INDEX OF ABUNDANCE to attain a relative measure of population size or density. While the actual number of birds will not be known, this index may enable detection of differences in populations among areas or years.

Counting the number of males calling *bobwhite* is an index of abundance. The usual approach is to establish a 20-mile (32-km) route on secondary roads. Stop every mile (1.6 km) and record the number of different males heard calling during a three-minute period. When finished,

Fig. 16. Biologists capture bobwhites for population analysis in wire cages with funnel entrances. The bait is some type of grain such as sorghum or corn.

calculate the average number of males calling at each listening stop. Ideally, this average will rise and fall as population numbers fluctuate.

Many biologists are leery of counting whistling males. Biologists once believed that only bachelors called; however, it has been learned that the breeding biology of bobwhites is a lot more complex than once assumed. Just who is calling and why they are calling remains a puzzle. Accordingly, one does not know if the counts mean anything; research results on this issue are mixed.

A better index, and one used widely by state game departments, is obtained by counting quail while driving slowly along secondary roads. The Texas Parks and Wildlife Department uses more than 200 roadside routes. Counts each August establish statewide and regional population trends, and provide data for setting season lengths and bag limits. The index derived from roadside counts is the number of quail observed per mile. This number should vary with population size and density — more birds per mile mean higher populations.

A different type of index can be obtained by driving to the quail pasture before dawn. Select a quiet area and then listen for the *hoy* or assembly call (see chapter 1, The Family Tree). You can identify different coveys based on the assembly call.

If the question is how many birds to harvest and 10 have been counted per mile, how many should be harvested? What about birds with home ranges that are not along roadsides?

With indices, one can say only that there are more quail in a particular area than another, or that there were more quail before than now. If that is all one needs to know, indices are the method of choice because they are cheap and fast. If one needs more precise information, then ABSOLUTE ABUNDANCE must be measured.

Absolute abundance is a measure of density (e.g., number per acre) or population size. If density is known, one can obtain population size easily by multiplying density times the size of the area. Some people have used bird dogs in an attempt to count all coveys in an area. Forest E. Kellogg, University of Georgia, Athens, has found that several coveys may be missed when counting with dogs. In fact, based on Kellogg's research in the 1970s, dogs miss an average of 50% of bobwhite coveys in larger areas. Dogs may flush as few as 20% or as many as 70%, depending on weather conditions and chance.

"Even dogs with desirable traits (e.g., excellent scenting ability, hunting desire, stamina, intelligence, experience, training) are not faultless in unfavorable circumstances," reported Kevin G. Gutzwiller of Baylor University, Waco, Texas, in 1990. "I have observed inconsistent performances by individuals during the same day and even during the same hour."

Bird dog performance varies because of environmental factors that affect the production and dispersal of scent. Human scent originates from RAFTS, which are small pieces of dead skin that support living bacteria on their surface, according to Gutzwiller. Bacteria metabolize dead cells and the body residues and secretions on them, thus producing a vapor (scent).

"People shed dead skin cells with bacteria continuously. Chickens, and presumably game birds, also slough off outer epidermal cells.

"Temperature, moisture, and air movements are the key physical factors influencing scent production and detection. Surfaces in direct sunlight may get hot enough to dehydrate and kill bacteria, stopping scent production. Freezing or near-freezing temperatures retard bacterial action, extending the decay period but reducing decay rate. Dew and light rain can rehydrate rafts and reactivate bacterial metabolism. Snow, via its temperature, moisture content, and density, influences bacterial activity and vertical scent movement.

"Strong wind may disperse rafts and scent to the point where they cannot be detected, whereas little or no wind may limit the area over which they are transported.

"Recently airborne birds are sometimes difficult to locate, presumably because not enough rafts have been deposited at the bird's landing location, insufficient time has elapsed for adequate vapor to accumulate around rafts, or both."

Other factors affect odor production and the ability of dogs to detect odors. Direct sunlight can kill the bacteria necessary for vapor production, regardless of temperature. Plants crushed while hunters search for a downed bird may release strong odors that mask quail scent. Some dogs will not search an area with human scent, possibly because they do not expect to find birds where they sense the recent presence of humans.

Kellogg has recommended systematic sweeps of the counted area for optimal counts using dogs. For example, work back and forth across the pasture every 100 yards (91 m) or so. Do not let the dogs quarter haphazardly through the pasture. If time permits, repeat the counts a few times and map the locations of coveys flushed. Then take the highest count and add mapped coveys that most likely were not flushed on the day of the highest count.

Ralph W. Dimmick, University of Tennessee, Knoxville, tested drive counts in 1982. With drive counts, a crew is sent through an area to try and flush all coveys. Each person counts birds that pass back through the drive line to his or her right. Spotters at the end of the area count birds flushing ahead of the crew. Spacing between members of the drive crew must be small to ensure that all coveys are flushed. In most habitats, the interval between counters should not exceed 10 yards (9.1 m). Wider intervals guarantee that some coveys will be missed. Obviously, drive counts are labor intensive and suited only for smaller areas. One could sample a portion of a large area and assume the sample is representative of the entire area. Unfortunately, uncertainty about population density increases as sampling intensity decreases.

Another sampling method that estimates population size is leg-banding. Before hunting season, biologists working under authorized permits will trap, band, and release quail. During hunting season, the biologists will keep track of the total number of birds bagged and the number with bands. These records provide a means of estimating the number of birds present before hunting season. For example, suppose 1000 quail are banded prior to hunting and 1000 are harvested. If 500 of the harvested

Fig. 17. Leg-banding captured bobwhites provides information on harvest rates, survival rates, movements, and population abundance.

birds are banded, this sample would indicate that 500/1000, or 50%, of the population was banded. Since 1000 birds were banded and this is half the population, there must have been 2000 birds before hunting season.

The last method commonly used to count quail is the one-person drive count. A single person walks, drives, rides horseback, or otherwise travels a straight line across a quail pasture. When a covey is flushed, a record is kept of the number of birds and the right-angle distance between the line being traveled and the point where the covey flushed. The counter knows two things: the distance traveled and the number of birds observed. At this point, one has an index of abundance (number of birds per mile). Using the distance measurements, the counter must estimate the width of the flushing band to obtain birds per acre. One-person drive counts are like traveling long, narrow rectangles from which all quail are flushed. The counts sample density in small areas that can be expanded to larger areas.

Before beginning a counting program, seek help from a professional biologist to design a sampling plan that will meet personal needs and give reliable results. A professional should assist in data analysis at the start of the program. He or she will be aware of the many pitfalls that can lead to misleading results and faulty interpretations.

 29 Pen-reared Bobwhites

WHEN AN OIL SULTAN FROM THE MIDDLE EAST VISITED A corporate hunting lease in south Texas, his bodyguards amused themselves by hand-capturing bobwhites released for the hunt. This highlights the poor performance shown often, but not always, by pen-raised bobwhites.

Artificial propagation and release of game birds for hunting has been carried on in the United States since the late 1800s. Early on, the practice was accepted without skepticism as a logical response to declining populations of quail. In the 1940s, however, state game departments began to evaluate the results of stocking activities. These evaluations revealed some rather appalling properties of artificial stocking:

- The recovery rate of released birds was generally quite low. In other words, few of the birds released ended up in the bags of hunters. Recovery rates approaching 20% were possible if game-farm birds were set loose in quality habitat and if heavy hunting took place soon after the birds were released. Typically, however, recovery rates hovered around 1%.
- Low recovery rates resulted in exorbitant costs per bird in the bag. For example, if it cost $3.00 to raise a bobwhite until release age and if only 1% of those released are recovered, the cost per bird recovered is $300.00.
- The release of pen-reared birds was inherently unfair to the average hunting license holder. The primary beneficiaries of game-farm birds were the relatively few individuals who hunted game-farm birds. It was easy for one person to take the number of birds intended for several hunters.
- Releases had trifling effects on a state's total harvest of a particular game bird; i.e., well over 98% of a state's take came from wild birds. This occurred because of a low recovery rate of game-farm birds, as mentioned above, and also because the total number of quail released in some states represented a trivial contribution to a state's population of native birds.

These outcomes, which were quite general throughout the United States, led to the wholesale closure of state game farms in the 1940s and 1950s.

Despite the wretched history of bobwhite releases, interest in artificial stocking remains high. Stocking is an established part of some hunting preserves and commercial leases that must provide hunting opportunities, regardless of trends in wild populations. This interest has prompted research into factors that affect the performance of released bobwhites. In particular, is poor performance due to genetics, upbringing (i.e., environment), or both?

Research by Darrell L. Ellsworth in 1988 at Southern Illinois University, Carbondale, indicates that the problem is not attributable to genetics. Biologists have suspected that several generations in captivity might result in a docile bird, genetically selected to perform well in pens. The research, however, showed that wild-trapped and game-farm bobwhites were similar in several measures of genetic fitness, such as heterozygosity.

"This suggests," wrote the researchers, "that early environment may be more influential than genetically programmed instincts in shaping pen-reared bobwhite performance in the wild. [Managers] should not assume that [crossing wild birds with pen-reared birds] will dramatically improve field performance of pen-reared bobwhites. We recommend that priority be given to developing rearing procedures that minimize contact with humans and promote natural behavior patterns prior to release."

What happens to bobwhites held in captivity? Research in 1995 by Shirley L. White of the Caesar Kleberg Institute indicates the answer may be loosely classified as "couch-potato syndrome." White set out to determine the extent to which masked bobwhites from Sonora, Mexico, differed from Texas bobwhites, the subspecies inhabiting south Texas. She obtained aged breeding birds from a captive flock of masked bobwhites. With assistance from the Texas Parks and Wildlife Department and quail hunters, she also obtained a sample of wild Texas bobwhites from the Chaparral Wildlife Management Area.

A dilemma arose immediately. The masked bobwhites had been raised in captivity, whereas the Texas bobwhites were wild. The difference she observed between races could therefore be due to confinement rather than race. To control for this problem, she also analyzed a race of bobwhites held in confinement but otherwise similar to Texas bobwhites.

White dissected 150 specimens, 50 of each type, and recorded data on the dimensions and weights of major organs. "Liver weight was much higher for domestic and masked bobwhites than for Texas bobwhites," White reported. "Heart weight, height, and width were larger for pen-raised birds than for wild birds."

The picture that emerges is one of lean, athletic bobwhites in the wild and "quail couch potatoes" in captivity. This outcome lends credence to the notion that upbringing is an important factor in the field performance of pen-reared bobwhites.

In *Hunting Preserves for Sport or Profit* (1987), Ed Kozicky emphasized the importance of total isolation in rearing bobwhites for sport-hunting qualities, noting that some breeders had been successful. He also pointed out the need for stringent and gentle handling methods in transporting birds from pen to field.

Even if husbandry could produce a sporty bobwhite, controversy will continue to plague pen-reared birds. The release of pen-reared bobwhites has been implicated in the decline of wild bobwhite populations through the introduction of diseases, displacement, increased mortality, and pollution of the gene pool.

Theodore DeVos, Jr., and Dan W. Speake of Auburn University, Auburn, Alabama, measured the effects of releases on the mortality rates of wild bobwhite populations in the early 1990s. In an area with pure populations of wild bobwhites, the 22-week survival rate was 41.4%; i.e., 41–42 of every 100 wild birds survived for 22 weeks. The survival of wild bobwhites in an area supplemented with pen-reared birds was 35.8% over 22 weeks. The similarity in these figures (41.4 vs. 35.8%) indicates that the pen-reared birds had statistically neutral effects on the mortality of wild birds in this study.

Pen-reared birds fared rather poorly. About 18 of every 100 birds survived for 22 weeks. This can be extrapolated as an annual survival rate of 1 to 2%, compared to a 20 to 30% annual survival for wild birds. "All groups of bobwhites exhibited reproductive behavior, and we observed successful cross pairing of pen-raised and wild bobwhites," reported DeVos and Speake. "We confirmed that due to low survival rates, pen-raised birds are unsuitable for restocking efforts; however, their use to supplement harvest may be justified where wild bobwhite numbers are low or hunter use is high."

Part Three

POPULATIONS
AND HARVEST

30 Changes in Latitudes, Changes in Attitudes

JIMMY BUFFETT OF *MARGARITAVILLE* FAME PENNED THE WORDS used as the title of this essay. The words provide a good conceptual backdrop for bobwhite managers.

The latitudinal range of bobwhites is immense: Guatemala at 15°S to Wisconsin at 45°N. This represents a span of more than 2000 miles (3200 km) that includes areas with harsh winters at high latitudes and tropical climates at low latitudes.

Changes in latitude are associated with physiological changes in bobwhite individuals and populations. The average mass of individuals increases from south to north. Birds from south Texas average about 160 grams (5.16 oz.) during winter, compared to more than 200 grams (6.45 oz.) in Wisconsin.

The larger size of northern birds is an adaptation to harsher winters. Bobwhites from the north carry two to three times more body fat than birds from the south, which helps northern birds survive periods of low food intake and fasting when snow covers the ground (see chapter 9, Fat Bobwhites).

Through the years, wildlife biologists have maintained records on the percentage of juveniles killed at various latitudes. This percentage does not reflect the true population condition, because birds hatched in the immediate past breeding season (juveniles) are more vulnerable to harvest than adults; however, the percentage of juveniles in the hunting bag is a good index of demographic (population) processes. The percentage at once provides information on survival and productivity.

Suppose a bobwhite population in an area shows no trend in terms of decline or increase through the years. Then the percentage of juveniles killed is a crude estimate of annual mortality rate, and the percentage of adults is a crude estimate of the annual survival rate. Moreover, by dividing the percentage of juveniles by the percentage of adults, an estimate of the average age ratio in juveniles per adult is obtained.

A population with an average of 80% juveniles in the hunting bag would be expected to experience 80% annual mortality and 20% annual survival with an average productivity of four juveniles per adult. (Remember, these figures are approximate, not exact, reflections of true population behavior.) *Bobwhites in the Rio Grande Plain of Texas* (1984) by Val W. Lehmann provides age-ratio data for a semiarid, subtropical climate. The hunting bag averaged 2.76 juveniles per adult during a 28-year period, which translates to 67.7% annual mortality and 32.3% annual survival.

Move northward about 500 miles (800 km) to north Texas, where A. S. Jackson recorded data on the hunting bag during the 1950s and 1960s. The average age ratio (3.9 juveniles/adult) indicates 79.6% annual mortality and 20.4% annual survival. Another 500 miles (800 km) northward leads into Illinois, another state in which long-term records on age composition of the hunting bag have been maintained. The data appear in *Population Ecology of the Bobwhite* (1984), an outstanding reference work by John L. Roseberry and Willard D. Klimstra. From 1950 through 1979, the hunting bag averaged five juveniles per adult. This ratio translates to 83.3% annual mortality and 16.7% survival.

Keep in mind that the numbers only apply to hunted populations, because inferences are being made about demographics from the age composition of the harvest. Bobwhites not subject to hunting would have higher survival rates and lower productivities. Nevertheless, an increase in mortality rate, a complementary decrease in survival rate, and an increase in productivity is observed from the low to high latitudes.

These simultaneous changes serve to balance a population's requirements to persist through time. A high-latitude bobwhite population might be stable at 20% annual survival and a productivity of four juveniles per adult, whereas a low-latitude population might persist with 30% annual survival and between two and three juveniles per adult.

What causes the differences between northern and southern populations? In northern latitudes with harsh winters and high winter losses, fairly stable conditions during breeding season and high average production are observed. Conversely, in southern latitudes subject to summer drought or deluges during breeding season, mild winters and high winter survival with low and variable production are seen. The bobwhite merely responds within a limited range of demographic possibilities.

A slight increase in annual mortality of birds in Illinois (e.g., from 83.3 to 90.0%) would necessitate a balancing age ratio of nine juveniles per adult. (Rate of production would cancel rate of loss at the balancing age ratio.) Production at this level is not possible over the long term, so any

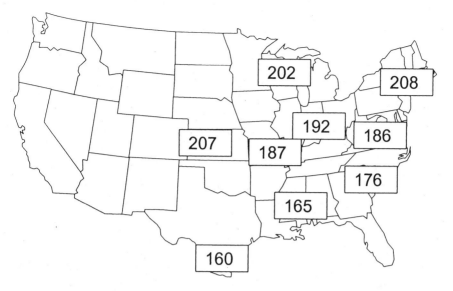

Fig. 18a. Average mass (grams) of bobwhites in various parts of the United States. Mass declines from northern to southern latitudes.

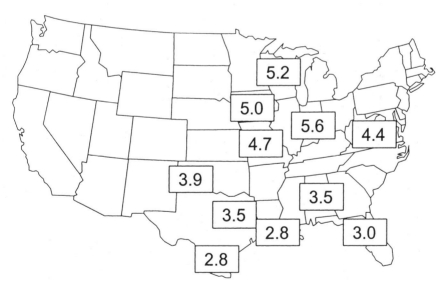

Fig. 18b. Average age ratio of bobwhites in various parts of the United States. The age ratio is the number of young birds divided by the number of old birds, based on samples collected in autumn. Bobwhites in northern latitudes are more productive than those in southern latitudes.

population that suffers 90.0% annual mortality will go extinct. By the same token, a slight decrease in production for birds in south Texas (e.g., from 2.1 to 1.1 juveniles per adult) would necessitate a balancing survival rate of 47.6%. This value cannot be expected over the long term.

The differences in population processes between northern and southern bobwhites alter attitudes on harvest management. Biologists in the Midwest have reported that 70% of a fall population of bobwhites can be harvested annually in a sustained yield setting. This is an impossibly high harvest based on all we know about bobwhite populations (unless birds move in from surrounding areas). It, however, points out that populations in northern latitudes, which suffer high annual mortality, can sustain relatively heavy harvests. Natural mortality and hunting losses compensate each other to a larger extent as natural mortality becomes higher (see chapter 43, A Trilogy on Quail Harvest Management: Fuzzy Logic).

In southern climes, a 70% harvest would drive bobwhite populations to extinction within a few years. In fact, with high winter survival, the entire spring-to-fall loss was attributable to harvest on some ranches in South Texas. Theoretical work on sustained yield indicates that, for maximum harvests through time, populations should not be hunted during drought years; however, a low harvest of 5 to 10% of the fall population during population busts has a minor effect on long-term yield.

 31 *Eight Hundred Million Heartbeats*

A BOBWHITE CHICK HATCHED ON MEMORIAL DAY PROBABLY will not live through Labor Day. One thousand such chicks dwindle to 100 or so within a year. Grown birds, although better at survival than chicks, also have short life spans. Why do quail die so fast?

Nature sets strict upper limits on life span. According to Stephen Jay Gould, a widely respected natural historian from Harvard University, all mammals except humans can be expected to live for about 800 million heartbeats. (Human heartbeats will number in the billions.) Rats and mice, with hearts like the engines in model airplanes, use up their allotted beats in short order. Elephants and hippos, with hearts like the diesels in

18-wheelers, expend their beats over decades and centuries. A canary heart would beat 4000 times while Roger Bannister ran a mile; at the mammalian rate of heartbeats, this bird would expire in 18 months.

Bobwhites living under ideal conditions live longer than canaries because their hearts beat at a slower rate. In captivity, bobwhites reportedly live up to nine years. Like the biblical Methuselah, who saw 969 summers, such long lives are rare. Shorter life spans in captivity probably are the rule rather than the exception, because quail life expectancy based on pulse rate is about four years.

The point is that even under perfect conditions, bobwhites have relatively high death rates. Paul L. Errington and F. N. Hamerstrom have speculated in 1935 that old age and accidents take about 23% of adult bobwhites each year. Herbert L. Stoddard reported in 1931 that a bobwhite held in captivity lived for seven years. From Stoddard's observation, one can infer that annual mortality could be at least 44%, even if the birds are pampered. Scientists report Coturnix (Japanese) quail die at an annual rate of 43% (males) to 49% (females); these rates occur with birds held in captivity and protected from predators and diseases. The bottom line is that quail experience high death rates (ca. 23–44% annually) even when protected from the rigors of nature and hunting.

Wild bobwhites rarely survive to old age. A banded bird was recovered in its fifth year—an extremely rare event. The chances of drawing a royal flush are better than the chances of bagging a five-year-old bobwhite. For every 10 thousand first-year adults, only three see their fifth summer; from one autumn to the next, a typical bobwhite lives six to eight months. All sources of mortality in the wild approximately double or triple the death rate compared to the pen environment.

So what happens to 540 million heartbeats? This is the deficit between the maximum potential in a perfect environment and what actually is expended. If natural mortality (but no hunting) is added to birds dying of old age, the annual mortality is tripled to 60%. Loren W. Burger, Jr., reported in 1995 that, predators caused at least 70% of nonhunting losses in Missouri. One, however, must be careful in evaluating predator losses. If a hawk kills a malnourished bobwhite or if a bobcat preys on a diseased bobwhite, what was responsible for the death? Predators can serve as garbage disposals, and in this capacity, have no effect on quail population numbers. Predators suppress quail numbers when they take healthy individuals that are unlikely to die of other causes.

According to a 1972 analysis by the Southeastern Cooperative Wildlife Disease Study at the University of Georgia, Athens, bobwhites from the Southeast suffer from 21 infectious agents and 101 parasites. In addition, birds in this region die from accidents and natural or artificial poisons. Based on carcasses submitted to the Wildlife Disease Study, avian pox was the most common disease. This viral infection is similar to the chicken pox that humans contract, resulting in blisters that turn into scabs. Outbreaks of avian pox apparently can cause high quail mortality in localized areas and time periods, but the percentage of a quail population infected usually is low. Parasites, internal and external, are thought to be minor causes of quail loss.

The impact of artificial toxins (i.e., pesticides and herbicides) on wild quail populations has been poorly documented. These chemicals can kill directly or indirectly by reducing supplies of insect foods, thus increasing chick losses. Agricultural chemicals are thought to be responsible for the worldwide decline in gray (Hungarian) partridge (*Perdix perdix*), because of their effects on chick survival.

The hunter, of course, is a source of quail mortality. Kenneth H. Pollock, North Carolina State University, Raleigh, analyzed long-term (1970–85) harvest data collected at the Tall Timbers Station in Tallahassee, Florida. Results suggested that fairly intense hunting (20–25% harvest) can raise annual mortality to about 80%. Recall that this number compares to at least 20% in a perfect environment and 60% when natural agents execute the harvest. Heavy harvest can reduce the average life span by one or two months over that expected without hunting.

The depressing statistics given above on death rates, life spans, and causes of death might lead one to the conclusion that no quail are to be found; the situation, however, is not that desperate. Suppose 1000 bobwhites are available at the start of hunting season. Even with intense harvest, one would expect 300–400 birds available for breeding; about 150 would be hens. Even slightly substandard production would bring the population back to 1000 by the start of the next hunting season.

Quail hunters, who must contend with shocking death rates in their quarry, should be thankful they are not mayfly hunters; mayflies hatch, breed, and die in the same day. Despite a life span of only 24 hours, the mayfly persists in abundance and provides a lesson in quail management: reproduction is just as important as death. If every bobwhite lived 800 million heartbeats, teeming hordes of *Colinus virginianus* would soon overrun farms, smother cities, and fill oceans. If they lacked natural checks on abundance, bobwhite populations theoretically have the capacity to increase in mass at an exponential rate.

Senescence (death from old age) seems to be important in management thinking. Senescence places an upper limit on the response of a population to some forms of predator management.

32 *Die-offs*

BILL WEBB FELT NO SENSE OF IMPENDING DISASTER AS HE checked bobwhite traps in late November of 1979. A graduate student at Texas Tech University, Lubbock, Webb was measuring quail response to management on a ranch in the Rolling Plains of King County, northwestern Texas. Trapping success and prospects for fast gunning were excellent. A covey could be flushed from every tall thicket of shinnery oak (*Quercus havardii*) in the sandy lands of King County. At dawn, the calling of myriad coveys sounded like a partridge pep rally. Quail density must have been at or slightly above a bird per acre.

In early December, a cold front moved through and deposited about five inches of snow that blanketed the ground for three or four days. When Webb returned to continue work after snowmelt, he could find scant evidence that quail once inhabited the area. Countless bobwhites had perished in a matter of days. King County had experienced a die-off, the loss of many quail in a short time; die-offs can occur anywhere in bobwhite range. They perhaps are most frequent in areas with severe winters or erratic rainfall, or both. These conditions typify the northern and western fringes of bobwhite range in the United States.

A. S. Jackson, formerly with the Texas Parks and Wildlife Department, documented a spectacular north Texas crash in the winter of 1943. Bobwhite abundance was high because of rainfall during the preceding two years. Forty-two inches (106.7 cm) had pelted the mesquite brushland in 1941, and 26 inches (66.0 cm) had fallen in 1942. These bountiful rains created ideal habitat conditions and quail irrupted. One 60-acre (24-ha) pasture yielded 100 bobwhites to harvest in 1942. With only 10 inches (25.4 cm) of rain between March and September of 1943, however, habitat quality rapidly deteriorated. Quail density was high because of production and carryover from the preceding two years. Jackson temporarily left the field to attend to office work on January 7, 1943. When he returned on January 15, he saw catastrophe.

"Everywhere," he reported, "the ground was littered with evidence that predation had been recent and terrific." Few coveys could be found; those remaining had fewer than half as many members as usual. Jackson believed that the major predators were northern harriers (*Cicus cyaneus*), red-tailed hawks (*Buteo jamaicensis*), and Cooper's hawks (*Accipiter cooperii*). He shot several to see if they had been preying on bobwhites. Some of the raptors had quail remains in their stomachs; some did not. (Today, it is illegal to shoot hawks. It probably was illegal then under the Migratory Bird Treaty Act of 1918, but it is assumed that Jackson was operating under an authorized collecting permit.) Predators apparently were responsible for the die-off, but were they the root cause? Hawks cannot be held responsible without exploring other possible causes.

Biologists speak of ULTIMATE and PROXIMATE mortality factors. Ultimate factors, like the judge and jury at a capital murder trial, pronounce the sentence. Proximate factors merely execute the sentence. Ultimate factors are the real concern in quail biology. Some die-offs probably do not occur at all; they only seem to occur. They could be called phantom die-offs. If bobwhites form larger coveys (which occurs in fall), or if they shift occupied range (reported for some areas), quail can seem to disappear. Numbers, however, could be remaining constant, with grouping or shifting belying catastrophe. (This explanation does not hold in Jackson's case, because he found ample evidence of "recent and terrific" predation.)

Another root cause could have been disease. Certainly, quail breeders see massive die-offs of penned birds. These people take precautions to prevent malady from running rampant through their facilities. Organic disease, although of much concern to hunters, probably only rarely is a root cause of quail die-offs in the wild. Healthy animals maintain immunity against diseases. If they get sick, the odds are that something made them unhealthy and disease organisms had a chance to flourish. That something is what doctors and quail managers must find.

Val W. Lehmann, studying the effects of Vitamin A on productivity, witnessed a south Texas crash in the winter of 1951. In this case, he suspected another root cause (i.e., ultimate factor): "Die-off was spectacular in February and March; quail appeared to be 'lighter' . . . than at most other times. [They] foraged continuously, almost frantically, on all but the coldest days of late winter; their search was undoubtedly for food *per se* rather than for food high in Vitamin A. Added together, these things suggest what might be termed 'simple starvation' was a potentially important factor in the February [and] March die-off."

Bobwhites, especially southern birds which carry less body fat than their northern kin (see chapter 9, Fat Bobwhites), can starve more rapidly than most people realize. The average Lone Star bob will survive less than two days at freezing temperatures with nothing to eat. Bobwhites burn out like rocket motors. Seemingly, the birds under Jackson's watchful eye perished with an abundant food supply. Greens (leafy foliage of forbs) were widespread and readily available.

Greens, however, are rather poor quail fare in many respects. They do have relatively high levels of protein and carbohydrates by dry weight (all water evaporated). Raw greens, however, contain 80–90% water, which provides no energy value. Furthermore, most birds species are incapable of digesting leafy plant material, extracting only 40% of the calories in these foods. A bobwhite that eats its weight in greens obtains about 0.2 ounce (5.7 g) of usable food. This provides perhaps 20 kilocalories, far too few for daily needs in the wild. By way of an analogy, if humans burned energy as fast as bobwhites and metabolized greens with equal efficiency, the San Francisco 49ers would have to eat more than 5.5 tons (5000 kg) of lettuce each day to maintain team weight.

In warmer climates, bobwhite populations living largely on greens, or those running energy deficits for whatever reason, may be prime candidates for die-offs. Suppose a fairly dense population enters fall with low supplies of quality foods such as insects and seeds. The population could maintain itself on low quality foods for as long as temperatures remained mild. Individuals might be running slight daily energy deficits, but immediate problems would not be apparent. Weight loss would not be obvious, because water tends to replace fat as fat is burned for body maintenance. Thus, even birds in poor to fair body condition would appear normal.

If a cold spell were to hit a population low on fuel, massive losses, as observed by Webb, Jackson, and Lehmann, could occur quickly. Cooler temperatures elevate daily energy needs. If snow covered food supplies, energy reserves (body fat) would drain rapidly. Under this scenario, it is easy to imagine massive starvation losses over large areas in only a matter of days. The quail population would be doomed, even if hawks, coyotes, foxes, or diseases played no role in mortality.

33 Key Variables in Quail Production

THE REMARKABLE INCREASES IN BOBWHITE POPULATIONS from spring to fall raise the question as to whether young birds produce broods the same year they hatch. This reproductive feat is accomplished by mourning doves (*Zenaida macroura*); chicks hatched early in the breeding season can lay and hatch eggs before the year is over.

A long breeding season, rapid development to sexual maturity, and a short period between laying and independence of chicks characterize the breeding biology of doves. These birds breed virtually year-round in southern climates, with peak hatching in May, June, and July. Males reach sexual maturity in 80 days and females in 93 days. Only 30 days elapse from the time an egg is laid until young birds can take care of themselves.

Bobwhites have a more daunting reproductive task than doves. It takes about 12 to 18 days to lay a clutch and 23 days to incubate the eggs. Thus, a female bobwhite will spend 35–41 days to hatch chicks, not counting time to find a nest site and construct a nest. Bobwhites also reach sexual maturity at a much slower rate than doves. A study reported in *Poultry Science* (1968) indicated that the average age to first egg production was 224 days (ca. 7.5 mo.). This time period was for captive birds with ample food; wild birds would face more rigorous conditions.

The earliest a bobwhite might hatch in south Texas, where some birds begin laying as early as mid-March, is about the first of May. Add 7.5 months until reaching sexual maturity, and the first possible eggs of a hatching-year quail would be laid about the middle of December. Laying at this time would be biologically foolish because cold weather, low insect supplies, and other factors would doom a brood. The biological evidence indicates that wild bobwhites cannot raise a brood in the same year that they hatch. Other variables must be considered to understand the productivity of this species.

An age ratio in autumn quail populations will indicate production per surviving adult. In general, the higher the ratio, the higher the production. The age ratio depends on several key variables important to quail production.

Fig. 19. Bobwhite nests are vulnerable to predators, trampling, abandonment, flooding, and high temperatures. The loss of a nest is counteracted by renesting.
PHOTOGRAPH BY DALE ROLLINS

- The proportion of hens that goes into laying condition. Generally, it is thought that all hens in a population attempt to lay at least one clutch. In drought years, some hens may not enter laying condition.
- The number of eggs in a clutch. Bobwhites in northern environments have larger clutches (i.e., more eggs in a nest) than bobwhites in southern environments. The average is about 12 viable eggs for the first nesting attempt; typically, the number of eggs will decline in second and third clutches.
- The probability of nesting success on any single attempt. As a general rule, 30–35% of nests initiated are expected to succeed (i.e., result in a hatch). A slight increase in the nest success rate (e.g., 50%) will increase age ratios in autumn dramatically.
- The number of renesting attempts. Hens that lose a clutch may renest up to four times in an attempt to have at least one successful nest. If renesting attempts decline, age ratios will decline.
- The number of days in the laying season. Because it takes time to find a nest site, prepare it for use, and lay and incubate a clutch (47–55 days), hens will have more opportunities to renest or have multiple broods with longer laying seasons. The laying season typically ranges from 90 days in

hotter, drier environments to 150 days in more temperate environments. Cold temperatures early in the laying season, or hot temperatures late, can reduce the number of days in the laying period.

- The survival rate of chicks. Chicks typically survive at a daily rate of about 0.9956. This means that 44 of every 10,000 chicks are expected to be lost each day. Higher chick survival rates lead to higher age ratios.
- The survival rate of adults. The daily survival rate of adults in summer is about 0.9967. Lower adult survival rates lead to higher age ratios and vice versa.
- The distribution of the hatch in time. Age ratios may be lower in years in which most hatches occur early in the nesting season and higher in years in which most hatches occur later. Generally, adults are expected to survive at higher rates than juveniles. Therefore, early hatches favor adults in the age ratio, and later hatches favor juveniles.

Managers may be able to increase the probability of nesting success by increasing the length of the laying period, thus permitting more renesting and attempts at raising multiple broods. Quality nesting cover should be available throughout the potential nesting season. Any practice, such as overgrazing, that reduces nesting cover later in the season is likely to reduce production.

34 *To Gemini and Cancer*

GEMINI AND CANCER STAND OUT AS IMPORTANT ASTROLOGICAL signs for bobwhites. If the planets should conspire to destroy a quail population, serious damage can be inflicted from May 21 to July 21. If Jupiter aligns with Mars, or whatever is necessary for a normal breeding season, then most bobwhites would hatch under Gemini and Cancer. On average, about 50% of nest initiation and 50% of hatching are expected to take place under these signs of the Zodiac.

The reproductive effort is an orderly process, barring a visit from Halley's Comet. In eastern south Texas, it begins shortly after the first of March, peaks in late May, June, and early July, and effectively ends in September. A few hatches take place in October.

If the breeding season progresses without catastrophe, about 85 to 90% of production will be completed by June 30. Late-season production (August, September, and October) cannot reverse damaging losses that take place earlier, at least in Texas. Late-season production may be relatively more important in other states. The month of June potentially accounts for one-third of nest production and two-fifths or more of chick production.

Flooding rains are the most likely catastrophe during breeding season. Herbert L. Stoddard, based on studies in the Southeast, reported in 1931 that about 30% of nest abandonment could be attributed to the elements.

"Many nests that are built in low areas during times of temporary drought are flooded during heavy rains," according to Stoddard. "Heavy rains likewise knock material from the nest roof down upon the eggs, or keep the nest in such a saturated condition that it is finally abandoned. Other nests may have mud washed down over the eggs during hard showers."

Summer deluges also exact a toll on young chicks. Stoddard reported that:

"Although loss of developing chicks by drowning appears likely to be of little consequence in the rolling types of country, and is largely confined to very young chicks, . . . it may become a serious factor in low, flat country with an impervious subsoil . . . , for birds caught in low ground would be forced either to swim or to perish.

"Very wet summers . . . are unfavorable to developing chicks in many ways, all of which contribute to the dwindling of the broods. While the main damage is undoubtedly caused by destruction and desertion of nests, the young chicks have their vitality lowered by wet and chilling; constant wetting may cause their death either directly or indirectly by making them more susceptible to disease.

"The general belief that wet summers are unfavorable to quail multiplication undoubtedly is only too well founded."

During the 1993-94 hunting season, a vast area between Corpus Christi and San Antonio, according to numerous eyewitness accounts, was largely devoid of bobwhites. The countryside was lush, flowers bloomed, insects buzzed, seedpods shattered. Few coveys, however, sang *koi-lee* at dawn. What happened to bird populations remains a mystery.

Nothing was particularly remarkable about the year, except for deluges in the middle of June. Some pastures received 12 inches (30 cm) of rain in one or two days. Low areas flooded and, in some cases, remained flooded for weeks. Even in rolling terrain given to rapid runoff, sheets of water reportedly tumbled down slopes. If a deluge in mid-June wiped out the month's hatch plus some younger chicks, autumn age ratios might be expected to drop from four young per adult to less than three. Typical expectations would be for populations with the latter age ratio to provide good hunting early in the season with hunting rapidly becoming poor as the season progressed.

Hunting, however, started poorly and remained so in the prairies and brushlands north of Corpus Christi. June rains seem to be an incomplete explanation for population failure. Perhaps lingering effects of the rains eliminated most production after the June deluges. Also, if breeding populations were low to begin with, a midsummer production catastrophe could make quail exceptionally scarce.

Heavy summer rains hit other portions of south Texas in 1993. In some cases, population failures ensued; in others, mysterious events occurred; in yet others, populations responded with vigor. A stretch of coastal prairie south of Corpus Christi reportedly had strong populations in early autumn, but when hunting season arrived, the quail had disappeared. Likewise, on the Bomer Wildlife Research Area, a 60-acre (24-ha) Kleingrass field teemed with bobwhites during summer, but only one or two coveys remained in November. The disappearances prompted concerns that an epidemic was sweeping populations in south Texas.

While disease cannot be discounted with the evidence at hand, one must be skeptical of the more or less random observations of quail abundance; the laws of chance guarantee the occasional sightings of many quail in weak populations and few quail in strong populations. Hunting and poker have the same theoretical underpinnings. If an epidemic had swept through south Texas, why did it miss some areas and what was the disease?

The explanation for quail disappearance in the Bomer Area was that bobwhites simply had moved a few hundred yards from the open Kleingrass field to habitats with more woody cover. The area supported an autumn density of about 3.0 birds per acre (7.5/ha) and yielded a harvest of 0.75 bird per acre (1.9/ha) (despite heavy summer rains).

Walter Rosene, like Stoddard, an eminent quail biologist from the Southeast, observed in 1969 both strong and weak populations following intense summer rains. He noted better production in areas with rolling topography versus flat topography; the latter physiography would foster flooding. Bobwhites inhabiting sites with sandy soils should better

ON BOBWHITES

withstand summer deluges than those on clays; rain percolates more rapidly into sands. The crash north of Corpus Christi generally occurred on clays, although extremely weak populations were reported on rolling prairie with sandy loams.

Convincing explanations are lacking for some of the mysterious happenings on south Texas quail range during 1993. A breakdown in reproduction probably was the general cause of the low densities, because bobwhite populations in subtropical climates wax and wane with production. Recalling the 12 signs of the Zodiac, perhaps the motions of heavenly bodies mediate quail phenomena on this planet. Astrological explanations are as good as anything science can provide at this time. Without supporting data, a mysterious disease is no better an explanation of quail disappearance than an eclipse on Neptune.

 ## 35 *The Great Wisconsin Quail Irruption*

WISCONSIN ONCE SUPPORTED BOBWHITE POPULATIONS THAT would match or exceed anything in the best quail range available today. If the historical record is accurate, those birds did not behave like bobwhites should.

In 1946, A. W. Schorger chronicled the "Great Wisconsin Quail Irruption" in the *Transactions of the Wisconsin Academy of Science, Arts and Letters.* "The quail within a period of ten years, 1845–1854, became extraordinarily abundant in Wisconsin," he wrote. "In Milwaukee they usurped the place of wild pigeons, and were used for trap shooting." In Madison, quail were said to be in every grove; good shots could easily bag 50–75 per day.

Naturally, the high densities led to some exaggeration. "Yes, in the early days," observed one wag, "if you wanted a meal of quails—all you had to do was take a club and let fly once or twice among the tall grass in the park, then go about with a wheelbarrow and gather up the slaughtered ones." Bobwhites were known to fly through the windows of the United States Hotel in Madison. One afternoon, it is said, the cook captured nearly a thousand.

Because no biologists were around to do formal counts, densities reached during the Wisconsin irruption were not determined. Two observations, however, provide a general idea of abundance.

"It was said that in Madison," wrote Schorger, "'a ten-minutes [*sic*] walk enables you to put up your first bevy of quails while every succeeding five minutes furnishes a fresh covey.'" With some assumptions, it can be estimated that a density of at least 2.5 birds per acre (6.3/ha) or about one covey per six acres (2.4 ha) would result in a flushing rate of one covey per five minutes. Schorger cited an early observer who said that, on average, there were "three bevies to every [ten-acre] lot." This would suggest a density estimate of 4.5 birds per acre (11.3/ha), or a covey per three to four acres (1.2 to 1.6 ha).

While the above densities are exceptionally high, they are not unprecedented in modern times. Densities of two to three birds per acre (5.0–7.5/ha) are known from Texas and other states; my students and I estimated nearly five per acre (12.5/ha) on a well-managed ranch in the Rio Grande Plains in 1987. We had flushed one covey per six minutes, without dogs, on a different South Texas ranch in 1986; hunters with dogs had flushed a covey every four minutes.

What perhaps differs between bobwhites of yesteryear and those of today is behavior at high densities. For example, bobwhites were believed to make long movements from summer to winter range during the nineteenth century. Schorger believed distances considerably greater than 25 miles (40 km) were covered. "A movement of quail in 1866 across the Ohio from Indiana to the vicinity of Louisville, Kentucky, began September 15 and was still in progress on October 26," Schorger reported. "It extended as far down the river as Owensboro, so that the front of advance was approximately 80 miles." Broad rivers blocked the paths of migrating bobwhites, causing quail congestion. Approximately 500–1000 birds were seen at the junction of the Ohio and Mississippi Rivers in 1839.

Given the bobwhite known today, long movements by populations are difficult to fathom. If the movements were made, they were made by walking rather than flying, because the maximum sustained flight of a bobwhite is about one mile (1.6 km). The birds would be exhausted after flying this distance. During historical irruptions, bobwhites also acted abnormally in other ways. An early observer from Iowa wrote: "We saw every hundred yards flocks numbering from twenty to two hundred. They seemed half deranged; they run into town, fill the streets, and even the barns, for they break numberless windows in their flight." In 1891, similar observations were made in Minnesota: "In the early part of the fall, . . . the quail generally have a crazy spell, during which they gather into large flocks, travel quite a distance and even go into town and butt their brains out against houses."

Why did Wisconsin bobwhites irrupt in the mid-1800s? The question is pertinent to modern quail managers. Aldo Leopold observed that bobwhites were somewhat restricted in distribution and abundance when Native Americans were the primary land users in North America. With the coming of Europeans and small-patch farming, habitat conditions became ideal for the birds. All or most of the land was fully usable (see chapter 27, Space, Time, and Relativity), and quail populations responded accordingly.

Leopold's model holds in general, but fits poorly in Wisconsin. Schorger estimated that only one-eight to one-fifth of the state was under tillage during peak populations. "It is difficult to believe," he said, "that so slight an extent of agricultural development could have affected greatly either an increase or a decline in quail."

Schorger observed that a decade of extremely mild winters coincided with the population irruption, and attributed the boom to this circumstance. Bobwhites are highly vulnerable to severe winters (see chapter 32, Die-offs). The elimination of high winter mortality because of mild weather would elevate breeding densities and, ultimately, lead to population irruptions. Bobwhites began to decline in Wisconsin during the severe 1854–55 winter. According to Schorger, populations crashed even where patchwork agriculture should have provided ideal habitat conditions.

The Great Wisconsin Quail Irruption offers two major lessons for the modern quail manager. First, the powerful influence of weather on population dynamics must be acknowledged. Second, and perhaps most important, models, such as the patchwork agriculture model of Leopold, must be employed within an environmental context. A final observation: if the green house effect (see chapter 48, Hot Habitat) is real, avid bobwhite hunters should start migrating to Wisconsin.

THE LONG-DISTANCE MOVEMENTS REPORTED BY SCHORGER are interesting. Lesser prairie-chickens (*Tympanuchus pallidicinctus*) were thought to be semi-migratory in Texas during the 1800s. Recently, biologists Alan D. Peoples and Steve DeMaso of the Oklahoma Department of Wildlife Conservation, have observed long-distance movements by bobwhites in their state. The maximum flight distance reported above (one mile= 1.6 km) is probably wrong (much too long). See chapter 2, Flight.

 ## 36 *The Occurrence of Multiple Broods*

"I DO NOT QUESTION THE OCCURRENCE OF SECOND BROODS for bobwhites," wrote Jack Stanford of the Missouri Department of Conservation in 1972. "The question is, how many occur, and under what specific conditions are they most likely to occur?"

Despite Stanford's claim, doubt remained in the late 1980s about double broods in one breeding season. The universities taught baby-boomer biologists that two broods were impossible. It takes 12–18 days to lay a clutch, 23 days to incubate and 120 days to rear a brood. This totals 5.5 months. A pair committed to one brood, it was argued, would lack the time to raise two broods; the breeding season would end before a second clutch could be laid.

Furthermore, laying alters the energy balance of hens. Ronald M. Case of Kansas State University, Manhattan, studied the energy requirements of bobwhites in the 1970s. He determined that the caloric intake of a hen doubles during laying. Although it can survive on a half-potato worth of energy (35 kilocalories) each day when not laying, the hen becomes a whole-potato (70 kilocalories) bird during laying. Each egg has 15–16 kilocalories, roughly the energy in one-fifth of an average potato. This demand for extra energy does not prevent having two broods. Second and even third clutches (usually smaller than the first) may be laid if an early clutch fails; however, the energy costs of laying dictate against rash expectations of producing a second brood.

The summer molt is another energy drain. It takes nutrients in excess of maintenance requirements and turns them into new feathers—not eggs. Although timing of the molt varies among individuals, this process places a definite time limit on second broods. It has become more clear, however, that factors limiting double broods are less severe than previously supposed.

Fig. 20. Bobwhite hens may be responsible for raising up to three broods in one nesting season. Multiple broods occur in bobwhite populations throughout the United States. PHOTOGRAPH BY R. D. WILBERFORCE

"My data show," wrote Stanford, "that a hen will renest within [eight] days after hatching brood number [one], and that the cock readily takes over brooding and rearing duties. The hen appears to lose all interest in the first brood at such times. Thus, by sharing care of the brood, quail pairs . . . have the physical and behavioral capabilities to rear [two] broods in [one] production year." Stanford worked with wild-caught bobwhites held in pens, and it was argued that double broods had not been observed in the wild.

Meanwhile, near Searchlight, Nevada, Gordon W. Gullion of the Nevada Game and Fish Commission was observing Gambel's quail (*Callipepla gambelii*) at guzzlers (rain-trapping devices). "Nesting [began] in February, 1952, with the first peak of hatching in mid-April," wrote Gullion. "This early hatching peak was at the height of productivity of the 1952 food crop, and apparently many adults took advantage of this condition to bring off another brood. The second nestings were just a week or two later than the normal nesting timetable for southern Nevada's desert regions, with the second hatching peak coming in early July.

"Adults had to free themselves of their earlier broods if they were to renest while feed conditions were still favorable. Two methods [were used] to achieve this end: (1) to delegate the care of broods to the males, or (2) to 'wean' the chicks and let them take care of themselves. This latter method seemed . . . most prevalent; even broods about four weeks old were 'weaned' and left in the 'care' of . . . older birds of the year. Of 979 young quail counted at five guzzlers . . . between June 28 and July 12, 1952, 59.9 per cent had been 'weaned' and were apparently . . . independent of any parental care."

In the 1980s, researchers first documented double broods in wild bobwhites. Dan W. Speake and William Sermons of the Alabama Cooperative Wildlife Research Unit, fit hens with radio transmitters and followed their activities. Some laid and hatched two clutches during the same summer.

A bobwhite hen in Jim Hogg County, Texas, laid and hatched two clutches during summer 1990, according to J. Scott Taylor, a graduate student with the Caesar Kleberg Institute. The hen, captured and fitted with a radio transmitter on April 7, began incubating its first clutch (seven eggs) on June 19. On July 12, three eggs hatched and three were infertile; one was pipped and partially ringed, but the chick had died inside. The chicks were no longer with the hen on July 30. They could have been adopted by a male or abandoned; they perhaps joined another brood, or died. Eight eggs in the second nest, initiated on July 25, were under incubation by August 1. The entire clutch hatched on August 22, and the hen was separated from these chicks by August 27.

Meanwhile, at the Packsaddle Wildlife Management Area in Oklahoma, Alan D. Peoples and Steve DeMaso were executing a telemetry study of bobwhite reproduction. "Some 'gypsy' hens have mated with a cock, laid a clutch of eggs, left that male incubating eggs, then mated with another male to go through the process again up to three times. We have observed up to 26 percent male incubation and brood-rearing."

Loren W. Burger, Jr., and co-workers studied the mating behavior of 112 female and 148 male bobwhites trapped and fitted with radio transmitters in north–central Missouri during the 1990s. "Females exhibited apparent monogamy during 60 percent of nesting attempts and apparent polyandry during 40 percent," Burger reported. Polyandry occurs when one hen mates with two or more cocks. The inference is that clutches and broods may have multiple sires. "All females and 87 percent of males that survived to 1 September were polygamous if associations between, as well as during, nesting attempts were used to classify mating systems."

"If the initial nesting attempt fails," reported Burger, "females lay a clutch that a male incubates, then immediately begin laying and incubating a third nest." Males incubated 29% of the successful nests in Missouri.

JACK STANFORD PROBABLY WAS THE FIRST BOBWHITE biologist to promote the concept of multiple broods. To a certain extent, he was right for the wrong reason. He studied the hatching phenology of bobwhites in Missouri using two methods: direct observation of broods and backdating to time of hatch based on wings collected during hunting season.

Stanford observed two hatching peaks when phenologies based on the two methods were compared. Stanford concluded that the two peaks indicated the production of double broods. Backdating, however, is a biased method of determining hatching phenology. Interestingly, the methods Stanford used will show two peaks even if one peak exists, and being right for the wrong reason is not unprecedented in science.

The production of multiple broods in bobwhites turned out to be an embarrassment to wildlife biologists. See the next essay.

37 Implications of Third Broods

THE RECENT CONFIRMATION OF MULTIPLE BROODS IN bobwhites certainly has rocked traditional thinking on quail production. Bobwhite hens can and do raise up to three broods in a single breeding season. This finding runs counter to about 60 years of orthodoxy. A false assumption (monogamy) had led to a false conclusion (single broods only).

The production of double and triple broods, however, need not be invoked to explain the behavior of bobwhite populations in the field. In 1975, John L. Roseberry and Willard D. Klimstra, two eminent research biologists, stated: "Productivity on our [Illinois] study area, with the possible exception of 1957, would seem not to have required that hens raise more than one brood per season although these data do not preclude the possibility that some individuals may attempt to do so on occasion."

How can the paradox that multiple broods are unnecessary even though they occur be explained? Bobwhite behavior, chance factors, and time must be considered. Bobwhite hens have evolved renesting behavior; i.e., if the hen is laying or sitting on a clutch, it may renest if predators, weather-related catastrophes, or some other agents destroy a nest. It is possible that a hen will make up to four nesting attempts. Without renesting, there would be few, if any, bobwhites, assuming annual mortality stays in a range of 65 to 80%. Renesting is a hedge against high nest loss rates.

The chance of a bobwhite nest leading to a brood, on average, is about 30% or slightly higher. Pick any 100 nests and about 30 would be expected to hatch per brood. This means that the chance of any nest getting destroyed is about 70%. The chances of nest success change from year to year and from area to area, but in general, bobwhite pairs are not very lucky when it comes to nesting.

Renesting, however, makes it much more likely that a hen will raise a brood. If it makes three nesting attempts, its chances of hatching a clutch leap to about 65%, despite a 70% likelihood of failure on any single attempt. Suppose the nest destruction demons relax during a breeding

ON BOBWHITES

season and chances of nest success increase to 50%. Then, with three attempts, about 88% of hens would be expected to hatch clutches, assuming no hen mortality.

At this point, an important discovery has been revealed—a method of estimating the percentages of hens that COULD raise two or three broods if all hens were to exercise three nesting attempts. Hens may raise two broods in three ways. They can fail on the first attempt and succeed on the next two, succeed on the first and third attempts and fail on the second, or succeed on the first two attempts and fail on the third. These outcomes will hold even if the hen turns over incubation duties for the second nest to a male. To raise three broods, hens must succeed on all three attempts.

If the chances of nesting success on any attempt are set at 30% and all hens make three nesting attempts, about 1 in 5 hens would raise two broods and 1 in 50 would raise three, *if all hens survive.* Hens will, however, suffer mortality. Thus, substantially fewer than 1 in 5 hens that started the laying season could possibly have multiple broods.

Now consider the time factor; it takes time to find a nest site, construct a nest, and lay and incubate a clutch. Walter Rosene estimated in 1969 the entire process to take 47–55 days, with a hen potentially spending more than 40 days in laying and incubation. The length of the laying period changes with region and year. In the western Rio Grande Plains of Texas and southern Illinois, the average laying period is 110–20 days. In the eastern Rio Grande Plains, hens lay over about 150 days. Changes in the weather in any given year, such as a late summer heat wave, may take 40–50 days off the laying period in a given region.

If 50 days is assumed as the time required for a successful nesting effort, then time alone limits a hen to two broods in much of the geographic range of bobwhites in the United States. Moreover, the opportunity for producing double broods accrues only in those hens that start laying early in the breeding season. A hen that started on day 50 of a 100-day laying season would not have time for a second brood. Most hens that fail on the first two attempts, or succeed on the first and fail on the second, would be incapable of producing multiple broods. The passage of time guarantees this outcome.

Consider a 150-day laying season. Suppose 10% of hens start laying early enough to raise three broods. By the time hen mortality and expected nest losses are deducted, only about 2 of every 1000 hens that started would be expected to raise three broods.

The effects of chance and time combine to make expected contributions to production from multiple broods rather meager. Take two quail populations living in the same environment with habitat of identical quality. Permit one population to produce multiple broods and restrict the second to single broods and three nesting attempts. If these populations were hunted, no difference in covey flush rates would be observed. The age ratio in juveniles per adult would be imperceptibly higher in the area with multiple broods. These outcomes would hold even if the time requirement for any successful nest were reduced.

The arguments above are based on average conditions, but nature is full of exceptional ones. If a production year came along in which hens started breeding at the same time, the probability of nest success was high, and the weather stayed cool and the ground moist into September, production from second broods might be worth mentioning. It appears that biologists who contend that management efforts should be focused on first broods have been vindicated. While the production of multiple broods is interesting, it does not seem to make much difference to bobwhite populations or sport hunting.

38 *The Mysteries of Density*

BOBWHITE POPULATIONS SEEM TO BEHAVE MYSTERIOUSLY. During summer, there might be a brood at every bend in the road; yet at the beginning of hunting season, birds become hard to find. Hunting season might begin with fast gunning and soon turn to slow action. There may appear to be no quail toward the end of hunting season; yet upon return to clean up camp in April, the brush would abound with bobwhites.

Much lore has been developed to explain these mysterious processes; e.g., the puzzling fall shuffle to explain the disappearance of birds between summer and fall. That the birds had moved into the brush is a commonly proposed explanation if hunting action slows after a couple of outings. That the birds came over from the next ranch is the explanation when singles and pairs appear out of the void during breeding season. One often fails to recognize that the simple link between the density of quail (number per acre) and the chances of seeing them largely explains their miraculous appearances and disappearances.

First, the density in birds per acre must be converted to density in coveys per acre to get a true picture of what goes on during hunting season. Assuming that the average covey contains 15 birds, if hunting season begins at the excellent density of 1.00 bird per acre (2.5/ha), this translates to a covey density of 0.07 bird per acre (0.18/ha); i.e., each covey would have about 15 acres (6 ha). (This represents a square area with 270 yards [246 m] on each side.)

Second, assume a density of 0.1 bird per acre (0.25/ha). This would result in 150 acres (60 ha) per covey, representing a square area with 852 yards (775 m) on each side. So a small decline in bird density can have a rather dramatic impact on the area allocated to a covey. The effects on hunting quality would be similar.

To get a more complete picture of the relationship between hunting quality and bird density, one might ask how far apart, on average, coveys are at a specified bird density. The closer together the coveys are, the faster they will be flushed, because of less travel from one covey to the next. The answer to the question of how far apart, on average, coveys are at different bird densities has rather alarming implications. Look at the graph accompanying this essay. The graph shows a Critical Zone in which the distance between coveys is extremely sensitive to a push toward the left (lower density) or right (higher density).

If one starts with a density in the Critical Zone and slides to the left (i.e., if density declines), then the distance between coveys takes off like a space shuttle; at the same time, hunting quality drops like a meteor. At a bird density of one per 100 acres (40 ha), coveys average more than a mile (1.6 km) apart. On the other hand, if one begins with a density in the Critical Zone and moves to the right (i.e., if density increases), the distance between coveys remains flat.

Aldo Leopold, in *Game Management* (1933), reported the highest density ever recorded for bobwhites, which was seven per acre (17.5/ha) on Round Island in the Mississippi River. During counts in autumn of 1987, Harvey W. Smith, Jr., and assistants flushed a covey of bobwhites every 10 minutes, without dogs, while sampling 29.3 miles (46.9 km) of walking transect. Smith's ranch is on red, sandy soils near Cotulla on the Rio Grande Plains of Texas. Estimated density was 4.8 birds per acre (12.0/ha). During the 1987–88 hunting season, Smith and guests bagged 1.24 birds per acre (3.1/ha).

More than 3.0 bobwhites per acre (7.5/ha) have been estimated at the Tall Timbers Research Station in Florida, and on Enrique Guerra's

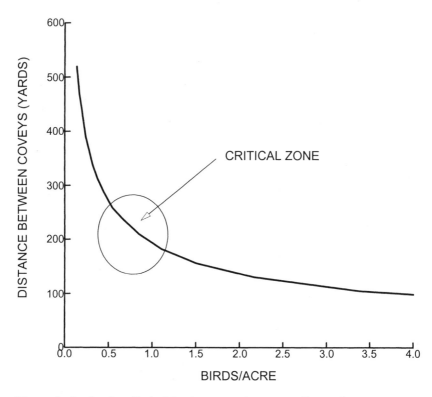

Fig. 21. As the density of bobwhites increases, the average distance between coveys decreases rapidly and then flattens out. Hunting quality is about the same, regardless of density, to the right of the critical zone. Hunting quality declines rapidly as density decreases to the left of the zone.

San Vicente Ranch in Hidalgo County, Texas. Portions of the San Vicente carried an estimated 3.9 birds per acre (9.8/ha) in autumn of 1985. The interesting thing about high densities is that hunting action will remain constant (roughly) as density increases. Hunting quality, or the rate at which coveys are flushed, will change little for densities greater than 0.5 birds per acre.

Now consider a more general type of quail density, namely group density. A group may be a covey, a brood, a pair, or a singleton. The natural behavior of bobwhites can cause group densities to cross the Critical Zone, going left or right, and bring about some of the mysterious population behaviors that are observed. Toward the end of breeding season (e.g., July and August), the countryside typically will contain a fairly high group density. Groups would consist of some pairs, a few single males, and broods of various sizes and ages. Bobwhites will seem to be quite common.

Entering autumn, however, coveys form; the several small groups coalesce into a few large groups. If covey formation moves group density left across the Critical Zone, bobwhites will seem to disappear. For example, if group density is 0.3 per acre (0.8/ha) and average group size is 5.0 birds at the end of breeding season, the distance between groups will average 275 yards (250 m). When coveys of 15 birds form, group density will drop to 0.1 per acre (0.31 ha) and the average distance between groups will increase to 475 yards (432 m). Herein lies at least a partial explanation for the puzzling fall shuffle. Covey formation lowers the density of groups. Therefore, it becomes less likely to see quail in autumn than in summer, even though the number of quail might remain constant.

Reverse reasoning shows that covey breakup in spring can move group density back across the Critical Zone. The average covey of 15 birds has about eight males and seven females. This covey might split into seven pairs and one single male (i.e., eight groups). Covey breakup, therefore, will increase group density eightfold. Beginning with a low late winter density of 0.1 group per acre (0.3/ha), the distance between coveys will average more than 0.25 mile (0.4 km). When these coveys split, however, the density of groups will increase to 0.8 per acre (2/ha). The average distance between groups will be about 185 yards (168 m). Quail will seem to appear out of the void.

If hunting season starts with a density in the Critical Zone, with harvest and natural losses, density will shift to the left and the distance between coveys will increase rapidly. Good gunning will decline rapidly. If, however, hunting season begins well to the right of the Critical Zone, fast action may hold up throughout the season. This effect also seems mysterious. How can quail continue to be harvested with no apparent effects on the population? Effects on the population are real, but not readily apparent from behind a shotgun. It is one of the mysteries of density.

THE LEARNING BEHAVIOR OF BOBWHITES ALSO INFLUENCES one's perceptions of abundance, especially during hunting season. There now is proof that bobwhites avoid hunting parties. See chapter 44, The Thinking Bobwhite.

39 *When 2 + 2 = 0*

PANGAEA, THE GREAT LAND MASS OF ANTIQUITY, BEGAN bearing continents 225 million years ago. Shortly thereafter, in terms of geologic time, about 52% of marine animals became extinct. The reasons why these extinctions occurred are not known, but a plausible explanation is that the birth of Africa, Eurasia, Australia, and the Americas fragmented shallow seas into areas that were too small for species survival.

The Pangaea event recurs on a much smaller scale throughout today's world. Wildlife habitats fragment into smaller and smaller islands as human populations and land use expand. The island analogy is a good one, because many of today's wild lands are like islands in a sea of civilization.

Bobwhites and other quail suffer the consequences of habitat fragmentation. Professor Leonard Brennan of Mississippi State University, Starkville, predicted in 1991 that bobwhites will be extinct in North America by the year 2005. This forecast is a projection of recent rates of decline. Habitat fragmentation may be a leading cause of quail decline in some areas (see chapter 53, Habitat Loss and Quail Decline).

All wild animals have minimum area requirements if they are to persist. When a habitable area becomes too small, swarms of biological hobgoblins threaten survival. Small populations deal poorly with catastrophes. It already is known that a few days of snow cover can decimate quail populations over large areas (see chapter 32, Die-offs). Large areas, however, have the advantage of large populations that help ensure the survival of some individuals. In a small area, a cataclysm is more likely to wipe out a population. Populations on island habitats can disappear with one ice storm, one fire, or one flood, perhaps never to return.

The heath hen, a race of greater prairie-chicken (*Tympanuchus cupido*), illustrates the point. Because of management, the heath hen population on Martha's Vineyard, Massachusetts, the birds' last stronghold, reached 2000 birds in 1916. A fire swept the island on May 12 of that year and the following winter was extremely severe. These events reduced the population to 150 birds; the population continued to dwindle until the last male died in 1931.

ON BOBWHITES

The island nature of fragmented habitat eliminates the possibility of replenishment through ingress from surrounding areas. A mile of plowed farmland, suburban development, or mall parking lot is intimidating to the bobwhite attempting to move between two islands of habitat.

Suppose that a catastrophe strikes and a few individuals from a small population somehow survive. The population may still be doomed. Extremely small populations are susceptible to inbreeding; this in turn could lead to the expression of undesirable genetic traits. Finally, individuals may become no better adapted to the wild than barnyard fowl; nature then would execute them swiftly and mercifully.

Even if no catastrophes strike and quail populations remain genetically vigorous, habitat fragmentation may unknit nature's fabric. Ecosystems may have keystone species upon which several other species depend for survival. If the keystone species vanishes because of habitat fragmentation, it takes into oblivion a suite of attached species.

To ensure the long-term survival of a quail population, how much habitat must be available? As a rule of thumb, population ecologists recommend that at least enough area for 500 individuals is provided (see the next essay). If areas fall below that size, management can take steps to perpetuate bobwhites; it may be possible to restock birds in areas where disasters have eliminated a population. Wild birds could be trapped and transplanted from a self-sustaining population elsewhere. Of course, transplantation is makeshift management because the problem of fragmentation would still exist.

Biologists have debated hotly the value of injecting new genetic material into an inbred population. New genes could be added by introducing birds from a different population; however, there is the danger that new material might be the wrong material for the environment. If, for example, a gene appeared that moved the breeding season to the wrong date, the consequences to the population could be disastrous.

Perhaps the most reasonable management approach to fragmentation problems would be the creation of corridors or stepping stones between habitat islands. Corridors are long, narrow strings of habitat along which animals can move between islands. Stepping stones are patches of habitat near enough to each other so that intervening dead zones do not thwart movement from island to island. Islands, corridors, and stepping stones imply the need for considerable cooperation among landowners, agency personnel, and private conservationists.

Somebody must take the lead—perhaps a Quail Unlimited chapter. This leader should seek expert guidance from a state or federal wild-life agency. The leader needs to convince concerned laypersons that quail management in fragmented countryside should be approached from a landscape perspective. Finally, and most importantly, it is critical to enlist the cooperation of ranchers and farmers, because their support is essential.

Hopefully, cooperative landscape efforts will characterize future quail management. In dealing with fragmentation, the unwary conservationist who tries to reverse the plight of populations with traditional management is bound to fail. It must be realized that two square miles (2.56 km²) of habitat here, and another two square miles (2.56 km²) over there, may in reality represent no quail habitat at all. The fragmentation demons work steadfastly to ensure that $2 + 2 = 0$.

40   *Minimum Requirements of Habitat and Population Size*

THIS ESSAY EXPLORES TWO IMPORTANT QUESTIONS IN QUAIL management: How many birds make a self-sustaining population (one that lasts for a long, long time)? How much area does this population need?

Another way to frame the first question is to ask, given a certain number of birds, what are the chances that the population will persist to some time in the distant future. The question would be irrelevant if the area occupied by quail is immense. Consider, however, a fairly large and isolated area, in which quail neither can leave nor enter from the surrounding countryside. The proper mental image is an island surrounded by unusable habitat. Under these conditions, which typify quail range in much of this great country, "how many" and "how much" are relevant queries.

Quail populations are remarkably unstable in many areas. Catastrophes such as blizzards or droughts can devastate their numbers. They have no defense against disaster except for their remarkable productivity, which itself is a source of instability. There exist no pat answers to the questions posed when dealing with boom-and-bust populations. There are few relevant data from the field. In such cases we could turn to a mystic or to the learned Dr. Sherman P. Glotz, IBM, P.C.

Glotz is somewhat eccentric. If told a lie, he will lie. If provided with flawed information, he will return the wrong answer. If one asks a million questions, all based on pure truth and sound logic, he will provide a million answers. Unfortunately, he will not reveal which answer, if any, is correct. For example, one tells him that the quail in question live in a relatively stable environment with only infrequent occurrences of catastrophes. He also is told that the population is about as stable as a quail population can be, and is asked if 500 birds are enough to ensure birds 100 years from now.

"Could be," says Glotz, "but the odds are not too good. A population of 500 living under the conditions you describe will go extinct about 10% of the time over that period. Some will go extinct within a few years." When asked how many he would recommend, Glotz, never one to give a straight answer, replies, "It depends. If you want to be certain the population persists, I recommend about 10 billion. If you are willing to gamble, you can get by with substantially fewer birds. What odds can you live with?"

Suppose 20:1 odds are acceptable. "Eight hundred. A population starting at this number has that chance of persisting for 100 years." When asked to consider a highly variable environment, one in which disasters occur frequently, Glotz replies, "This is hard to call. I need more information. What is the average population on the area? How does the starting population compare with the average? Are populations able to increase productivity and survival at low numbers? Do they suffer higher mortality at high numbers? If I were to take a wild guess, I would say 3000–4000 birds."

Glotz is asked to clarify that if a quail manager in an erratic climate wants to ensure that his great, great grandchildren have bobwhites, space for 3000–4000 birds must be provided right now. "That is my answer," says Glotz. "It is the best I can do with the information you have provided." Glotz, in his arrogance, will not admit that his answer is not as direct as it seems. His answer does not guarantee that a bobwhite population will last 100 years if it starts with at least 3000 birds.

Consider a coin flip. Even though the odds are 1:1 that the next flip will be heads, one would be imprudent to bet the farm on one flip. What will happen in the next 100 years is no more predictable than what will happen on the next flip of a coin. If, however, the coin is flipped 100 times, one would expect to see heads 40–60% of the time. Glotz's answer is predicated on 100 flips.

Glotz raised the issue of space. A population of 800, 3000, or 4000 bobwhites has definite requirements for some amount of area, with that amount depending on minimum density. If a population drops to 1 bird per 10 acres (4 ha) at a low point, then 800 birds would need 8000 acres (3200 ha) of secure, permanent habitat. This is a square area about 3.5 miles (5.6 km) on each side. At the same low density (1 bird/10 ac.), 3000–4000 bobwhites would need 30,000–40,000 acres (12,000–16,000 ha). Square areas of this size would be 7.0–8.0 miles (11.2–12.8 km) on each side.

The area requirements of self-sustaining bobwhite populations are surprising. Of course, one must be skeptical of the Glotz predictions. If, however, those predictions approximate the situation in nature, the management implications are equally surprising. Populations can be expected to disappear on what seems to be a large amount of habitat if the area is island-like. In fact, populations probably already have disappeared in this type of setting. Some populations will last several decades; others will be gone in less than a decade. No amount of habitat management will make much difference.

SEE ALSO CHAPTER 53, HABITAT LOSS AND QUAIL DECLINE. The above essay deals with what is called population viability analysis. Dr. Sherman P. Glotz is a computer model.

The Stiff Spring of Density Dependence in Quail Populations

41

THERE IS A MYSTERIOUS FORCE AT LARGE IN QUAILDOM. IT may act like the benevolent Dr. Jekyll at one time and the malevolent Mr. Hyde at another. Without the force, though, quail populations would suffer booms and busts of untold magnitude.

Consider the elegant research during the 1950s, 1960s, and 1970s on bobwhite population dynamics done by John L. Roseberry and Willard D. Klimstra in southern Illinois. Based on a detailed analysis of mortality rates in populations with and without hunting, these researchers showed that fall-to-spring mortality should have been about 73% in an area of Illinois; i.e., 73 of every 100 birds SHOULD have died from fall to

ON BOBWHITES

spring. About 66% of the birds actually died. The mysterious force reduced mortality below expectations.

The force also acted on breeding populations. When hunting reduced breeding populations below that expected without hunting, the surviving birds produced more young per adult. The net effect was that hunting did not have as much impact on populations as might be expected in the absence of the force. The force generally seems to be present in chicken-like game birds. It is known in grouse (*Tetronidae*) in Canada and gray partridges (*Perdix perdix*) in England, and probably acts on all species of quail.

Biologists call the force DENSITY-DEPENDENT POPULATION PROCESSES. This term describes the processes in which key population variables, such as survival and production, vary with density. Density is the number of animals in an area (e.g., number per acre or number per square kilometer). The term DENSITY-DEPENDENT SURVIVAL describes the phenomenon whereby survival decreases as density increases. For example, a bobwhite population at an average density of 0.5 birds per acre (1.3/ha) would experience lower survival than one at 0.2 birds per acre (0.5/ha). The difference in survival rates between these two populations would be small but important.

When lower density populations are more productive than higher density populations, DENSITY-DEPENDENT PRODUCTION is described. Like density-dependent survival, density-dependent production often is weak (but important) in quail population dynamics. One can compare annual fluctuations in quail abundance to a weight hanging on a weak spring. If the spring is stretched and the weight is released, it will fluctuate up and down violently and erratically. If the spring is stiffer and the weight is pulled with the same intensity and released, fluctuations will be less violent and erratic. That is why density-dependent processes are like a stiff spring in quail populations. For another homely analogy, a bobwhite population without density dependence is like a pickup truck with worn shock absorbers; a population with density dependence is like a pickup with new shock absorbers.

The malevolent Mr. Hyde operates on quail populations at high densities. High densities cause social stress in animals; that is why there are minimum per-bird area requirements for pen-reared quail. For whatever reasons—antagonism, conflict, aggressive behavior, competition for space—the stress ultimately weakens an individual's defense against other problems. For example, a bobwhite may become more vulnerable to diseases and parasites that would cause few problems in populations at lower densities. Humans experience the same breakdown of defenses under stress; the death of a loved one, a divorce, or pressure at the workplace are factors that can lead to illness.

Predators may focus on prey species with higher densities, given a suite of species from which to select. It makes sense for a predator to take the path of least resistance when hunting. A predator attempts on each hunt to balance the energy cost of hunting against the energy return from prey capture. Therefore, aside from prey captures due to chance, it will catch the more abundant prey animals. The predator may hunt certain types of prey selectively because of rewarding past hunts.

Time also plays a role. In time, any population is guaranteed to decline during nonproductive periods. If this population starts with individuals that vary in survival abilities, those individuals with lower likelihoods of survival will disappear first. The net result will be that the average survival rate in the population increases as time passes.

Finally, at higher densities there are fewer resources (e.g., food, water, and cover) per individual. If habitat quality varies—some poor, some mediocre, some good—individuals in high density populations will occur in weaker habitat. This could reduce their survival rate.

The benevolent Dr. Jekyll returns at low densities. Social stress diminishes, predators shift to other species, and time takes on less stature because of higher average survival rates among individuals. Individuals are awash in resources.

Quail populations would be more sensitive to harvest without density-dependent processes. Roseberry and Klimstra have shown that if a bobwhite survives hunting season, its chances of survival between the end of hunting season and the beginning of breeding season increase. As density declines, survival will increase. A breeding population reduced through hunting will be more productive on an individual basis (see chapter 43, A Trilogy on Quail Harvest Management: A Devious Beast, Indeed); i.e., the average hen will produce more chicks. As density declines, production will increase. The stiff spring of density dependence adds bounce to a hunted bobwhite population.

That same bounce is crucial for quail populations not subject to hunting. A blizzard in Oklahoma can devastate bobwhites. The stiff spring will push population numbers upward after a catastrophe. The same stiff spring will push them down after a series of years in which weather patterns are favorable and numbers grow. Without the stiff spring, population irruptions and crashes would be evident that are much more violent than those seen now. In fact, without the stiff spring, there may not be any quail to talk about.

42   *From Austin and Other Capitols*

A RECENT ARTICLE IN A MAJOR METROPOLITAN NEWSPAPER lambasted the Texas Parks and Wildlife Department, headquartered in Austin, on the manner in which the department conducts its business. From the perspective of the author, the department used timeworn, if not downright goofy, technology in evaluating game abundance and setting harvest regulations. I here assess the merit of this opinion.

Personnel in state game departments are a diverse lot. They are drinkers and teetotalers, left-wingers and right-wingers, two-steppers and boogalooers. They hold in common, by legal mandate as well as by moral conviction, a desire to protect and perpetuate a state's wildlife resources. To that end, they execute annual surveys of game abundance. The conduct of these surveys occasionally seems foolish.

Suppose a shopping mall is built on a survey route that has been used for several years. Biologists may continue counting along the route, even though it passes through Baskin and Robbins. Why? This is because a key piece of information upon which state game departments base management is the trend in wildlife abundance. A state does not need to know how many animals are present. Indeed, it is not economically feasible to determine this number.

Trends in abundance over the years provide most of the information necessary to establish harvest regulations. If a downward trend is detected for some species, then harvest regulations might be restricted or seasons closed. An upward trend could provoke the opposite response. No trend, or stable populations, provides evidence that past harvest regulations are acceptable for maintaining the state population.

The only valid way to determine a trend in wildlife abundance is to sample the same areas every year. That is why biologists continue to count along survey routes that pass through ice cream parlors.

Harvest regulations, particularly bag limits and season length, generate conflicts between the sporting public and state game departments. If a quail population crashes because of drought, departments seem to ignore their own trend data; regulations may not change, which flies in the face of common sense.

Common sense, it turns out, may fail to hold from a state perspective. Take bag limits, for example. If trend data indicated that a bobwhite population declined by 50%, a logical response would be to reduce the bag limit by 50%. A massive body of historical evidence shows that the total number of birds harvested in a state responds weakly, if at all, to changes in daily bag limits. A change in the daily bag from 1 to 2 birds would not double the kill, nor would a change from 1 to 4 birds quadruple the kill. A change from 10 to 15 birds would have virtually no effect on the total number harvested in a state. The average hunter in Texas bags 2–4 bobwhites on a hunt and 7–10 for the season. These same numbers accrue with daily bag limits of 12 to 15 birds. Whether the daily bag is 5 birds or 500 birds will have little effect on the averages.

Then why have bag limits at all? The reason is more political than biological; a tradition of bag limits for quail is being preserved. Why not reduce bag limits during population lows simply to appease the sporting public if bag limits do not matter? For one thing, the state departments want to maximize the opportunity for recreation. For another, simple and consistent regulations are more likely to be understood and followed.

Season length falls in the same general category as bag limits — it does not make too much difference. Most public hunting takes place on opening weekend, closing weekend, and holidays such as Thanksgiving and Christmas. Any season that starts, ends, and brackets the holidays will have about the same effect on total harvest, regardless of its length.

Another factor in determining season length is the self-limiting nature of recreational hunting. Self-limitation operates from three directions. First, the mere mention of low quail populations will cause many hunters to plan other activities for autumn. Second, during years in which quail are sparse, their very sparseness will limit the harvest. Any effort, such as a day of hunting by two people, becomes less and less efficient from the hunters' standpoint as populations decline. Third, the lack of reward from effort expended will cause active hunters to reevaluate their immediate goals. Hunting all weekend and seeing no birds rates about a 2 on a fun scale ranging from 1 to 10. Low quail populations will lead the average hunter to other leisure activities, like watching football. Season length is not too important if you give a hunting season and nobody comes.

The dynamics under which states legitimately operate do not necessarily hold on farms and ranches. In these smaller areas, reliable knowledge of quail population size is essential to manage the harvest efficiently. The number of quail harvested is important in any year to maximize the long-term yield. Generally, state harvest regulations provide a liberal framework within which the private manager can operate.

The state approach toward surveying game abundance and setting harvest regulations may not be pretty. It may even evoke chuckles. The methods are old-fashioned. In the days of lasers, state biologists still use spotlights. Spy satellites have not replaced Chevy pickups for counting wildlife along the byways. Nevertheless, the old-fashioned methods are valid and the harvest regulations established are based on long experience that has proven reliable.

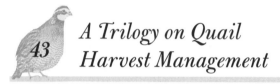

43 A Trilogy on Quail Harvest Management

THE NEXT THREE ESSAYS WILL ATTEMPT TO MAKE SOME SENSE of the conflicting opinions and recommendations on quail harvest management. Some biologists and hunters believe harvest does not affect bird population numbers, while others believe it does. Who is right? Why do beliefs differ? Are the correct principles being employed? Can unified thinking on quail harvest management be achieved?

The first essay deals with foundation research and thinking and the evolution of beliefs. The next addresses the fuzz that develops when, to draw an analogy, cups are regarded as half empty or half full. Paradoxes are fuzzy and they occur in management of the quail harvest. The third essay shows how the devious beast of harvest management makes anything under the sun seem possible. Certain hotly debated issues in quail harvest management will be found not to deserve the attention they receive, and it will be revealed that quail harvest can be managed scientifically to meet population objectives set by the harvest manager.

The Mismeasure of Management

Stephen Jay Gould wrote a book, *The Mismeasure of Man* (1981), wherein he showed how the scientists of yesteryear mismeasured, misread, and misinterpreted data on human beings. The outcome was a set of false beliefs that persists today. False beliefs do not improve the lot of humankind or the competence of the quail harvest manager. The title of this section reflects certain parallels between the mismeasure of humans and the mismeasure of the effects of harvest on quail populations.

In the United States, original thinking on the management of wildlife began to flourish in the 1930s. These must have been heady times for wildlife biologists, because new ideas were pouring forth from Aldo Leopold and Paul L. Errington, among others. Back then, almost everyone in wildlife management was a hunter by avocation, and all of them loved the wildlife they hunted.

Errington believed early on that harvesting quail did not affect their population numbers. He hypothesized that there would be no more or fewer quail whether they were harvested or not. He accepted the existence of a DOOMED SURPLUS, which, if not taken through recreational harvest, would be reclaimed by nature. The Errington concept must have been reassuring to hunters who managed wildlife; they had theoretical justification for hunting the very animals so dear to their hearts.

One assumes that Erringtonism was discussed over bracing toddies at many a gathering of wildlife professionals. If an idea is repeated enough, it becomes a belief. Somebody once said, "I wouldn't have seen it if I hadn't believed it with my own eyes." Beliefs have this effect.

A historical chronology examines how the belief that "harvest does not matter because it takes only surplus birds" has corresponded with facts.

About 1930. Paul L. Errington observes what he calls a THRESHOLD OF SECURITY in Wisconsin bobwhite populations. He finds fairly constant densities (the threshold) of bobwhites in spring. Mortality from predators seems to relax after populations reach the threshold level; i.e., few quail die from predation after numbers reach the threshold.

1935. The term DOOMED SURPLUS relative to quail first appears in print in "Bob-white Winter Survival on Experimentally Shot and Unshot Areas," by Errington and F. N. Hamerstrom, Jr. They had conducted field tests in Iowa to determine if the threshold concept operates when human harvest is added to predator losses. The research was poorly designed by present-day standards and the article is of little general value.

1944. Ben Glading and Roy W. Saarni publish an article in *California Fish and Game.* These authors conclude that more than 25% of California quail can be harvested with little effect on the average fall population.

Fig. 22. The extent (if any) to which harvest affects bobwhite populations remains a contentious issue in population management despite more than 60 years of research. PHOTOGRAPH BY R. D. WILBERFORCE

Now wait a minute. California quail in the hunted area experienced an average fall–spring mortality of 47.0%, whereas quail in a check area (not hunted) experienced mortality of 28.9%. Harvest mortality was almost a direct addition to natural mortality. The check area, it turned out, butted up against and partially surrounded the hunted area. Quail from the check area could and did, by Glading and Saarni's observations, move into the hunted area. These authors did not realize the power ingress has in minimizing the effects of harvest mortality and stabilizing harvested populations. From another perspective, every quail from a population can be harvested every year if replacements move in from surrounding areas; i.e., a 100% harvest could be recommended.

Wildlife researchers design experiments to achieve results that can be trusted. The Glading–Saarni study had an unacceptable design, with results that are unacceptable according to any known principle of logic.

1944. F. M. Baumgartner compares bobwhite populations on hunted and check areas in Oklahoma. He concludes that removal of 20 to 55% of the fall population has no conspicuous effect on the breeding population from year to year.

What is this? Baumgartner's data showed 55.5% mortality from fall to spring in the hunted area versus 26.5% in the check area. Harvest doubled the winter mortality rate. The only way that spring densities could have been equal in the hunted and check areas was if fall densities started higher in the hunted areas. Baumgartner, in fact, admitted that the hunted area had a "more favorable distribution of food and cover" than the check area. Strictly interpreted, Baumgartner's results showed that spring populations in hunted areas with better habitat were about the same as spring populations in check areas with poorer habitat.

1945. Errington admits in print that he is wrong about the constant threshold concept. The threshold is variable; moreover, catastrophes such as blizzards are not considered in his theory.

This admission by Errington should have laid the doomed surplus concept to rest. The belief, however, had been formed. It spread like a computer virus on the internet through the minds of wildlife managers, outdoor writers, and hunters. Researchers "found" support for the belief, just as nineteenth century anthropologists had "found" an association between the heaviness of eyebrows and criminal behavior.

The results of field research in the past two decades do not support the early thinking on harvest management. A consensus is developing among wildlife biologists that harvest, to some degree, adds to natural mortality. The early workers, however, lacked the luxury of hindsight, and were, without doubt, dedicated and honest; the nature of this essay in no way is meant to question their integrity. Moreover, present-day researchers, including myself, undoubtedly are laboring under many false beliefs.

Fuzzy Logic

Fuzzy logic is a new way of thinking about truth. Fuzzy logicians argue, for example, that a statement on the effects of harvest on quail populations is most likely to be partly true and partly false, and unlikely to be completely true or false.

Consider these fuzzy statements: Quail harvest mortality is compensatory. Quail harvest mortality is additive. Compensatory mortality occurs when the losses due to harvest and the losses due to natural agents compensate for each other. If losses due to harvest increase, losses due to natural agents will decline. If this mutual compensation is absolute, harvest will have no effect on total losses. The shooting of one bird will generate life miraculously to another. Additive mortality occurs when losses due to harvest add to losses attributable to natural agents. If additivity is absolute, each bird shot will reduce the postseason population by exactly one bird.

Whether harvest mortality is compensatory or additive has important implications toward harvest management. If it is compensatory, harvested and unharvested population numbers will be about the same. If it is additive, harvested populations may be lower than unharvested populations.

Absolute compensation or absolute additivity is possible. Absolute compensation would occur if a harvest is completed and all surviving birds die from some catastrophe. In this case, the population would be the same—zero—with or without harvest. Absolute additivity would occur if no birds died from natural causes. Between these extremes, compensation and additivity are fuzzy concepts.

Here is an example of the fuzziness. Suppose a population of quail is expected to experience 50% winter mortality if it is not hunted. Suppose further that a manager decides to harvest 50% of the birds present at the start of hunting season. The total mortality rate, with the harvest, would be about 75%. If harvest mortality is absolutely compensatory, the total mortality would be 50%; if absolutely additive, the total mortality would be 100%. The total mortality of 75% indicates that the harvest is at once compensatory and additive.

Considering the statement that harvest mortality is compensatory, one might conclude the statement to be about 50% true and 50% false based on the above example. The cup of quail harvest theory is half empty and half full, and it gets worse.

The natural mortality rate without harvest will influence conclusions on additivity and its topsy-turvy counterpart, compensation. Here is a remarkable outcome of harvest management theory. Considering the time from start to end of a normal hunting season, one can say that the net loss to the population for each bird shot roughly equals the survival rate in the absence of harvest.

Suppose a population would experience 50% mortality with no harvest. Then 50% of the birds would survive without harvest. Moreover, only 50% of the birds shot would debit the postseason population; e.g., the harvest of 100 birds would result in a net loss of 50 birds at the end of hunting season. Therefore, the degree of truth in the statement that hunting mortality is additive, increases as natural survival rate increases. The degree of truth for compensation increases as the natural survival rate declines.

Time also enters the picture. Suppose hunting season lasts one second. Hunters arrive early, find coveys, level their shotguns and blast away when season opens. The statement that harvest mortality is additive would hold 99.99999% true with a one-second season. The degree of truth in the statement will decrease as length of the hunting season increases. On the flip side, the degree of truth in the statement that harvest mortality is compensatory, will increase as the length of the season increases. Neither statement ever becomes 100% true except in the extreme circumstances discussed above (100% survival or 100% mortality).

Notice that up to this point additivity and compensation have been treated as intertwined concepts relating to the hunting period. If the period of consideration is expanded, more fuzziness is added to the additivity – compensation issue. For example, if a quail population is harvested in only 1 year and the effects of harvest are measured 10 years later, the concept of compensation would be found to have a high degree of truth.

The above example is deliberately outrageous. It merely illustrates that when a biologist, sportswriter, or hunter talks about additivity or compensation, one must know the exact time frame. A second important time frame is the start of one hunting season through the start of the next. When some people address additivity – compensation, they are referring to this period (see the next section, A Devious Beast, Indeed).

Here are some conclusions:

- Additivity and compensation of harvest mortality are hopelessly intertwined. The degree of truth in either concept varies with the period of reference and quail survival rates.
- Generally, but not always, quail populations subject to harvest will have lower postseason densities than populations not subject to harvest. This premise holds based on theory and field research.
- Perhaps the concepts, additivity and compensation, are like Don Quixote's windmills.

With density-dependent survival (see chapter 41, The Stiff Spring of Density Dependence in Quail Populations) and the passage of time, it is possible (in theory) for the death of a quail to generate the equivalent of another quail's life.

A Devious Beast, Indeed

If one reads the popular and technical literature on quail harvest management, utter confusion may result. One sees statements like: eighty percent of bobwhite populations are going to die from various causes so harvest does not matter; bobwhite populations can sustain 70% harvest; harvest is more additive than compensatory; harvest should be reduced during population lows. Conflicting opinions about harvest may appear in the same issue of an outdoor magazine.

Does chaos prevail, or do these conflicting opinions suggest something about the very nature of the beast of harvest management? First, some definitions must be established. The word "hunting" does not necessarily mean the killing of quail. A management biologist from a state wildlife agency might say that hunting season regulations do not make much difference, regardless of the number of quail, or that hunting does not make any difference. These statements have been time-tested and are largely true (see chapter 42, From Austin and Other Capitols). In contrast, the word "harvest" means the killing of quail.

The annual cycle of a quail population includes three periods that are relevant to harvest management: the start to the end of hunting season; the end of hunting season to the start of breeding season; and the start of breeding season to the start of hunting season. To simplify this essay, it will be assumed that hunting season ends at about the time breeding season begins. The assumption, which holds for states such as Texas, eliminates the second period from consideration.

In the second part of the trilogy, it was concluded that harvest of quail generally reduces the number of breeders, but not necessarily in a one-to-one fashion. An example demonstrated that the harvest of 100 quail might reduce the breeding population by 50 quail.

What does the size of the breeding population have to do with the number of quail available at the start of the next hunting season? Upland game birds—grouse, pheasants, quail—show a general tendency of breeding populations with lower densities to be more productive than breeding populations with higher densities (see chapter 41, The Stiff Spring of Density Dependence in Quail Populations).

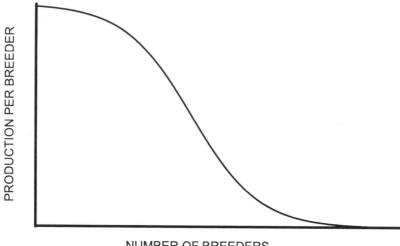

Fig. 23. Paul L. Errington discovered in the 1940s that individual bobwhites were more productive at lower breeding densities. In Iowa and Wisconsin, the relationship between production and density was found to follow a reverse-S pattern.

Paul L. Errington reported this effect in 1945 in bobwhite and ring-necked pheasant (*Phasianus colchicus*) populations; his research showed a reverse-S relationship between breeding density and percentage of summer gain. Here are some examples of how the reverse-S pattern might work.

- If breeding density is 500 quail, summer gain will be 273%. The population at the start of hunting season will be 1865 quail.
- If breeding density is 750 quail, summer gain will be 191%. The population at start of hunting season will be 2182 quail.
- If breeding density is 2000 quail, summer gain will be 0.02%. The population at the start of hunting season will be 2040 quail.

According to Errington's reverse-S pattern, one may end up with about the same number of quail at the start of hunting season, given reasonable variation in breeding density.

The reverse-S pattern is stronger in northern than in southern latitudes, which leads to mixed opinions about harvest management. Many catastrophes, such as flooding rains, cold spells, heat waves, or simple bad luck, can undermine a production season. The reverse-S pattern represents an average tendency of quail populations.

Now imagine a group of lonely wildlife biologists—field glasses on neck, clip board in hand, a copy of *A Sound County Almanac* in hip pocket. The group is studying how the previous year's harvest affects populations the following year. The studies take place at different times and places, and none lasts more than a few years. A sampling of conclusions that might be reported in *The Journal of Wildlife Management* and *Quail Unlimited* magazine are as follows:

- Harvest reduces quail populations in direct proportion to the percentage of the population harvested.
- Harvest reduces quail populations but the reduction is less than one would expect from the harvest rate.
- Harvest has no effect on quail populations.
- Harvest stimulates quail populations; i.e., the shooting of birds this year will increase the population next year.

Errington's reverse-S pattern will permit any of the conclusions to be true at a given time and place. The different outcomes arise when breeding populations start at different points along the reverse-S curve. The beast of harvest management is a devious beast, indeed.

One can defeat the devious beast with sustained yield management of the quail harvest. Many quail hunters would prefer MAXIMUM sustained yield management, which has the goal of maximizing the number of quail that can be harvested from a management area down through the years. Under sustained yield management, the fuzzy notions of additivity and compensation take a background role. In fact, one can ignore them completely, as the goal will be to achieve a harvest that will leave a desired density of breeders. That density will be chosen based on information contained in Errington's reverse-S pattern; the proper density is the one that maximizes the spring-to-fall increase in population size.

Maximum sustained yield management in a specific area imposes certain burdens on the manager. He or she must develop a scientific harvest management program that will entail censusing the quail population during fall and spring and measuring the total harvest in detail. These records will permit adapting harvest management to a specific area to acquire the maximum yield.

Hunters who protect smaller coveys to preserve breeding birds may not accomplish the objectives of maximum sustained yield. John L. Roseberry and Willard D. Klimstra have shown in *Population Ecology of the Bobwhite* (1984) that decline in covey size is related only weakly to winter

Fig. 24. Under maximum sustained yield management of the harvest, bobwhite populations are harvested to a spring density, which is expected to maximize production during any breeding season. Not only do hunters benefit from this type of management, some contentious issues (additivity vs. compensation) in harvest management become irrelevant. PHOTOGRAPH BY DALE ROLLINS

losses in bobwhites. Thus, covey size could remain fairly constant from fall to spring while the population suffers a high death rate. In general, covey size will decline at a much slower rate than population size during winter.

There is likely an optimum covey size that will promote survival. Perhaps 12 birds, for example, is the best number for a roosting disc (circular formation of bobwhites). If so, birds from small coveys would have a tendency to join birds from another small covey, thus creating the ideal size. This process would mask the effects of hunting losses based on covey size alone.

44　The Thinking Bobwhite

BEFORE ENTERING THE MINDS OF BOBWHITES, ONE FIRST must address the troublesome issue of whether or not animals think. The operating assumption has long been that they are incapable of thinking. Rather, orthodoxy holds that all animal behavior represents unconscious responses to genetic wiring. Genetic dictates may yield simple and powerful survival rules for bobwhites:

- Freeze when a threat (e.g., a hawk) is in the air overhead.
- Run or freeze when a threat (e.g., coyote or fox) is approaching on the ground.
- Fly when a ground threat gets within a critical distance.

Debate rages among animal behaviorists as to whether animals can enhance simple survival rules with thoughtful exploration of alternatives responses. In his book *Animal Minds* (1992), Donald R. Griffin points out the common sense view that "animals are likely to think about what they are doing and the results they expect from their actions, especially when these are adapted to varying and often unpredictable circumstances." He further states that it is impossible with current technology to prove or disprove the possibility of animal thought.

Nevertheless, bobwhites would be well served by an ability to recognize the nature of unexpected or unusual threats, and to freeze, run, or fly, depending on which behavior maximizes the chance of survival. This would require the ability to learn from experience and, in a most primitive sense, anticipate the future outcomes of alternative responses. The development of behavioral traditions in bobwhite populations could develop if experienced individuals are able to train naive individuals. Primitive thinking would add enormously to the repertoire of responses to danger, adding to the list of survival rules:

- Ignore the approach of a cow; cows do not kill.
- Ignore helicopters; they never attack.

- Run like hell at the approach of one or more slobbering dogs followed by a highly modified pickup truck.

Hunters have wondered if a much discussed but unproven increase in the propensity of bobwhites to run might be an outcome of genetic selection. The argument goes: if the propensity to run is genetically based, and if runners are less likely to be shot than holders, then hunting creates populations of runners. Runners beget more runners, and holders end up in gravy.

Dr. Steven D. Lukefahr, a geneticist at Texas A&M University–Kingsville, stated in 1996 that it was possible (in principle) for hunting to create genetic runners. Hunting, however, is not the only mortality agent for bobwhites. Can genetic runners deal effectively with other threats? When a hawk circles overhead, for example, the bobwhite that runs is at extreme risk. It would be better to remain hidden in the ragweed, because running could be (quite literally) a dead-end behavior. One now is confronted with the unlikely proposition that hunting mortality must be selective for birds that run from humans but hold for hawks.

Suppose running is a learned behavior and hunted populations develop a stock of wary birds to deal with hunters. (Wariness is the ability to recognize new threats and respond in a manner that increases the chance of survival.) A population may start hunting season with wariness reserves near zero, because most of the population will be unschooled juveniles. As hunting season progresses, many birds will be exposed to hunting pressure, and some will be killed. For the stock of wariness to grow, individuals must be able to associate a behavior (holding tight) with an undesirable fate (death). If bobwhites are capable of thinking in a primitive manner, they may decide to try a new behavior—running for better cover. Also, if bobwhites can associate hunting parties with undesirable fates, they probably can associate certain areas with hunting parties and may begin living where hunting parties are less likely to occur.

Now the stock of wariness begins to grow and feed upon itself. Birds with the baccalaureate in Hunter Avoidance start running at the approach of setters and pointers. Naive birds associate running and hunting, and by imitation, become runners. Birds begin to occur where hunters are not present. Wariness spreads through the population like an epidemic of coccidiosis in north Texas.

The ring-necked pheasant is a case in point. During the late 1970s, my students and I at Texas Tech University, Lubbock, were estimating pheasant numbers on dry lake beds. Spotters were positioned at the far side of a lake bed; then a drive crew swept through the cattails (*Typha* sp.) and rushes (*Juncus* sp.), flushing the birds. Before hunting season, spotters positioned themselves at a leisurely pace. After hunting season, spotters had to sprint to their positions. Pheasants had come to associate vehicles and humans with undesirable fates, and had found that running was a good response. Reliable counts could not be obtained unless spotters beat pheasants to the far side of the lake bed.

Meanwhile, as wariness grows in bobwhites, the recompense for some fixed hunting effort, such as one hunter in the field for one day, will decline. The decline would be due in part to removal of birds from the population by hunting and natural agents. Fewer birds mean lower encounter rates. Hunting quality may deteriorate faster than can be explained solely by removal of birds; it may decay more quickly because the population has accumulated a large stock of wary birds that has learned how to foil humans and dogs.

It is likely that an experienced hunt manager, through trial and error, would develop protocols to deal with the thinking bobwhite. In some intensely hunted areas, a rule of thumb is to never hunt a course more frequently than once every week or two. This policy would at first make sense on the basis of distributing harvest throughout an area. If bobwhites think, the policy also makes sense in terms of dealing with learned behaviors.

To conclude this essay, recall the 1967 movie, *Planet of the Apes.* These were exceptional apes, for they had literature, culture, and medicine. They were thinkers. The apes also had a Forbidden Zone in which no ordinary ape was free to tread. Orthodox apes thought it best to keep some concepts concealed from the average simian citizen.

We have been walking the Forbidden Zone, dear reader. Thinking bobwhites? What next?

The Role of Random Variation
in Population Dynamics

45

THE SOUTH TEXAS BRUSH COUNTRY TEEMED WITH BOBWHITES during the excellent 1987–88 hunting season, and the 1992–93 season was even better. The years in between, however, were poor to mediocre. Why are not more seasons like 1987–88 or 1992–93?

The answer lies in demons and imps that harry the best laid management plans. Trolls periodically emerge from terra incognita and wreak havoc on quail populations. The unrelenting specter of time tantalizes the slavering quail hunter, only to award a kick in the teeth.

Imagine perfect bobwhite management in a perfect environment. Woody cover is well distributed, ground cover provides freedom of movement while concealing birds from their enemies, and foods are readily available and highly nutritious. There are no blizzards, droughts, or floods. Rain falls at exactly the right time in precisely the proper amounts. One would expect, under these conditions, high and stable quail populations. The expectation of high populations would be reasonable, although busts are possible. The expectation of stable populations, however, would not be reasonable.

The imps of chance work to impose ups and downs in quail numbers. Suppose one could base population trends on the flip of four fair coins. Four tails beget a population bust, three tails a mild decline, two tails a stable population, one tail a mild increase, and no tails (all heads) a population eruption. After 100 years of management, one would expect 6 years with population busts, 25 years with mild declines, 38 years with stable populations, 25 years with mild increases and 6 years with booms. Remember, these trends take place in a perfect environment with perfect management.

Nature is rife with the imps of chance. The genetic composition of quail populations can drift randomly from one state to another, and perhaps affect production and survival. Accidents, purely chance events, will vary in frequency from year to year. Simple luck will affect the rate at which predators find and depredate bobwhites. Despite their diabolic properties, the imps of chance are minor pests in the grand scheme of quaildom. They become major pests when they mature into the trolls of tragedy.

Now imagine perfect bobwhite management in a less than perfect environment—one with trolls. An extended period of snow cover could devastate quail populations; a hard drought could reduce production to near zero, causing numbers to plummet. Pity hunters whose quarry endures both blizzards and droughts. Back-to-back occurrences of such catastrophes could render vast areas largely barren of quail for some time.

The specter of time enters the quail population equation every breeding season. The reproductive juices begin to flow as days lengthen in spring. These juices dry up as days shorten in autumn. A hen must commit 47–55 days, to finding a nest site, constructing a nest, and laying and incubating a clutch. Clearly, the time available in summer limits its potential production.

Time also is contained in the rate at which populations can grow after a catastrophe. Imagine hunting somewhere in the Rolling Plains of north Texas. Drought limits production during a particular summer; during the next winter, a foot of snow covers the ground for two weeks. The bobwhite population suffers widespread and massive death, leading to a density of one bird per 1000 acres (400 ha). It will take at least 10 years for the population to return to a respectable level (e.g., 1 bobwhite/ac., 2.5/ha). Time to recovery will exceed 10 years if any catastrophes occur, or if the imps of chance contrive against the population. So even with faultless management, the specter of time can make any management efforts seem ineffective for the better part of a decade.

Demons struck south Texas quail in the mid-1980s. The winter of 1984 was a hard one (by standards of the subtropics); a short, stiff drought followed and hunters in the 1985–86 season spent most of their time playing dominoes. The trolls went back to their caves during the breeding season of 1986. Rain fell as if the Rio Grande Plains had been translocated to Mississippi. Everybody expected a banner year for hunting, and everybody was disappointed when they went afield. What had happened?

The specter of time knew. Extremely low quail densities cannot go to high densities in one year. That is not enough time. The weather remained favorable for bobwhites, and by the 1987–88 hunting season, the population had irrupted. The trolls of tragedy, however, waited in the wings.

The reason for not having more hunting seasons like 1987–88 or 1992–93 is that powerful factors beyond management control influence bobwhite numbers (see chapter 35, The Great Wisconsin Quail Irruption). As one cannot manage the weather, repeal the laws of chance, or increase the speed of light, one simply has to accept imps, trolls, and specters in quail population dynamics.

Managers, however, can take steps to thwart the demons by maintaining numerous species of plants and animals that are consistent with the habitat needs of bobwhites. Providing diversity will help reduce the effects of catastrophes.

The management of small populations should be of special concern. Should hunting be allowed during a drought? Should livestock be excluded during drought so that quail will have more cover? The more birds that live through a catastrophe, the less influence the specter of time has when the situation returns to normal.

Perhaps most importantly, space can be provided; the more usable habitat quail have, the more quail there will be, even after a drought or a blizzard (see chapter 27, Space, Time, and Relativity). The more quail there are, the faster populations will return to normal levels after some troll has done its dastardly work.

THE IMPS OF CHANCE CAN BE REGARDED AS RANDOM variation. For example, if a coin is flipped five times, and this is repeated several times, the number of heads in a run of five will vary. The variation arises from random processes. This same type of variation occurs in nature and, in this essay, was attributed to fictitious imps.

Part Four

ISSUES AND
PHILOSOPHIES

"'GAME' ANIMALS ARE 'CREATED' . . . BY SELF-STYLED 'wildlife managers' who cut, burn, flood our forests and land in a pattern of ecological havoc that upsets nature's balance and eliminates 'nongame' animals." So said the Fund for Animals, Inc., in a 1973 survey by the National Shooting Sports Foundation. The statement is propaganda—or is it?

Herbert L. Stoddard, the father of modern bobwhite management, strongly advocated the burning of forests to improve bobwhite habitat. Clear-cutting would be a good management prescription for dense and old forests. Grazing, discing, and mechanical brush management may be simple, cost-effective methods of producing more bobwhites. None of these management techniques is delicate. Some people, especially those with an antihunting bias, would say the practices wreak ecological havoc.

The outbreak of antihunting and animal rights sentiments in recent years has jolted the fraternity of hunters and wildlife managers. Animal rights advocates have challenged the basic precepts of the wildlife management–hunting system.

Daniel J. Decker and Tommy L. Brown of Cornell University in Ithaca, New York, described in 1987 how animal rights advocates, the most fervent antihunters, view the system as a "you pat my back, I'll pat yours" loop: wildlife managers create surplus animals for hunting and hunters pay (license fees and excise taxes on arms and ammunition) wildlife managers to create the surplus. They reported that "[o]verall, wildlife management is depicted as a process to maintain ecological imbalance by manipulating habitat and hunting, thereby ensuring a harvestable surplus of game for hunters to shoot and guaranteeing a flow of revenue to subsidize the agencies that carry out wildlife management."

The animal rights movement challenges traditional wildlife management on four fronts: education, performance, methods, and motives. According to the movement, education overemphasizes wildlife populations and underemphasizes individuals in those populations. From their perspective, a healthy, self-sustaining population of game animals neither justifies nor counterbalances hazards to individual animals. Performance, they say, runs counter to sound principles for dealing with nature, charging that wildlife management creates an imbalance and distresses individuals and populations of nongame species. The animal rights philosophy holds that certain methods of population management are heinous. They believe harvest to be an inhumane method of population management that abrogates the rights of individual animals. These activists want no less than full civil rights for animals. Motives, they argue, are self-serving, and ask if wildlife managers would be so intent on creating imbalances if they were not getting paid to do it.

Some criticisms from the animal rights groups merely pit one set of human values against another. Should populations or individuals be the focus of management? Do animals have rights equal to those of humans? Let your conscience be your guide.

One can evaluate, with objective data, the merit of other criticisms. Does habitat management in general, and quail habitat management in particular, cause stress to nongame animals? My research group at the Caesar Kleberg Institute recently completed a five-year analysis (1986–90) of the response of nongame birds to bobwhite habitat management. The work took place in a typical brush country setting, with honey mesquite being the most common tree.

The first concern was to determine if intense food and water supplementation might alter the composition and abundance of nongame bird populations. On one hand, supplementation might benefit nongame species that eat seeds and drink water. On the other, it might disrupt the organization of bird communities by attracting huge numbers of unpopular species, like blackbirds—grackles (*Quiscalus* spp.), starlings, and other birds of ebony hue. Neighborhoods that have endured roosting concentrations of blackbirds can attest to their unpleasantness.

My technicians and I set out a feeder and waterer for each 20 acres (8 ha). Sorghum (milo) was fed from August through March and water was supplied year-round. Nothing happened. With or without food and water supplementation, areas we studied had 40 or 50 species of birds. No one species was affected consistently by the availability of food and water. Blackbirds did not invade.

As another part of bobwhite management program, we wrought a pattern of ecological havoc with a bulldozer and rangeland disc; 50% of the mature brush was ravaged. We, however, preserved narrow brush strips every 100 yards (91 m) and broad strips every 200 yards (182 m). Shortly

Fig. 25. Less than delicate treatments may be necessary to rejuvenate habitat for bobwhites. This area shown had too much brush; management removed most of it but left widely dispersed brush plants. The soil was ripped to allow infiltration of rainfall, which in turn will promote vigorous stands of grasses and forbs.

after treatment, about half the countryside looked like a combat zone. No changes, deleterious or otherwise, were observed in nongame bird populations. With or without brush eradication, these bird populations were healthy and diverse. Bobwhite numbers roughly doubled with brush management.

Do not take these results to indicate that game management is always compatible with nongame animals. Had we cleared more brush, we would have seen a shift in abundance and a decline in the number of bird species. Woodpeckers, for example, require mature mesquite and might have disappeared from the immediate area.

Our results showed that game management can be compatible with nongame wildlife. Whether wildlife managers flood a green-tree reservoir for mallards (*Anas platyrhynchos*), plant a food plot for mourning doves (*Zenaida macroura*), chain a dense stand of piñon–juniper (*Pinus* sp.-*Juniperus* sp.) for mule deer (*Odocoileus hemionus*), or disc a mature brush community for quail, some nongame species will always benefit. If treatments occur over large areas, wildlife managers have the technology to design programs with multiple wildlife benefits. The design may not be ideal for the game animal under consideration, but it will preserve—and perhaps increase—the richness of wildlife that society desires. In a sense, we can have our cake and eat it too.

Despite compatibility between game management and nongame animals, fervent antihunters are not going to rest their case. Decker and Brown stated that the basic antihunting strategy had two preliminary phases: "(1) stop expansion of hunting (e.g., no new seasons or new areas) and (2) increase restrictions (e.g., fewer species legal for hunting, shorter seasons, fewer hunting areas or less acreage, and tightened eligibility requirements for hunters).

"Three avenues seem to be keys to restricting hunting: restriction of opportunity, access, and eligibility. Opportunities to hunt can be restricted by diminishing the duration of open seasons and the number of species hunted. Access can be restricted by curtailing acquisition of additional public lands for hunting, decreasing the amount of public land currently available for hunting, and encouraging posting of private lands by increasing landowners' liability to trespassers. Eligibility can be restricted through more difficult and time-consuming hunter education courses and by increasing the cost of participation in hunting."

Meanwhile, most people are ambivalent about the issue. These neutrals, who total 80% of the population in Texas, represent the swing vote. Pro-hunting individuals and organizations, when setting out to "wreak a pattern of ecological havoc" for the benefit of game, should see to it that the nonhunter is not forgotten, or worse, slighted. It is easy enough to design multiple wildlife benefits into any management program.

 ## 47 *Perspectives on Grazing*

MATAGORDA ISLAND, SEVEN MILES FROM THE TEXAS MAINLAND out of Port O'Connor, once quaked from the explosions of 500-pounders (227-kilogramers). Crews from B-52s honed their bombing skills at this U.S. Air Force facility.

Beef cattle were an integral part of the wildlife management program on the island. Grazing modified the structure and composition of vegetation in a manner favorable to game, particularly bobwhites. The management formula—cows plus some 800 brush shelters—was simple and effective. Hunters took up to 5000 bobwhites during good years.

In 1972, Staff Sergeant McCoy managed the island's abundant game—deer, waterfowl, and quail. The Air Force encouraged recreational hunting, and McCoy ran a smooth operation that catered to the needs of people and wildlife. Sergeant McCoy left Matagorda Island when the Air Force closed the facility in the 1970s. The Winn family, who ranched about 11,000 acres (4400 ha) south of the bombing range, sold to the Nature Conservancy, which in turn sold the property to the U.S. Fish and Wildlife Service. Today, Matagorda is wholly public land, the administration of which is subject to political crusades. Cows have been banned. The motivation behind beef-free public lands is, in part, commendable. Cattle can cause serious problems (see chapter 50, The Misleading of America).

When Aldo Leopold, one of America's greatest conservationists, worked for the U.S. Forest Service in the Southwest, he early encountered livestock damage. In mountainous country, cattle camp along rivers and streams. These relatively level, easily grazed riparian sites contain the most abundant supplies of succulent, nutritious forage. Removal of the forage potentially can lead to erosion. During the early 1900s, Leopold saw entire valley bottoms washed away in a matter of years.

Such soil losses are tragic, because nature builds soils over eons—millions of years. When the soil goes, so go ecological options. Grazing that accelerates soil loss curses the future; it should not be tolerated by environmentalists, quail hunters, or cowboys. Removing cattle from fragile landscapes may be a sound policy.

On robust landscapes, however, grazing is an issue fraught with conflicting personal values and misconceptions. The issue of grazing being right or wrong becomes a matter of personal opinion, often lacking foundation in philosophy or science. A common misconception is that grazing lands in **GOOD** or **EXCELLENT** condition are necessarily better for wildlife than those in **POOR** or **FAIR** condition. According to 1989 observations by Dr. E. Lamar Smith of the University of Arizona, Tucson:

"The general public assumes that (1) ranges in poor to fair condition got that way as a result of overgrazing by livestock, (2) these ranges are deteriorating, and (3) reduction or removal of livestock will improve range condition. . . . Economists often assume that range condition is related to livestock production or wildlife values and that greatest return will come from improving poor condition ranges. . . . All these assumptions are logical, but incorrect.

"Range condition is a technical concept." The adjectives poor, fair, good, and excellent describe departures from vegetation conditions that existed when Comanches, Apaches, and Sioux were the dominant land users in North America. The words deliver a semantic impact that can distort opinions about grazing. If Sitting Bull's favorite hunting area somehow had remained untouched during the last 200 years, it would be said to be in excellent condition; i.e., the composition of plants would have changed little since the days of the Native American chief.

To use words with less emotional baggage, the hunting area could be described as being in LATE SERAL condition. Had the area been grazed subsequent to the altercation at Little Bighorn, it might be determined to be in poor range condition; i.e., plants different from those observed by Sitting Bull now would dominate the site. To be more objective, the area could be described as being in EARLY SERAL condition.

Range condition merely describes plant composition relative to that of yesteryear. That is all. With respect to range condition, "poor" does not mean "poor" in an everyday sense; neither does "excellent" mean "excellent." Perhaps much of the controversy over grazing would vanish if the terms early seral and late seral were used to describe range condition.

Wildlife species respond differently to range condition classes. Some, like the Great Plains harvest mouse (*Reithrodontomys montanus*), are adapted to virgin conditions. The plow and the cow, applied recklessly, are among its greatest enemies. Other wildlife species do best under non-pristine conditions. In some areas, popular species like deer and quail are favored by poor to fair range condition.

Another concern about grazing is competition between wild and domestic animals. Domestics have a distinct advantage when food supplies are low, because their owner will supply a load of hay. Such husbandry would be impractical with wildlife. Thus, wildlife die when crunches hit and cattle survive with supplementation. Had cattle been absent before the crunch, perhaps wildlife would have had better food supplies and higher survival.

The above scenario, however, does not always hold. Livestock grazing can and often does increase food supplies for wildlife by changing range condition (i.e., plant composition) from excellent to fair or poor. The main effects arise from the consumption of plant species that are most palatable to livestock, but more subtle effects are also present.

According to research published in 1987 by J. R. Brown and Steve Archer, plant ecologists with Texas A&M University, College Station, dung deposited in autumn rapidly breaks up, leaving patches of bare ground. By the end of the next growing season, the dunged spots most likely will support Scribner's dichanthelium (*Dicanthelium oligosanthes*) and thin paspalum (*Paspalum setaceum*). These grasses are members of the panic grass family, which includes such notable game bird foods as Texas millet (*Panicum texanum*), browntop millet (*Panicum ramosum*), and barnyard grass (*Echinochloa crusgalli*). In fact, Brown and Archer found these two grasses growing only on plots with dung. Thin paspalum is a good food for doves and quail. Its seeds are among the first vegetable matter eaten by quail chicks, and adults eat them frequently. Mourning doves like seeds from most species in the panic grass family.

Dr. Phil Urness of Utah State University, Logan, has spent several years studying the ecology of mule deer in the West. He found in the 1980s that cattle grazing increased the abundance of browse plants crucial to the winter survival of deer. In fact, Urness cautiously advocated CON-TROLLED OVERGRAZING as a habitat management tool.

If grazing reduces populations of a particular wildlife species, it will simultaneously increase populations of other species. Take any piece of land, change it in almost any way, and it will benefit some species and harm others. This is a law of nature. Matagorda Island, in accordance with natural law, will experience shifts in the composition and abundance of wildlife when the last cow is ferried across Espiritu Santo Bay to the mainland. Vegetation changes will drive the wildlife changes.

Without grazing, taller grasses such as seacoast bluestem (*Schizo-chyrium scoparium*) will take over upland sites. The competitive blue-stems will smother many species of forbs, especially annuals. Leaf litter will build up and bare ground will diminish. The diversity of plant life (i.e., the number of species) will decline. Likewise, the diversity of mi-crohabitats will decline; the plant community will become structurally monotonous.

How will wildlife populations respond? Ecological theory predicts a general decline in abundance and diversity of migrant and resident wild-life on the island. As grasses replace and suppress forbs, insects would be expected to decrease. As insects decline, reptiles and birds that feed on insects will diminish. Nongame birds that feed on forb seeds will decrease. Any animal, cold- or warm-blooded, that cannot abide tall, dense ground cover, will decline or avoid using Matagorda.

Some of the above predictions are already coming true; portions of the island have not been grazed in five years. Biologists familiar with Matagorda have observed fewer peregrine falcons (*Falco peregrinus*), for example, on ungrazed versus grazed pastures. They believe peregrines eschew ungrazed pastures because of lower prey abundance and greater difficulty in finding prey.

The bobwhite's fate on Matagorda is straightforward. If one were to write a prescription to rid an area of quail, one hardly could improve on a no-management scenario in a productive habitat. Much of the island will become uninhabitable to bobwhites because of rank vegetation and low food supplies. These birds may persist only along the gulfward sand dunes, where wind and soil movement create lower successional conditions, and along roads on which traffic maintains low vegetation.

The interactions between grazing animals and wildlife are complex. There are no pat answers, panaceas, or fixed policies that will apply equally well under all circumstances. Undoubtedly, there are situations in which the presence of cattle is inappropriate. Just as surely, there are circumstances in which grazing serves a purpose in wildlife management.

 48 Hot Habitat

THE BIG BANG THAT CREATED THE UNIVERSE TOOK PLACE about 20 billion years ago. The earth has been around for about 4 billion years. In those 4 billion years, there have been countless warming and cooling cycles, arising from periodic changes in the earth's orbit around the sun and the earth's tilting upon its axis.

Bobwhites have survived warming and cooling trends for the last 12 million years, give or take a few million years. So why all the agitation over global warming? The past success of quail does not necessarily indicate future success. Landscapes transformed slowly during the first 11,999,700 years of quaildom, but have changed abruptly in the last 300 years.

Whether or not one accepts global warming as real depends somewhat on one's political outlook. Generally speaking, many on the political right view global warming as an imaginary bogeyman; many on the left see it as a real one. The laws of physics and chemistry, however, remain immutable to political persuasion.

David M. Gates, a biophysicist and author of *Climate Change and Its Biological Consequences* (1993), has pointed out that cyclic temperature changes on earth are nothing new; however, the RATE of current warming is unprecedented. Temperatures are rising as the concentrations of carbon dioxide and other greenhouse gases increase in the atmosphere. These gases trap sunlight, just as greenhouses trap sunlight. Hence, the atmosphere heats up.

Projecting current temperature trends into the future is risky. Indeed, somebody once said that little difference would be observed if meteorologists predicted the economy and economists forecast the weather. It must be recognized that meteorologists deal with an extremely complex issue—weather. Nevertheless, Gates held that certain outcomes of global warming are certainties and other outcomes are highly probable.

From 1860 to the present, the average temperature at the earth's surface has increased about 1.1°F (0.6°C) This estimate is reliable, having been based on 200 million temperature readings. "The decade from 1980 through 1990 had seven of the warmest years on record for the world as a whole," Gates reported. While a general understanding is lacking of how these warm years have affected the thermal environment of quail, there have been some alarming measurements.

My students and I from Texas A&M University–Kingsville, in collaboration with the Callaghan Ranch and Peyton M. Lake, began a study of blue (= scaled) quail habitat management near Laredo in May of 1996. One objective was to study the thermal environment of blue quail and determine how this environment affected production. Hourly temperatures in a brush motte (thicket), about 350 square yards (284 m²) in size, were determined in June.

Quail respond to the OPERATIVE TEMPERATURES in their immediate vicinity; an operative temperature is air temperature less the cooling effects of wind plus the heating effects of the sun's rays. Operative temperature generally is higher than air temperature. Operative temperatures at ground level within the motte started at 82°F (27.8°C) (0700 h) and rose steadily to a maximum of 142°F (61.1°C) (ca. 1400 h). The lowest maximum temperature recorded within the motte was 118°F (47.8°C). Operative temperatures throughout the motte declined to about 105°F (40.6°C) by 1900 h.

Temperatures in the motte were high enough to cause thermal stress in quail for five to six hours during the day. Thermal stress means that the body gains heat and body temperature rises. Quail die if body temperature reaches 116.7°F (47.1°C). The highest temperature recorded would kill an average quail in about 10 minutes. Keep in mind that the temperatures described above occurred at ground level. Also, the researchers did not sample all points in the motte. Blue and other quail undoubtedly find cool refugia on hot days.

My students and I sought to determine in 1996 how ground temperatures at nesting sites might compare in droughty versus rainy years. We set up artificial nesting frames, some of which were covered with screen on the tops and westward facing sides. The screen reduced the intensity of sunlight by 60% and simulated a nesting site with good grass cover. In addition, some plots were watered to simulate a rainy year with good grass cover.

Drought conditions prevailed during the artificial nest study. Operative temperatures on the control plots (no shade or water) reached 113–31°F (45.0–55.0°C) during May and June. Temperatures remained below 105°F (40.6°C) at nesting sites with artificial shade and water. The results showed that temperatures in the nesting environment may be associated with lower production in drought years and higher production in rainy years. Moist soil with grass cover (rainy year) was cooler than dry soil with no cover (drought year). The artificial nest coverts, however, did not reduce temperatures enough to prevent thermal stress. Thermal stress periods were brief (less than one hour), if they occurred at all under the artificial coverts.

Gates stated that continued warming of the earth's surface was highly probable. Computer projections have indicated that the average surface temperature will increase by 2.7 to 8.1°F (1.5 to 4.5°C) by the year 2060, the most likely outcome being an increase of 5.4°F (3.0°C). These increases seem trifling. Could they possibly be meaningful to quail?

To answer that question, compare the temperatures near Laredo and Corpus Christi to see how temperature differences affect bobwhites. Classical south Texas brush country surrounds Laredo. This area is close to being a desert. Corpus Christi takes on more of a marine flair, with the Gulf of Mexico nearby. The average daily maximums during July and

Fig. 26. Steve Kopp, a former graduate student at Texas A&M University–Kingsville, conducts an experiment on the effects of shade and soil moisture on the nesting environment of bobwhites. His results revealed that high temperatures at ground level reduce bobwhite production during drought.

August are 99–100°F (37.2–37.8°C) in the Laredo area and 90–91°F (32.2–32.8°C) in the Corpus Christi area.

Now compare the length of the laying season for bobwhites in these localities. The season is about 90 days near Laredo and 150 days near Corpus Christi. The high temperatures near Laredo are associated with a 60-day decline in the length of the laying season. Accordingly, bobwhites near Laredo have fewer opportunities to renest if a nest is destroyed or to produce multiple broods if a nest is successful.

Production is lower near Laredo than near Corpus Christi. Hypothetically adding 5.4°F (3.0°C), a reasonable estimate of global warming by the year 2060, to the temperatures near Laredo will effectively limit the laying season to a month or so and bobwhites will go extinct in the general area. Reproduction cannot possibly balance mortality with such a short season. Birds near Corpus Christi may persist, but they will be less productive because the length of the breeding season will shrink.

Perhaps a short digression into bobwhite reproduction and temperatures is in order. Maximum egg production occurs at a temperature of about 70°F (21.1°C). Laying begins to taper off at 85°F (29.4°C) and essentially ceases at 95°F (35.0°C).

Some people wonder if quail might adapt to higher temperatures through the process of natural selection. Might nature select for birds that can somehow deal with rising temperatures?

One scenario permits an evolutionary response by quail to global warming. Birds that breed earlier in the year are likely to be more successful than birds that breed later in the year. Therefore, one could see a shift to earlier starting dates for the laying season as time passes. Gambel's quail (*Callipepla gambelii*) made this shift as an adaptation to deserts.

The shift, if it occurs, will have negative effects on the quality of hunting, assuming the opening dates of hunting season remain as they are now. Earlier hatches yield poorer hunting, and later hatches yield better hunting. This occurs because early-hatched birds must survive for longer periods than late-hatched birds. Survival to hunting season would be lower in early versus late hatches. Thus, if global warming fosters earlier hatching, fewer birds will be available at the start of hunting season.

The second scenario does not permit the adaptation of quail to higher temperatures. Poultry scientists have tried unsuccessfully to breed heat-tolerant chickens. There is an absolute limit to heat tolerance, the basis of which lies in the laws of physics and chemistry; the limit cannot be breached through genetic selection.

Of course, changes in the distribution of quail could occur; populations may retreat from traditional areas that become too hot and move into areas that were formerly too cool (e.g., quail in Fairbanks, Alaska). There are two problems, however, with the distribution-shift outlook. First, habitats change at a much slower rate than animal populations. If quail go where temperatures are acceptable but the habitat is not, the habitat may not become suitable for years. Quail will perish; a few years to quail is a millennium to humans. The second problem is one of landscapes. Modern landscapes separate acceptable natural habitat by broad stretches of sterile habitat. In many areas, it simply is no longer possible to have meaningful shifts in quail distribution.

JIM HEFFELFINGER, A BIOLOGIST WITH THE ARIZONA GAME and Fish Department, pointed out a flaw in the logic of this essay. Comparing the reproductive behaviors of bobwhites in Corpus Christi and Laredo has confounding issues. Not only is the climate hotter near Laredo than Corpus Christi, Laredo also receives less rainfall. Thus, temperature and rainfall are confounded, meaning it is not logical to ascribe differences in reproduction to temperature without isolating and separating the effects of rainfall.

Nevertheless, the fact remains that reproducing quail are sensitive to temperatures, and higher temperatures inhibit production. High temperatures during July and August can reduce the breeding season of bobwhites in Illinois by 45 days, according to research published in 1975 by John L. Roseberry and Willard D. Klimstra.

T. S. Robinson observed in a 1955 paper that bobwhite production varied with rainfall and temperature in Kansas. If a certain threshold of rain occurs, temperatures will govern production; i.e., if the rainfall threshold is reached and temperatures are high, production will be substandard. I saw the same effect in bobwhites of South Texas, based on my 1996 analysis of long-term records collected by Val W. Lehmann. Collaborative work published in 1999 by Heffelfinger and me indicates that the production in Gambel's quail is sensitive to rainfall and temperature. Higher temperatures can reduce production below that expected with a given quantity of winter rain.

49 *La Perdiz Mascarita*

SUNSETS IN THE HEART OF SONORA, MEXICO, ARE magnificent. Dusk washes the western sky with red–orange neon that rises high into the heavens. Distant mountains etch a rugged, black horizon, sometimes broken by haunting fingers of saguaro cactus (*Carnegiea gigantea*).

Dusk in Sonora marks the opening of business for night animals, such as coyotes (*Canis latrans*), and the close of business for day animals, such as bobwhites. Bobwhites in the Sonoran Desert? A race known as the masked bobwhite—la perdiz mascarita—inhabits certain broad valleys in the region between Santa Ana and Hermosillo.

The masked bobwhite (*Colinus virginianus ridgwayi*) is both typical and unique as bobwhites go. It whistles *bobwhite* during the breeding season, forms roosting circles at night, and eats seeds, insects, and greens. The rangeland habitat it occupies resembles that of the Texas bobwhite

(*C. v. texanus*). Coloration of the male provides the most striking contrast between masked bobwhites and other races. The head is black as if hooded by an executioner's mask. In fact, "hooded bobwhite" would be more descriptive. The breast feathers of males are a solid reddish brown, a hue that matches the adobe bricks manufactured in Sonora. Females are colored like other races.

A unique life history feature of the masked bobwhite is timing of the breeding season. In the hotter, drier portions of the Rio Grande Plains, some Texas bobwhites are ready to lay by mid-March. The laying season ends for most females by mid-July, although limited reproduction may extend into September. Just as the laying effort wanes for Texas bobwhites, it begins for masked bobwhites. Laying usually starts in July and peak activity may occur in August or September. Broods hatched in October are not uncommon.

The delayed breeding season is a consequence of the rainfall pattern in Sonora. Annual rainfall averages only 13 to 14 inches (33.0 to 35.6 cm), but 10 inches (25.4 cm) come during July and extend through September. These late summer rains stimulate greenery, which in turn serves as habitat for insects. These animals are essential foods of laying hens and younger chicks. Masked bobwhite production coincides with the availability of insects and cooler ground temperatures.

The breeding season of masked bobwhites is brief, initiated by undependable rainfall and terminated by short days and low temperatures. For bobwhites, a species that depends more heavily on reproduction than on survival to maintain populations, limited breeding can lead to a precarious existence, especially if habitat quality declines. Accordingly, the masked bobwhite is an endangered species (see chapter 50, The Misleading of America). The bird was thought to have gone extinct about 1950, but a remnant population was discovered in Sonora during 1964.

Efforts to save masked bobwhites from extinction center at Buenos Aires National Wildlife Refuge, Arizona, and Rancho El Carrizo, Sonora. The current population at Buenos Aires resulted from an innovative reintroduction program. Borrowing from the observations of Herbert L. Stoddard, biologists John Goodwin of the Arizona Game and Fish Department and David H. Ellis and Steve Dobrott of the U.S. Fish and Wildlife Service, developed a foster parent program of reintroduction in 1977.

Two-week-old masked bobwhite chicks are obtained from a captive flock at the Patuxent Wildlife Research Center, Laurel, Maryland. This captive flock originated from wild birds captured on Rancho El Carrizo during 1968 and 1969. Mate selection is computer controlled to minimize inbreeding. Starting on the first of July and continuing at two-week intervals into October, 300 chicks are flown by commercial airline to Tucson. These birds are transported to Buenos Aires Refuge and, in lots of 10, placed in brooders that contain a wild (and presumably wily) Texas bobwhite.

The Texas birds are males that have been surgically sterilized to prevent genetic dilution of masked bobwhites. These males either accept or reject chicks placed under their care. Acceptance is indicated by two behaviors: brooding (i.e., huddling of chicks under the adult for warmth) and protective behavior (e.g., attacking a foreign object held near the brooder). The absence of these behaviors indicates rejection. After a week in the brooder, acceptors and their chicks are transferred to outdoor runs, where they remain for 7 to 10 days. When weather conditions are appropriate, the chicks and adult are released gently into habitats having a diversity of forbs and grasses.

Biologists from the United States and Mexico keep track of wild masked bobwhites on Rancho El Carrizo. This ranch was established by the five Camou brothers who had immigrated to Mexico from Canton de Azasp, France, during the early 1800s. The original ranch stretched from Nogales to the Gulf of California—a spread of 4 million acres (1.6 million ha). Revolution and land reform have pared El Carrizo to a small fraction of its original size; yet it remains large and impressive.

Gustavo Camou, a graduate of the University of Arizona, Tucson, admits to being obsessed with saving the masked bobwhite. Speaking for the family, he laments the extinction of the pronghorns (*Antilocapra americana*) in the 1940s and wants no further losses. This commitment has translated into grazing and brush management practices that maintain or improve habitat.

The number of livestock placed in pastures that harbor masked bobwhites is limited to ensure adequate cover. Mature woody plants, primarily velvet mesquite (*Prosopis juliflora*), are controlled mechanically to increase forage production for livestock and improve habitat for bobwhites.

Hopefully, the sunset that opened this essay is an inapt metaphor for the future of masked bobwhites, and with the dedicated efforts of biologists from the United States and Mexico, the strong commitment of the Camou family, and timely rainfall, this rare bobwhite will persist in the wilds of Mexico.

LA PERDIZ MASCARITA

SINCE THIS ESSAY WAS WRITTEN, SEVERAL DEVELOPMENTS have occurred in the recovery program for masked bobwhites. The captive propagation facility has been moved from Maryland to southern Arizona. A critical assessment of the foster parent program by Sally Gall and William P. Kuvlesky, Jr., Buenos Aires Refuge biologists, revealed some problems. These problems included abandonment of broods by Texas bobwhites and poor chick survival in general. As a result, foster parenting has been phased out and replaced with the gentle release of more mature masked bobwhites. This change has been associated with increased survival rates of released birds.

Meanwhile in Sonora, Mexico, Gustavo Camou and other Mexican ranchers have continued their efforts to preserve masked bobwhites. Gustavo, with financial assistance from the Turner Foundation, has installed a grazing system to promote desirable ground cover. He also has used discing and aeration to manage the structure of brush and facilitate infiltration of rainfall. Several ranchers from Mexico have requested and received technical guidance from the U.S. Fish and Wildlife Service on the management of masked bobwhites, mule deer, and other species.

50 *The Misleading of America*

NBC NEWS AIRS A WEEKLY SEGMENT TITLED "THE FLEECING of America," which purports to expose waste of federal tax dollars. Tom Brokaw, anchor and member of Trout Unlimited, solicits tips from concerned citizens and those with axes to grind. A recent segment dealt with federal expenditure to save the masked bobwhite from extinction.

In this essay, I ignore the question of whether tax dollars should be used to help endangered species. The answer is a value judgment to be resolved by the democratic process. Rather, I explore the nature of facts as presented in "Fleecing" and facts as determined in the mesquite savannas of Arizona and Mexico.

The plight of the masked bobwhite began with the introduction of cattle to the virgin grasslands of southern Arizona. Overgrazing soon destroyed the ground cover necessary in this hot environment; by 1885, masked bobwhites were in serious trouble.

Herbert Brown described conditions during a drought in the 1890s. "During the years 1892 and 1893 Arizona suffered an almost continuous drouth, and cattle died by the tens of thousands. From 50 to 90 percent of every herd lay dead on the ranges. The hot sun, dry winds, and famishing brutes were fatal as a fire to nearly all forms of vegetable life. Even the cactus, although girdled by its millions of spines, was broken down and eaten by cattle in their mad frenzy for food. This destruction of desert herbage drove out or killed off many forms of animal life hitherto common to the great plains and mesa lands of the Territory. Cattle climbed to the tops of the highest mountains and denuded them of every living thing within reach." Accordingly, the masked bobwhite vanished from Arizona around 1900.

In 1985, the Buenos Aires Ranch on the border with Mexico was purchased with revenue from the Land and Water Conservation Fund, generated from taxes on offshore oil leases. The ranch became the Buenos Aires National Wildlife Refuge, with a goal of reestablishing masked bobwhites in southern Arizona. The reintroduction program involved the captive propagation and release of masked bobwhites originally obtained from Mexico (see chapter 49, La Perdiz Mascarita).

The NBC commentator averred that each masked bobwhite cost U.S. taxpayers $23 thousand. The accounting methods for this estimate were not explained, but the commentator provided some figures from which the accounting was possible. He said the total expenditure on the masked bobwhite program has been $8 million during the past 10 years. Dividing $8 million by $23 thousand per bird yields 347.8 birds.

The commentator reported that refuge biologists estimated 300–500 bobwhites on the refuge; this range accurately reflects the opinion of refuge personnel. So the "Fleecing" analysts set the surviving population at about 350 birds. An objective analyst would have selected the median (400 birds). Strictly speaking, the TV program gave an estimated cost per surviving bird.

The commentator also reported that more than 23 thousand bobwhites have been released. This yields a cost of $347.83 per bird released. Wayne Shifflett, the refuge manager, stated in an interview that between 5 and 10% of costs for refuge operations go to the recovery of masked bobwhites. This indicates, using the median of 7.5%, that about $600 thousand have been spent on masked bobwhite recovery in the past decade. An additional cost of $800 thousand was reported for propagating the birds in Maryland, for a total cost of $1.4 million over 10 years.

Now the estimate of cost per surviving bird becomes $3500, based on the objective estimate of 400 birds in the population. The cost per bird released drops to $60.87. Whether one chooses the "Fleecing" estimate of $23 thousand per surviving bird or the derived estimate of $3500 per surviving bird, both are biased upward because of the cash value of existing facilities used in the reintroduction program.

"Critics charge," the commentator stated, "that if this fleecing of America continues, the biggest benefactors will continue to be the hawks and other predators who [*sic*] are getting fat on government quail." Who are these nameless critics and why should we believe them? The predators at Buenos Aires are not getting fat on masked bobwhites released by the government. The refuge has 117 thousand acres (46.8 thousand ha) and about 2300 chicks are released each year. This represents less than 0.02 ounce (0.6 g) of lean meat per acre per year.

One scene in "Fleecing" showed a distribution map for masked bobwhites superimposed on a covey of live birds. The distribution map was perfectly accurate, and indicated a huge range from southern Arizona deep into Sonora, Mexico. The commentator, however, neglected to mention that the map was accurate for 1850 and earlier.

"The quail has always lived in Mexico," the commentator stated, "and still thrives there today." The formerly vast range of the masked bobwhite has shrunk from millions of acres to a few thousand. Wild populations now occur on two or three ranches in Sonora. The ranch families there, particularly the Camous of Hermosillo, have made financial sacrifices to save masked bobwhites from extinction. They have sought and received management advice from the biologists at Buenos Aires Refuge and elsewhere. (The South Texas Chapter of Quail Unlimited sponsored a tour of bobwhite management in Texas for a rancher, Gustavo Camou, and biologist, Florentino Garza, from Mexico.) Despite the earnest efforts of these families, masked bobwhites in Mexico remain near extinction.

Also, there are facts of omission: Buenos Aires Refuge provides habitat for more than 300 species of birds and several reptiles and mammals; the refuge attracts thousands of visitors each year for birdwatching, hiking, and hunting; expenditures by these visitors contribute to the economy of southern Arizona.

The U.S. Fish and Wildlife Service has done a remarkable job of maintaining a captive flock of masked bobwhites for reintroduction purposes. The flock originated from a few birds captured in Mexico; inbreeding becomes a concern when starting with a small population. Analyses by independent researchers, however, indicate that the captive flock is more healthy genetically than some populations of wild bobwhites in the United States.

The program at Buenos Aires has been a testing ground for reintroduction techniques. Populations of bobwhites in most of the United States have been declining for the past decade or more (see chapter 53, Habitat Loss and Quail Decline). Reintroduction may become a routine management practice in the future, and the federal experience with masked bobwhites will help identify the most effective techniques.

AS A RESULT OF THE ABOVE ESSAY, I RECEIVED CRITICAL mail from NBC's nameless critics in Arizona. I was accused by them of having no shame. It is fine to debate human values; that is a great part of being human. It is unethical to me to use fabrication as a basis for arguments in these debates.

51 *Spike Memes*

A SPIKE MEME SEEMS TO BE REPLICATING IN THE MINDS OF quail thinkers throughout this great country. A meme is a thought that takes on a life of its own, passing from mind to mind and perpetuating itself through human generations. Meme first appears in Richard Dawkin's *The Selfish Gene*. A spike meme, symbolically like a spike gene in a deer herd, is a bad thought—one that fosters neither good quail science nor good quail management.

The spike meme comes in many guises, such as: "Your research results are interesting, but the results don't apply here"; "Our quail are genetically different from your quail so we must study quail at all times and places"; "We cannot accept your management practices because this is a different place." These guises generalize to: "There are no patterns in our knowledge of the biology and management of quail."

Consider the spike meme extinct in this essay. There is a dazzling (although incomplete) knowledge base with beautiful patterns available for bobwhites. First, consider an individual bobwhite. In a previous essay (chapter 30, Changes in Latitudes, Changes in Attitudes), it was shown that individuals do indeed vary in body mass at different geographical places. Bobwhites in southern climates weigh about 160 grams (5.6 oz), whereas those in northern climates weigh about 200 grams (7.1 oz). There is a general pattern that holds for many wild animals: body mass increases with latitude (Bergmann's rule). This outcome has a basis in body temperature regulation. Does the outcome lend credence to the spike meme?

A branch of biophysics deals with body temperature regulation. Body temperature remains constant when calories gained (food) is equal to calories lost (heat). The goal of any warm-blooded animal, including bobwhites, is to maintain a constant body temperature. The relationship between calories gained and calories lost at different air temperatures is known with some precision, thanks to the work of Professor Robert J. Robel of Kansas State University, among others.

A 180-gram (6.4-oz) bobwhite may be considered a typical bobwhite. If the number of calories needed by a 180-gram (6.4-oz) bobwhite at some air temperature is calculated, one will find that the result is quite close to the calories needed by a 160-gram (5.6-oz) or a 200-gram (7.1-oz) bobwhite. Geographic differences in body mass have trivial effects on calorie flow.

From Sonora to southern Illinois, bobwhites whistle *bobwhite,* gather broken coveys with covey calls, lay clutches of 12 to 15 eggs, incubate eggs at 37.5°C (99.5°F), have a body temperature of 41.5 to 42.0°C (106.7–107.6°F), and generally behave as bobwhites. The poetic conclusion is this: "A bobwhite is a bobwhite is a bobwhite is a bobwhite." If one knows how an individual responds to something in Tallahassee, Florida, one can be reasonably certain that the response will be about the same in Tyler, Texas. This is an animal that can be taken as a CONSTANT in the development of management theory and practice. The spike meme does not hold with respect to bobwhite individuals.

Turning now to populations, the latitude-attitude article pointed out that population processes also vary with latitude (another nice pattern). Bobwhite populations in southern climes tend to be weaker producers and better survivors, whereas those in northern climes tend to be stronger producers and poorer survivors.

In a numerical perspective, an average bobwhite population in south Texas survives at a rate of about 30% annually and produces about 2.3 juveniles per adult. One in southern Illinois survives at about 17% annually and produces about 5.0 juveniles per adult. A population in southern Oklahoma has intermediate survival and production rates. These average rates permit populations that vary from year to year to persist throughout the years.

Taken at face value, geographic effects on population behavior seem pronounced. The spike meme seems to hold with respect to populations. The above conclusion, however, is shallow. Knowing there is a latitudinal pattern in population processes, we can use information from one area to predict survival and production rates in another.

Moreover, taking the geographic effects at face value does not give the complete story. Suppose the question is the amount of life (i.e., the number of quail days; one quail living one day results in one quail day) that the average bobwhite must contribute for a population to persist. The contribution of life from one quail is the life it lives plus the life it contributes by producing offspring. The condition that a bobwhite population, wherever it occurs, persists through time is imposed.

Under the conditions given above, the contribution of life ranges from 280 to 290 quail days per year, regardless of where bobwhites occur. Geographic variation in survival and production is permissible only if it leads to a fairly constant life contribution of about 285 quail days. The spike meme does not hold for populations if populations are viewed relative to life contributions.

This essay could lead to much moaning and gnashing of teeth, because it challenges a cherished assumption of wildlife management. Therefore, quail researchers are invited to mount rebuttals on their computers and study areas. Note that the content of the essay in no way diminishes the value of research. One cannot recognize patterns unless one has data that may contain patterns. Indeed, this essay is based on research results.

Quail managers are invited to view management as a set of principles that hold approximately wherever quail are present. They may take comfort in knowing that knowledge gained in Brownsville, Texas, has applications in Boca Raton, Florida. While their environments may vary, management of these birds can be approached as if individuals and populations were similar everywhere.

52 *Watercolor Equations*

ALDO LEOPOLD WAS MISLEADING WHEN HE DEFINED GAME management as "the art of making land produce sustained annual crops of wild game for recreational use." What is art, and what does it have to do with game management in general and bobwhite management in particular?

Arts and sciences are taught at the universities. The arts involve such matters as literature and music. Teaching quail biologists how to write poetry or play flutes, however, is not what Leopold had in mind. Turning to a dictionary for help, it defines art as any "craft, trade, etc., or its principles: as, the cobbler's *art.*" It goes on to say, "craft implies ingenuity in execution, sometimes even suggesting trickery or deception; in another sense, craft is distinguished from art in its application to a lesser skill involving little or no creative thought."

When Leopold published his definition in 1933, game management perhaps was best described as an art. It was still in its infancy, and Leopold was taking the first wobbly steps toward science. Science is a process, a search for patterns in nature; it is the explaining of these patterns with hypotheses, theorems, and laws that allow reliable predictions about future events.

Clearly, science is not management, although management can use the knowledge developed by science. When this happens, one has applied science or technology. For quail management to be considered a technology instead of an art, it must have in the background a massive body of sound knowledge. That body exists and it is a glorious body indeed.

Since Leopold's time, biologists have been collecting data on the natural history of bobwhites. Biologists have been asking what they eat; how far they move; what type of habitat they use for nesting, loafing, and feeding; how many eggs they lay; how much they weigh; what their language is; what their nutritional requirements are; how they spend their time; and how their populations behave through time. The scientific papers and graduate student theses addressing these topics most likely would fill a moving van. Thomas G. Scott listed about 3000 papers on bobwhites in his *Bobwhite Thesaurus* (1983).

Descriptive natural history is regarded by some as the least rigorous kind of science, but it provides essential information, not only for more elegant science, but also for management. If the properties of grass cover within which a bobwhite nests are known, management action can be taken to foster nesting cover. If the suite of habitat types that a bobwhite needs to persist is known, areas can be analyzed and deficiencies corrected as necessary. If the timing of pair formation, laying, and brood rearing are known, land management can be timed to do minimal harm to populations. If population behavior is known, harvests can be planned to accomplish many different goals.

The descriptive literature also includes an impressive store of knowledge on the more esoteric aspects of bobwhite biology. For example, thanks to the research of bobwhite biologists, as well as those working on other species, the daily energy requirements of a bobwhite can be calculated. Given the air temperature and the time that a bobwhite walks, flies, and rests, the number of calories that the bird will burn can be determined. How long it takes for a bobwhite to starve to death with heavy snow cover and how long it takes for one to die of hyperthermia on a hot summer day can be delimited. The laws of physics and chemistry form the basis for the knowledge outlined above; it is not art.

The knowledge arising from pure biology allows the formation of sound management decisions. Foods that provide the necessary amounts of metabolizable energy are planted. The causes of low quail populations are known. One's perspective on habitat and populations is clear.

Knowing descriptive natural history and pure biology, one can begin to formulate abstract concepts pertaining to the quail–habitat interface; models can be developed to ascertain what populations need and how they will respond to habitat management. Such models already are in place.

My students and I demonstrated in South Texas in 1993 that it is possible to measure a few habitat variables in summer, check records on rainfall for the past two years, and, using an equation, predict from these data how many bobwhites will be present at the start of hunting season. The predictions will not be perfect, but they will be surprisingly accurate.

Quail managers can borrow from the powerful theorems of mathematics to execute their technology. Harvest management is a case in point; it basically is based on the laws of probability. Scientifically, managers can prescribe harvest quotas in small areas based on these laws. If equations can be formulated that show how to accomplish a management objective, as in the case of harvest management, art is not being practiced—even if the equations were painted in watercolors.

Theorems in ecology are relevant to quail management. Perhaps the most powerful for applied management is the theory of ecological succession. Research has shown that bobwhites are generally (but not always) associated with lower successional stages; i.e., they do best in habitats that have been recently disturbed by grazing, brush management, fire, or small-scale farming. Leave the habitats undisturbed, and with the passage of time, they will become unsuitable for bobwhites. The implication for management is clear: periodically, havoc must be wreaked on portions of the countryside if quail numbers are to be maximized.

One of the greatest scientific achievements in all of human history can be used to guide the understanding and management of bobwhites. Sir Isaac Newton, Albert Einstein, and Charles Darwin provided a legacy of knowledge that is unmatched by all other scientists. It is the natural historian Darwin's theory of natural selection, however, that provides the very foundation for understanding wildlife.

The argument here is not whether humans evolved from monkeys or vice versa—simply that bobwhites are the current product of some 40 million years of artfully dodging the talon and the fang. When a question arises about the bird or its management, one should pause and reflect: Is the bobwhite adapted to this or that based on its evolutionary history, the outcome of which stands in plain sight before us?; How will this or that affect its chances of surviving and reproducing?

Management practices are enacted in those situations in which the answers are or appear to be yes, the bobwhite is adapted, and yes, the practices will increase survival and productivity. The most effective decisions, however, will not always be made if management is decided from a strictly Darwinian perspective. Sometimes the answer will seem to be yes, when in fact it does not matter. At least it will be less likely to form damaging decisions with natural selection as a guiding principle.

Based on the massive body of descriptive information that has accumulated since the 1920s, the theorems and principles of ecology, and the awesome power of natural selection, Leopold's definition can be revised. Today, quail management can be defined with confidence as "the applied science of making the land produce sustained annual crops of bobwhites for recreational use."

THE SUCCESSIONAL STAGE TO WHICH BOBWHITES ARE BEST adapted changes with climate. These birds clearly are lower successional species in rich environments—those with high rainfall, good soils, and long growing seasons. Higher successional stages, however, work best in poorer environments.

53 Habitat Loss and Quail Decline

CONSIDER QUAIL POPULATION TRENDS FROM A CONTINENTAL perspective. Start south of the border, head northward to the western United States, loop eastward, and finish in the American Southwest.

Mexico has 15 species of quail, some of which are not familiar in the United States (e.g., spotted wood quail [*Odontophorus guttatus*] and elegant quail [*Callipepla douglasii*]). Other species are well known (e.g. bobwhite [*Colinus virginianus*] and blue [= scaled] quail [*Callipepla squamata*]). There are no count data for Mexico as a whole; however, biologists have estimated that 14 species are probably secure from extinction in the near term and one species, the bearded tree-partridge (*Dendrortyx barbatus*), should be designated a critical status. The masked bobwhite of Sonora, a subspecies of bobwhite, is endangered (see chapter 49, La Perdiz Mascarita).

Quails of the western United States include Gambel's, California (*Callipepla californica*), and mountain (*Oreortyx pictus*). Kevin Church and associates from the Kansas Department of Wildlife and Parks analyzed breeding bird surveys for these species in 1993. Populations were more or less stable during the period 1966–91. Church and associates also analyzed survey data for bobwhites in the eastern half of the country and blue quail in the south–central and southwestern United States. From 1982 to 1991, bobwhites declined at a rate of 3.5% per year and blue quail at a shocking 8.3% per year.

Leonard Brennan with the Tall Timbers Research Station in Tallahassee, Florida, analyzed continental trends of bobwhites (1961–88) based on Christmas Bird Counts conducted by members of the National Audubon Society. Here are some quotes from his 1991 findings: "If the current population trend continues, we are likely to lose bobwhite hunting opportunities across the majority of this quail's geographic range by the year 2000." Based on Brennan's projections, Christmas Bird Count trends will hit zero by 2005. According to Brennan, "[t]he irony of this projection is nearly unfathomable because effective habitat management techniques have been known for bobwhites for over half a century." Brennan had data from 31 states, and bobwhites were declining in 24 states (77% of those surveyed). States with stable populations included Colorado, Iowa, Kansas, Missouri, Nebraska, Oklahoma, and Texas. Bobwhites also occur in Oregon, Washington, and Hawaii, where they have been introduced.

Bobwhite populations may be likened to an Olympic gymnast performing on a balance beam. The populations can execute demographic pirouettes and backflips, but they are still landing on a four-inch (10.2-cm) beam. Any subtle influence can throw bird populations out of kilter and cause them to crash to the floor, like a gymnast who loses concentration.

Why are bobwhites and blue quail declining and what can be done about it? A number of conjectures have been put forth. Here are the main ones with respect to bobwhites. Bobwhite populations in the southeastern quarter of the country have declined with the establishment and spread of the red imported fire ant (*Solenopsis invicta*). Fire ants reportedly depredate chicks emerging from eggs at the time of hatching. In principle, chick losses could lead to dwindling populations of bobwhites.

The hypothesis that fire ants could reduce quail production enough to cause population declines through time has at least two problems. First, biologists have observed stable, moderate-to-high density bobwhite populations in the presence of fire ants. Second, bobwhites are declining in areas in which no fire ants are present (northern portions of the United States).

A second hypothesis on the cause of the quail decline relates to predator–prey dynamics. The long-term records reviewed by Kevin Church revealed that some populations of hawks have increased as populations of bobwhites have declined. Could there be a cause and effect association?

During the first half of the twentieth century (1900–50), complex predator–prey systems were evident; i.e., there were many species of predators and many species of prey involved. This complexity created a robust, resilient system (see chapter 3, Death Webs). On average, quail populations were about the same everywhere, regardless of the types and numbers of predators.

As landscapes became simpler in modern times, predator–prey systems began to lack resiliency. It is known that in agricultural landscapes, predators can suppress game bird populations; however, the question remains if the new predator–prey system is the problem, or did a landscape problem foster the new predator–prey system?

Global warming is a third problem facing quail populations. The temperature of the earth has been rising for the past 15–20 years. Through its effects on production, global warming could be contributing to the factors that are causing quail populations to decline in the eastern and southwestern United States.

Breeding seasons start about the same time in a particular geographic area; the ending date, however, is variable. Higher temperatures in late summer reduce the number of days available for breeding. This reduction, in turn, reduces renesting and the production of multiple broods; this in turn lowers production and may throw a quail population out of balance (see chapter 48, Hot Habitat). Global warming may contribute to declines in warmer parts of the country, but is an incomplete explanation of the quail decline in all parts of the country.

Loss of habitat undoubtedly remains the key cause of the quail decline. A bobwhite population requires 10–30 thousand acres (4–12 thousand ha) of stable, permanent cover to persist (see chapter 40, Minimum Requirements of Habitat and Population Size). This cover may be grassland with brush, brushland with grass, or open forests with low brush and grass. The cover must be in a block or a set of small blocks that are well interconnected with permanent travel corridors. Cropland of almost any type is a debit to usable space, as are urban environments.

Bobwhite populations are volatile; i.e., numbers can change dramatically from one year to the next. These populations also are vulnerable to catastrophes such as heat waves, droughts, and blizzards. Any volatile wildlife population subject to weather catastrophes requires a substantial amount of permanent cover if the population is to persist.

Lacking enough permanent cover, two circumstances will arise: zombie populations and graveyard habitat. Zombie populations are those too small to persist indefinitely; the indifferent laws of chance foretell their doom. Graveyard habitat is acceptable (even excellent) habitat in parcels

Fig. 27. The smoke plume from burning wheat stubble casts a pall over an agricultural landscape that is unsuitable for maintaining bobwhites. The main reason for quail declines in the United States remains loss of habitat.

too small to support viable quail populations; graveyard habitats once supported zombie populations.

The main problem facing bobwhite populations in our great nation seems to be loss of habitat. Quail need space to live in, which is permanent native cover. The more space they have, the broader the balance beam upon which to land after a particularly demanding population exercise.

THE MODERN QUAIL DECLINE IS MERELY A PROJECTION OF the decline that started near or before the turn of the nineteenth century. This is a statement made by Herbert L. Stoddard in 1931: "It is becoming a difficult matter in the Eastern United States to find areas where quail are living under natural conditions, unaffected by man and his works. The great bulk of the open woodland of the coastal plain has been lumbered off, and the prairie portions brought under the plow."

Aldo Leopold, writing in the late 1920s and early 1930s, was ruing the continental decline of bobwhites some 70 years ago. E. Lowell Sumner, Jr., said this of California quail in 1935: "During the last fifty years the California quail . . . has suffered a marked decline in numbers throughout the state."

 54 Falling into Cracks

DIGGING A POSTHOLE IN VICTORIA CLAY WILL TEST ONE'S resolve. When moist, these black gumbo soils of the Gulf Coast Prairie stick to shovels like feathers to glue. More time will be spent scraping the blade and gooey clods off the scraper than will be spent excavating the hole. When dry, the soil hardens like concrete. Shovels and posthole diggers must be augmented with crowbars to chisel deeper. If one is lucky, the set will fall on a wide crack in the soil; cracks characterize Victoria clays.

According to popular theory, those same cracks that may ease the toil of fence builders imperil the lives of bobwhite chicks. This risk must be an overstatement. My daughter's hamster, although nearly sightless, gives wide berth to the edges of couches and chairs when roaming free in the living room. My frisbee dog has better sense than to dive into a garbage can while chasing a fetching stick. Does any animal, young or old, lack an innate sense of danger about falling?

Perhaps quail chicks are an exception. They certainly behave like genetically programmed robots. If the mother jumped over a crack and called, the whole brood might fall into a clayey crevice. This would be possible only during the first few days of life. Perhaps quail enthusiasts fall into more cracks than quail chicks. Upon seeing one event and then an associated event, an assumption is reached that the two are related: (1) there are few quail this year and (2) there were a lot of cracks in the soil during brood season. Therefore, a lot of chicks must have fallen into cracks.

Could it be, given dry conditions during brood season, that a high percentage of hens failed to lay? In 1987, a rainy year, 10 of 12 hens collected and dissected in south Texas were laying. In 1988, a dry year, none of 8 hens was laying. Could chicks have starved? With a lack of greenery, there were no insect foods. These causes of the lack-of-production effect are more plausible than the crack-in-the-soil hypothesis.

Another example of erroneous reasoning involves fire ants (see chapter 13, Fire Ants): (1) there were many quail in the past and (2) now there are a lot of fire ants. Therefore, fire ants must be causing the quail decline. Although native and imported fire ants damage individual bobwhites, and perhaps whole clutches on occasion, there remains little scientific evidence that ants affect bobwhite population numbers. Of course, there is little evidence that fire ants do not damage bird populations. The problem is that fire ants are too convenient an explanation of quail declines to be fully credible.

Consider an area in east Texas infested with fire ants. The area consists of large, Bermuda grass pastures, kept free of weeds with periodic doses of herbicides. Brushless fence lines are maintained in that condition. The only woody cover is an occasional large post oak (*Quercus stellata*) or blackjack oak (*Q. marilandica*). The area has no quail. Remove fire ants from the picture, and the area still would have no quail. The fundamental problem is land management that has failed to consider wildlife. This above-described land use has led to unsuitable habitat.

The belly-dipping premise is perhaps another crack into which quail enthusiasts have fallen. The premise holds that in semiarid environments, incubating bobwhites dip their bellies in water. The ostensible purpose of this behavior is to carry water back to the nest on feathers to provide humidity for incubation. Embryos die if humidity becomes too low—

Fig. 28. The cracks that develop in clay soil as it dries may swallow a few bobwhite chicks. In the text, clay soils symbolize misconceptions of quail life processes that are based on erroneous assumptions of cause and effect.

they simply dry up before hatching. If the belly-dipping premise holds water, so to speak, it makes sense to put out dipping dishes for bobwhites.

The origin of the premise is obscure but may be tied to lore about sandgrouse (*Pterocles* spp.), which are related more closely to pigeons than to grouse or other game birds. The 15 or so sandgrouse species inhabit arid lands in Eurasia and northern Africa. Like native North American pigeons—mourning doves (*Zenaida macroura*) and white-wings (*Zenaida asiatica*)—sandgrouse require surface water for drinking. Most species make daily flights to water holes; they may cover maximum one-way distances of 38 miles (60.8 km). Sandgrouse may dip their bellies in water to carry moisture to chicks in the nest.

The first known reference to belly-dipping bobwhites appeared in 1953 in the *Transactions of the North American Wildlife Conference*. During that time, the transactions consisted largely of papers by research biologists. According to Val W. Lehmann: "It was not until August, 1951, . . . when three active [bobwhite] nests located one-half mile or less from a water hole hatched every egg successfully, this despite severe drought, that we realized the possible significance of surface water in promoting yield. These particular females . . . daily flew to a nearby water hole and bathed for periods of from seven to ten minutes prior to afternoon feeding; moisture important to hatching was almost certainly carried back to nests in their plumage."

If the above quote is the basis for the belly-dipping premise, the premise is largely without foundation. It is unlikely that a bobwhite would fly 0.5 mile (0.8 km) to water (see chapter 2, Flight). It may not be possible for them to fly this far, unless they are dropped from an airplane. How would the author know that the same quail was observed? Individual bird identifications would have been necessary. The author needed to be at the nest when the bird flew off and at the water hole when it arrived; simultaneous observations of two or three birds would have been required if incubation periods overlapped.

Why would quail want to carry water back to the nest in the afternoon? Relative humidities are higher at night than during the day. If belly-dipping is to make sense, hens should bathe in the morning and carry water back for the heat of the day. Quail feathers, indeed most birds' feathers, are carefully maintained to repel rather than absorb water. The uropygial gland on the upper tail secretes an oily substance for waterproofing feathers. How could these hens possibly have carried water back to the nest, given water-repellent feathers, especially if they fed for two or three hours after bathing.

What may have happened is that the biologist quoted above saw quail standing in water and the first explanation that jumped to mind was humidity control at the nest. Equally plausible is a simpler explanation: the birds simply were cooling their feet. Based in part on a questionable premise, large numbers of dipping dishes are scattered throughout semi-arid rangeland. Yet there is no reason to believe that providing such water promotes incubation success.

Making progress in quail conservation is like digging a posthole in Victoria clay. One must chisel away at the hard problems (ignorance of life processes) and scrape off the gumbo (misconceptions about quail biology). Gumbo besmudges one's outlook when wrongly assuming that two events are related in a cause and effect manner.

55 The Value of Mistakes

IN 1931, HERBERT L. STODDARD PUBLISHED HIS CLASSIC book, *The Bobwhite Quail.* Do the same controversies in quail conservation persist? What has been learned, if anything? Has science helped to resolve questions, or has it generated more confusion?

"There is a wide belief among sportsmen and gamekeepers," wrote Stoddard, "that inbreeding is one of the important factors in the decline of upland gamebirds." Hunters of this mind-set reasoned that hunting and scattering coveys would be good for the genetic health of quail populations. The "shoot-'em-up-for-genetics" notion still lives—and remains farfetched. Quail inhabited this planet for tens of thousands of years before shotguns became a feature of their environment. They evolved behaviors that help ensure genetic vigor. Young birds may leave their home areas and carry genes to new areas. The covey itself, contrary to popular opinion, is not necessarily a family group, but rather a mixture of birds from different family groups. Birds from neighboring ranges also exchange genes.

Although inbreeding was not a concern during Stoddard's time, and scatterguns are not necessary to ensure genetic diversity, it is ironic that inbreeding is of potential concern today. Loss of habitat reduces populations to smaller and smaller levels in some portions of the United States. Lower populations are more likely to suffer inbreeding than higher populations, especially when distances between habitat islands increase (see chapter 39, When 2 + 2 = 0). Modern landscapes suppress gene exchange among local populations.

Another issue that Stoddard wrestled with, one that has not gone away, relates to bobwhites and surface water. Many people believe that a supply of water, such as a pond or stream, is a necessary component of bobwhite habitat. Stoddard kept penned birds "in perfect physical condition for several months" without providing any water. The birds gained their requirements from dew, succulent vegetation, and insects. Modern research supports Stoddard's assertions about water (see chapter 11, The

Question of Water and chapter 12, Another Shot of Water). For a corroborative narrative, harken back to 1884 and the words of Amory R. Starr:

"In September . . . I went on a bear-hunt to what is known as the Nueces Canyon . . . in the southwestern portion of Texas. It was during a severe drought. Water was to be found only on the Nueces River and a few of its tributaries, and while the cattle had eaten all the grass within several miles of the stream along part of our road, in other places we found it quite abundant, because the cattle would not go so far from water to graze upon it, and yet in those very places I saw more bobwhites . . . than I ever saw before or since. They were just as abundant miles from water as they were upon the banks of the steam."

All those aspiring to be quail scientists, including the author of this essay, have made biological blunders. Consider a gaffe by Herbert L. Stoddard, the master himself: "While it is possible that bobwhites may in some parts of their range attempt occasionally to bring off a second brood while the first is developing, no case came to light during the course of our work, and we believe that in the Southeast it rarely if ever happens."

Stoddard undoubtedly would retract this statement if he could. While his observation was accurate, given the state of knowledge at that time, history has shown that he operated under false assumptions (see chapter 36, The Occurrence of Multiple Broods and chapter 37, Implications of Third Broods). Because of modern radiotelemetry equipment, which Stoddard and his peers lacked, double broods of bobwhites have been documented in Alabama, Florida, Iowa, Oklahoma, Texas, and Missouri. Apparently, the behavior is common under certain circumstances.

"The bobwhite may live for a few weeks without free water, but this bird thrives only where rain is adequate for its needs," wrote Walter Rosene in *The Bobwhite Quail: Its Life and Management* (1969). Adequate rain, according to a map on pages 22 and 23 of Rosene's book, must exceed 40 inches (102 cm) per year. He portrayed the western portions of Oklahoma and Texas as a region in which rainfall is deficient during all seasons. Yet certain portions of the Rio Grande Plains carry high bobwhite densities year after year, with rainfall that fluctuates around an average of 20 to 25 inches (50.8 to 63.5 cm).

Seemingly low amounts of rainfall are sufficient for bobwhite populations if the rain occurs when it is effective—spring and autumn. Moreover, short, stiff droughts in summer, an annual occurrence in south Texas, probably benefit bobwhites by reducing vegetation growth. Runaway plant production in rainier environments creates management problems.

"In the absence of evidence to the contrary, we can be reasonably sure that fall densities seldom exceed 1 quail per 2 acres of the best [South Texas] range," wrote Val W. Lehmann in *Bobwhites in the Rio Grande Plain of Texas* (1984). Based on my research in the 1980s, it is known that the range that Lehmann addressed routinely carries more than a bobwhite per two acres.

On one ranch, my students and I with the Kleberg Institute of Texas A&M University–Kingsville, documented more than two birds per acre (5/ha) during four consecutive years. In the boom year of 1987, harvest exceeded a bird per acre (2.5/ha) on some ranches, and one carried an estimated density of almost five birds per acre (12.5/ha) (see chapter 38, The Mysteries of Density).

What had prompted Lehmann to make this erroneous assertion? He may have collected data during periods of population lows, or used an unreliable technique for counting bobwhites. He had driven from brush motte to brush motte in the rangeland and had counted birds in mottes. If he had failed to check every motte, if coveys had moved away from mottes when the pickup approached, or if some coveys had been away from mottes, he would have arrived at a low estimate of density. Modern counting methods, not available in Lehmann's time, avoid these problems.

"Another thing to consider is the consistency of the annual average, regardless of its value. Most of Texas experiences wide variation in rainfall from 1 year to the next. As the frequency of below-normal years increases, so does the potential value of watering in bobwhite management," wrote Fred S. Guthery in *Beef, Brush, and Bobwhites* (1986). Suppose average annual rainfall is zero inches with no variation from year to year. No years would be below normal; however, assuming quail could exist in this environment, one might want to provide water (but see chapter 12, Another Shot of Water).

While Guthery must have had indigestion when he held forth on rainfall averages and watering, the other authors made honest mistakes based on the best available data at the time. Mistakes are expected in science and indeed necessary. Knowledge advances as mistakes are identified.

The lesson for quail conservationists is to read books or articles on quail biology and management with a jaundiced eye; maintain at least mild skepticism. Follow your intuition when something appears odd; watch for nonlinearities. As much as possible, keep up-to-date on the facts, and recognize that the facts change as knowledge grows.

The path to sound knowledge in any endeavor resembles the main highway out of Kuwait City after Desert Storm. Notions that seemed as invincible as Russian T-72s become burned-out wreckage as truth assaults misconceptions.

Index

abnormal behavior, 130
Acacia farnesiana. See huisache
accidents, 15–16
Accipiter cooperii. See Cooper's hawk
Accipiter striatus. See sharp-shinned
   hawk
aflatoxin, 64–66
age ratio, 86, 115–17, 124
airspace, 7, 9, 10, 69
alarm call, 6
Allen, Craig R., 45
Amaranthus retroflexus. See redroot
   amaranth
Ambrosia psilostachya. See western ragweed
Ambrosia trifida. See giant ragweed
anacahuita, 18
Anas platyrhynchos. See mallard
animal rights, 169, 172
antihunting sentiments, 169
Antilocapra americana. See pronghorns
Archer, Steve, 175
artificial propagation. *See* pen-reared
   bobwhites
aspergillosis, 64
assembly call, 5
avian pox, 120

Baccharis salicina. See willow bac-
   charis
Bannister, Roger, 119
Barnes, Thomas G., 72
barnyard grass, 175
bathing, 198
Baumgartner, F. M., 153
Baumgras, P. S., 68
Beasom, Sam L., 14, 77

Beckwith, Stephen L., 36
belly-dipping, 198
Bergmann's rule, 188
Bermuda grass, 37, 73, 91, 198
Bhatkar, Awinash, 47
blackhead, 64
blackjack oak, 198
black locust, 54
black-throated bobwhite, 3
blue panic, 74
blue quail: age as species, 3;
   broomweed in diet, 70; compara-
   tive nutrition, 38; effects of heat on
   production, 33; hybridization with
   bobwhites, 5; in Mexico, 193; and
   predator control, 81
bluewood. *See* brazil
bobcat, 11, 12, 15, 81
body fat: and food supplies 35; and
   rainfall, 81; regional variation in,
   34–36; and reproduction, 30; and
   winter survival, 61
body mass: and latitude, 115, 117; and
   temperature regulation, 4
Bomer Wildlife Research Area, 15, 74,
   101, 128
boom-bust fluctuations, 28
Brackenridge Field Laboratory, 48
Brassica sp. *See* rape
brazil, 18, 20, 58, 74
Brennan, Leonard, 142, 193
bristle grass, 58, 73
Brokaw, Tom, 184
brood abandonment, 134
brooding, 183
Brown, Herbert, 185
Brown, J. R., 175

Brown, Tommy L., 169
browntop millet, 60, 175
brush control patterns. *See* brush
 management
brush management: canopy coverage,
 21, 94; costs and returns, 76, 83;
 patterns, 21, 70, 76, 94, 170; techniques, 76, 82, 83, 171, 184
brush piles, 22, 83, 85
Buenos Aires National Wildlife Refuge,
 182, 185
Buenos Aires Ranch, 185
buffel grass, 73, 75, 78
Buffett, Jimmy, 115
bullsnake, 11
Burger, Loren W., Jr., 119, 135
burning. *See* fire
bur oak, 17
Buteo jamaicensis. See red-tailed hawk

California quail, 3, 24, 33, 152, 193
Callaghan Ranch, 177
Callipepla californica. See California
 quail
Callipepla douglasii. See elegant quail
Callipepla gambelii. See Gambel's quail
Callipepla squamata. See blue quail
calls: intensity, 6; types and purposes,
 5-6
Camou, Gustavo, 183, 186
Canis familiaris. See dog
Canis latrans. See coyote
Cannabis sativa. See marijuana
Cantu, Ruben, 46
Carnegiea gigantea. See saguaro cactus
Carya illinoensis. See pecan
Case, Ronald M., 35, 132
Cassia sp. *See* partridge pea
catastrophes, 128, 142, 144, 148, 165,
 195
caterwauling, 6
cattail millet, 36, 38
cattails, 163
Celtis pallida. See granjeno
Cenchrus ciliaris. See buffel grass

chachalaca, 3
chaparral. *See* roadrunner
Chaparral Wildlife Management Area,
 19, 110
Church, Kevin, 193, 194
Circus cyaneus. See northern harrier
coachwhip, 11, 13
Coleman, Joe, 23
Colinus cristatus. See crested bobwhite
Colinus leucopogon. See spot-bellied
 bobwhite
Colinus nigrogularis. See black-
 throated bobwhite
Colinus virginianus, 3
Colinus virginianus ridgwayi. See
 masked bobwhite
Colubrina texensis. See hog-plum
Commelina sp. *See* dayflower
common broomweed, 70
common lespedeza, 53
competing risks, 14
Condalia obovata. See brazil
Condalia obtusifolia. See lotebush
condition. *See* body fat
cone of vulnerability, 69
confounding of management practices,
 85
Conservation Reserve Program, 72-75,
 101
Cooper's hawk, 11, 14, 122
copulation call, 6
Cordia boissieri. See anacahuita
corn, 60, 64, 67, 73, 93
corridors, 143, 195
Corvus spp. *See* crow
costs of management, 75-77
cotton rat, 13
cottontail, 99
Coturnix coturnix. See Japanese quail
counting, 86, 102-108
covey breakup, 141
cowpea, 74, 93
coyote, 11, 15, 81, 123, 181
Crawford, Keith R., 96
crested bobwhite, 3

crickets, 37, 47, 55
Crotalaria spectabilis. See showy
  crotalaria
Crotalus. See rattlesnake
croton, 16, 18, 35, 38, 58
Croton spp. *See* croton
crow, 11
CRP. *See* Conservation Reserve
  Program
Cynodon dactylon. See Bermuda grass
Cyrtonyx montezumae. See Mearns
  quail

Darwin, Charles, 192
Dawkins, Richard, 187
dayflower, 18, 38
Decker, Daniel J., 169
deluges, 127
DeMaso, Steve, 131, 135
Dendrortyx barbatus. See tree-partridge
density: and apparent population behavior, 138–41; of coveys, 140; in
  early Wisconsin, 130; in presence of
  fire ants, 48; and soils, 17–19
density dependence, 14, 146–49
density estimation. *See* counting
Desmanthus illinoensis. See Illinois
  bundleflower
DeVos, Theodore, Jr., 110
Dewberry, Oscar, 45
dialects, 5
Dicanthelium oligosanthes. See Scribner's dicanthelium
die-offs, 121–23
Dimmick, Ralph W., 106
Dipodomys. See kangaroo rat
diseases, 120, 122
distribution, 3, 92, 115
Dobrott, Steve, 182
Doerr, Ted B., 19, 64
dog: efficiency of, 105–106; use in
  counts, 105
doomed surplus, 152
Douglas, William O., 92
doveweed. *See* croton

drive counts, 106
drought, 13, 17, 18, 31, 42, 44, 78, 83, 84

Echinochloa crusgalli. See barnyard
  grass
ecological succession, 54, 82, 192
economics, 75–77
eggs: energy content, 132 ; energy requirements for laying, 35, 132; formation process, 30; laying rate, 43;
  mass and chick survival, 39
Einstein, Albert, 99, 192
Elaphe obsoleta. See Texas rat snake
elegant quail, 193
Ellis, David H., 182
Ellsworth, Darrell L., 109
energy requirements, 36
Errington, Paul L., 103, 119, 152, 158
escape cover, 9, 10
Euphorbia marginata. See snow-on-
  the-prairie

Falco peregrinus. See peregrine falcons
fall shuffle, 138, 141
Feather, Carol, 69
feeding, 63–68, 83
feeding cover, 10
Festuca arundinacea. See tall fescue
fight call, 6
fire: in comparison with food plots, 61;
  incompleteness in management, 17;
  and Conservation Reserve Program,
  73; management considerations,
  68–71; and usable space, 99
fire ants, 45–49, 194, 198
flameleaf sumac, 17
flight, 7–10
food call, 6
food plot, 59, 61, 77, 85
foods: competition with kangaroo rats,
  12–13; detection of energy content,
  39; important species, 16; management for chicks, 56–59; preferences,
  36–39
Food Security Act, 72

fossils, 3
fox, 81
foxtail, 58, 60
fragmentation, 142
free water, 41
Frye, Roy, 63
fuzzy logic, 154

Galactia sp. *See* milkpea
Gall, Sally, 184
Galliformes, 5
Gambel's quail, 3, 24, 29, 33, 41, 134, 180, 181, 193
Garza, Florentino, 186
Gates, David M., 177
Gene Howe Wildlife Management Area, 12
Geococcyx californianus. See road-runner
geographic races. *See* subspecies
geographic range. *See* distribution
Geomys spp. *See* gophers
German millet, 36
giant ragweed, 38
Gilbert, Lawrence E., 48
Giuliano, W. M., 38
Glading, Ben, 152
global warming, 176–81, 195
Glycine max. See soybean
goatweed. *See* croton
golden crownbeard, 35
Goldstein, David L., 24
Goodwin, John, 182
gophers, 16
Gould, Stephen Jay, 118, 151
grackle, 11, 170
granjeno, 18, 20, 21, 22, 58, 74
graveyard habitat, 195
gray fox, 11
gray partridge, 120
grazing, 75, 77, 172–76
greater prairie-chicken, 142
Great Plains harvest mouse, 174
greens, 29, 40, 42, 58, 123
Griffin, Donald R., 161

grit, 37
ground-cherries, 18
ground squirrel, 11
Gruver, Brad, 64
Guerra, Enrique, 19, 139
gular flutter, 26–28
Gullion, Gordon W., 134
Guthery, Fred S., 203
Guttiérrez, R. J., x
Gutzwiller, Kevin G., 105
guzzler, 134

habitability, 82
habitat quality, 91
half-cutting, 83
Hamerstrom, F. N., Jr., 103, 119, 152
Hanselka, C. Wayne, 83
harvest: additive vs. compensatory, 78, 154–57; bag limits, 149–50; and covey size, 159–60; and density-dependent production, 158; history of research, 152–54; maximum sustained yield, 159; rates, 79, 118, 120; season length, 150; self-limitation, 150; success rates as population index, 87; take per acre, 19, 83, 121, 128, 139; time effects, 156; vulnerability of age classes, 115
heath hen, 142
heat stress. *See* temperature
Heffelfinger, Jim, 180
hegari, 37, 67
Helianthus sp. *See* sunflower
hemp, 54
herbicides, 120
hog-plum, 18, 20
Hooke, Robert, 27
Hooke's Law, 27
house cat, 11
Howard, Ronnie, 29, 61
huisache, 74
hybridization, 4

Ilex vomitoria. See yaupon
Illinois bundleflower, 38

inbreeding, 143, 183, 186, 201
index of abundance, 103
Inglis, Jack M., 12
ingress, 153
interbreeding. *See* hybridization
irruptions, 121, 129–31, 149, 165

Jackson, A. S., 116, 121
Japanese quail, 66, 119
Johnsgard, Paul A., *x*
Johnson, A. S., 45
Johnson, Dave, 20, 25
Johnson grass, 38
Juncus sp. *See* rushes
juniper, 17, 23, 70, 71, 171
Juniperus sp. *See* juniper

Kane, Arlo H., 64
kangaroo rat, 12
Kassinis, Nick, 8
Keeler, James E., 63
Kellogg, Forest E., 105
keystone species, 143
Khan, Genghis, 59
Kleingrass, 53, 72, 73, 74, 101, 128
Klimstra, Willard D., 33, 116, 136, 146,
     159, 181
kobe lespedeza, 37
Koerth, Ben, 58
Koerth, Nancy E., 43, 81
Korean lespedeza, 54, 73
Kozicky, Ed, 110
Kuvlesky, W. P., Jr., 82, 184

La Copita Research Area, 82
Lake, Peyton M., 177
La Paloma Ranch, 69
law of dispersion. *See* principle of
     edge
leg-banding, 106
Lehmann, Val W., 18, 29, 46, 103, 116,
     122, 181, 199, 203
Leif, Anthony P., 70
Leopold, Aldo, 15, 87–91, 97, 99, 103,
     131, 139, 152, 173, 190, 197

Lespedeza stipulacea. See Korean
     lespedeza
Lespedeza striata. See common les-
     pedeza
Lespedeza thunburgii. See Thunberg
     lespedeza
lesser prairie-chicken, 131
Lewis, Carl, 9
life span, 118, 120
lime prickly ash, 18, 20, 21
Linnaeus, Carolus, 3
live oak, 17
loafing coverts, 20–23
Lochmiller, Robert L., 38
longevity. *See* life span
lotebush, 58
Lukefahr, Steven D., 162
Lutz, Scott, 47
Lynx rufus. See bobcat

Macartney rose, 20, 21
mallard, 171
marijuana, 54
mark-recapture estimates, 106
marsh hawk. *See* northern harrier
masked bobwhite, 82, 110, 181–87,
     193
Masters, Ron, 70
Masticophis flagellum. See coachwhip
Mearns quail, 33
Meinzer, Wyman, 11
Meleagris gallopavo. See wild turkey
memes, 187–89
Mephitis mephitis. See striped skunk
mesquite, 17, 20, 21, 22, 74
metabolic water, 40
metabolizable energy, 37, 54
Michael, Victor C., 36
milkpea, 18, 58
millet, 35, 58
milo. *See* sorghum
Mitchell, M. R., 46
molt, 34, 132
morning covey call counts, 5–6, 104
mortality: die-offs, 121–23; due to

mortality (*continued*)
    harvest, 153–54; from senescence, 119; ultimate and proximate factors, 122
mountain quail, 193
mourning doves, 7, 42, 64, 124, 171, 199
movement, 130, 131
mule deer, 171, 175, 184
multiple-brooding, 132–38

natural selection, 39, 192
Neotoma sp. *See* woodrat
Nestler, R. B., 37
neural networks, 97–99
Newton, Sir Isaac, 27, 192
Nice, Margaret, 60
North, M.O., 31, 33
northern harrier, 122
nurse plant, 22
nutrition: amino acids, 38, 57; of chicks, 56–59; crude protein requirements, 38, 56; energy requirements, 37, 39, 132; value of greens, 123; water requirements, 43, 201

Odocoileus hemionus. See mule deer
Odocoileus virginianus. See white-tailed deer
Odontophorus guttatus. See spotted wood quail
old age. *See* senescence
Opuntia leptocaulis. See pencil cactus
Opuntia sp. *See* prickly pear
Oreortyx pictus. See mountain quail
Ortalis sp. *See* chachalaca
overgrazing, 173, 184–85
oxidative water, 40

Packsaddle Wildlife Management Area, 135
paisano. *See* roadrunner
panic grass, 58
Panicum antidotale. See blue panic
Panicum coloratum. See Kleingrass
Panicum miliaceum. See proso millet
Panicum ramosum. See browntop millet
Panicum texanum. See Texas millet
Panicum virgatum. See switchgrass
parasites, 120
Parkinsonia aculeata. See retama
partridge pea, 18, 37, 58
paspalum, 58
Paspalum setaceum. See thin paspalum
Paspalum sp. *See* paspalum
patchwork agriculture, 88–89, 91, 131
Patuxent Wildlife Research Center, 182
pecan, 17
pencil cactus, 83
Pennisetum glaucum. See cattail millet
pen-reared bobwhites, 108–11
Peoples, Alan D., 38, 77, 131, 135
Perdix perdix. See gray partridge
peregrine falcons, 7, 176
pesticides, 120
Phasianus colchicus. See ring-necked pheasant
phorid fly, 49
Physalis sp. *See* ground-cherries
Pitchfork Ranch, 83
Pituophis catenifer. See bullsnake
Platanus occidentalis. See sycamore
Pollock, Kenneth H., 120
Polygonum sp. *See* smartweed
populations: growth rates, 165; rates of decline, 193; sources of variability, 164–66. *See also* catastrophes
population viability, 144–46
Porter, Mike, 61
Porter, Sanford D., 47
post oak, 198
predation ecology, 11–16, 69
predator control, 80–81
predators: avoidance of, 9; fitness of quail, 119; hunting tactics of, 148; list of, 11
preformed water, 40
prescribed burning. *See* fire
prickly pear, 18, 69
principle of edge, 89, 97, 99
Procyon lotor. See raccoon

production: age at first breeding, 124; and body fat, 30; clutch size, 125; density-dependent effects, 147; effects of heat, 31, 178; effects of time, 30, 148; factors affecting, 28–33, 182; geographic effects, 15; key variables affecting, 124–26; multiple-brooding, 132–38; phenology, 126–27; time required for laying and incubation, 124, 125; and timing of hatch, 126

pronghorns, 183

proso millet, 60

Prosopis glandulosa. See mesquite

Prosopis juliflora. See velvet mesquite

Prunus sp. *See* wild plum

Pterocles spp. *See* sandgrouse

quail decline, 15, 193, 197

queensdelight stillingia, 38

Quercus havardii. See shinnery oak

Quercus macrocarpa. See bur oak

Quercus marilandica. See blackjack oak

Quercus shumardii. See Texas oak

Quercus stellata. See post oak

Quercus virginiana. See live oak

Quiscalus spp. *See* grackle

raccoon, 13, 64, 81

radiation, 24

Rancho El Carrizo, 82, 182, 183

range condition, 173–74

rape, 37

rattlesnake, 11, 13, 64

redroot amaranth, 38

red-tailed hawk, 11, 122

Reithrodontomys montanus. See Great Plains harvest mouse

relativity in management, 100

renesting, 125, 132, 136

reproduction. *See* production

resonance, 27, 28

restocking. *See* stocking

retama, 74

Rhus aromatica. See skunkbush sumac

Rhus copallina. See flameleaf sumac

Rhynchosia sp. *See* snoutbean

ring-necked pheasant, 158, 162

roadrunner, 11–12

roadside counts, 104

Robel, Robert J., 26, 37, 54, 55, 56, 61, 68, 188

Robinia pseudo-acacia. See black locust

Robinson, T. S., 44, 181

roosting disc, 160

Rosa bracteata. See Macartney rose

Roseberry, John L., 33, 72, 116, 136, 146, 159, 181

Rosene, Walter, 46, 128, 137, 202

running, 162

rushes, 163

Saarni, Roy W., 152

saguaro cactus, 181

sandgrouse, 199

San Tomas Hunting Camp, 61

San Vicente Ranch, 19, 42, 139

scaled quail. *See* blue quail

scent, 105–106

Schizachyrium scoparium. See seacoast bluestem

Schorger, A. W., 8, 129

Schroeder, Richard L., 93

Scott, Thomas G., 191

Scribner's dicanthelium, 175

seacoast bluestem, 175

seed requirement, annual, 60

seed values, 53–56

senescence, 14, 119, 121

seral stage, 174

Sermons, William, 134

sesame, 37, 74

Sesamum indicum. See sesame

Setaria italica. See German millet

Setaria sp. *See* foxtail

sharp-shinned hawk, 12

Shifflett, Wayne, 185

shinnery oak, 121

showy crotalaria, 37

Shupe, Tom, 5

Sigmodon hispidus. See cotton rat
Simpson, Ron, 46
skunkbush sumac, 74
slack zones, 94–96
Sloan, Denise, 13
smartweed, 54
Smith, E. Lamar, 173
Smith, Harvey W., Jr., 19, 139
Smith, Loren M., 70
Smith Ranch, 19
snoutbean, 18, 58
snow, 121
snow-on-the-prairie, 16
soils: and food supplies, 18, 19; temperatures, 25, 31
Solenopsis invicta. See fire ants
sorghum, 35, 36, 37, 53, 60, 64, 67, 73, 93, 170
sorghum almum, 38
Sorghum halepense. See Johnson grass
Sorghum vulgare. See sorghum
Southeastern Cooperative Wildlife Disease Study, 120
soybean, 54, 93
space-time, 100
space-time saturation, 100
Speake, Dan W., 110, 134
species-habitat models, 92
Spermophilus sp. *See* ground squirrel
spiny hackberry. *See* granjeno
spot-bellied bobwhite, 3
spotted wood quail, 193
Spring, A. J., 13
Stanford, Jack, 31, 132, 135
Starr, Amory R., 202
starvation, 30, 35, 36, 37, 123
stepping stones, 143
Stewart, Robert Gregory, 66
Stillingia sylvatica. See queensdelight stillingia
stocking, 109, 143
stockpiling, 79
Stoddard, Herbert L., 8, 9, 10, 13, 45, 46, 68, 102, 119, 127, 169, 182, 197, 201, 202

strip discing, 83, 85
striped skunk, 11
Strophostyles sp. *See* wild bean
subspecies, 3, 6–7
succession. *See* ecological succession
Sumner, E. Lowell, Jr., 24, 197
sunflower, 18, 35, 68, 74
supplemental feeding. *See* feeding
surface water, 41
survival: of adults, 126; of chicks, 126, 127; density-dependent effects, 147; geographic effects, 15, 116–17
Swank, W. G., 82
switchgrass, 37, 74
sycamore, 17
Sylvilagus sp. *See* cottontail

tall fescue, 72
Tall Timbers Research Station, 120, 139, 193
Taylor, J. Scott, 134
temperature: of body, 24, 177; and flight, 10, 25; important temperatures, 26; and length of laying season, 33, 179; at loafing coverts, 20; and maximum egg production, 95; operative, 177; regulation of body temperature, 26–28; role in bobwhite ecology, 23–26
tepee shelters, 22, 74, 101
Texas millet, 175
Texas oak, 17
Texas rat snake, 13
thermal cover, 25
thermal stress. *See* temperature
thin paspalum, 18, 58, 175
threshold of security, 152
Thunberg lespedeza, 37
tree-partridge, 193
trichomoniasis, 64
Triticum aestivum. See wheat
Tympanuchus cupido. See greater prairie-chicken
Tympanuchus pallidicinctus. See lesser prairie-chicken

Typha sp. *See* cattails

Urness, Phil, 175
Urocyon cinereoargenteus. See gray fox
uropygial gland, 200
usable space, 61, 90, 99, 166, 195

Valentine, Gary, 45
velvet mesquite, 183
Verbesina sp. *See* golden crownbeard
Vigna unguiculata. See cowpea
vitamin A, 29, 122
vocalizations. *See* calls

wariness, 162
water: effects of deprivation, 41; effects of supplementation, 44, 83; requirements for laying, 43; sources of, 40–41
weather catastrophes. *See* catastrophes; drought
Weaver, Laura, 58
Webb, Bill, 121
weight. *See* body mass
Welder Wildlife Foundation Refuge, 13
Wells, Roger, 24

western ragweed, 16, 35, 38, 68
wheat, 36, 54
whistle counts, 103
White, Shirley L., 110
white-tailed deer, 22, 42
white-winged dove, 42, 199
wild bean, 38
Wild Horse Desert, 18
wild plum, 74
wild turkey, 11, 22, 42, 64
willow baccharis, 74
woodrat, 69

Xanthocephalum dracunculoides. See common broomweed

yaupon, 16

Zanthoxylum fagara. See lime prickly ash
Zea mays. See corn
Zenaida asiatica. See white-winged dove
Zenaida macroura. See mourning doves
zombie populations, 195